LOCAL GOVERNMENT AND URBAN POLITICS

LOCAL GOVERNMENT AND URBAN POLITICS

William Hampton

LONGMAN
London and New York

LONGMAN GROUP UK LIMITED
Longman House, Burnt Mill, Harlow
Essex CM20 2JE, England
and Associated companies throughout the world

*Published in the United States of America
by Longman Inc., New York*

© Longman Group UK Limited 1987

First published 1987

BRITISH LIBRARY CATALOGUING IN PUBLICATION DATA

Hampton, William
    Local government and urban politics.
    1. Municipal government—Great Britain
    I. Title
    352′.0072′0941   JS3115

ISBN 0-582-29638-2

LIBRARY OF CONGRESS CATALOGING IN PUBLICATION DATA

Hampton, William, 1929–
    Local government and urban politics

    Bibliography: p.
    Includes index.
    1. Local government—Great Britain. I. Title.
JS3111.H25 1986   352.041   86–2962
ISBN 0–582–29638–2

Set in 10/11pt AM Compedit Times Roman
Produced by Longman Singapore Publishers (Pte) Ltd.
Printed in Singapore

To Hazel Hampton

CONTENTS

ILLUSTRATIONS AND TABLES

LIST OF FIGURES

LIST OF MAPS

LIST OF TABLES

PREFACE

Since 1963 I have taught local government and urban politics to a wide range of audiences: undergraduates, postgraduates, local government officers, prospective councillors, and members of university extra-mural classes. Throughout the writing of this text I have kept these audiences firmly in the front of my mind. I have tried to anticipate the needs of those who must enter examinations; but at the same time I have been aware of the interruption from the extra-mural student if technical terms are introduced without explanations, or if the tutor strays too far from the practical relevance of his or her subject. This book is written, therefore, for those who would understand, for whatever purpose, one of the most exciting and contentious areas of present political affairs. At the same time, I have tried both to eschew writing from current headlines and to present the material within a proper historical and academic framework. Some recent controversies are dealt with in discussion sections at the end of various chapters.

The writing of a textbook is in some ways an exercise in licensed plagiarism. My students have provided many of the questions and my colleagues in the Urban Politics group of the Political Studies Association have provided most of the answers. In mitigation I may only argue that in the past they in turn have been kind enough to make use of my own work. The friendly co-operation implied in these remarks is, I hope, fully acknowledged in the references in the text and in the bibliography. There are some, however, who deserve a more specific mention. Bernard Crick made some helpful suggestions to improve an earlier draft; I am also grateful for his support over many years. Stuart Lowe and Rod Rhodes were kind enough to lend me typescripts of their own books before publication. Michael Goldsmith and John Gyford sent me unpublished research reports. Howard Elcock, Pat Seyd, David Regan, Noel Boaden and Arthur Midwinter answered specific questions for me when I was stumped for an answer. Within my own university, I was granted research funds to support the preparation of the book. The library staff both in the university and in Sheffield City Polytechnic were most helpful; in particular I am grateful to David Jones who conducted a literature search for me on the economic activities of local authorities. Several members of the town hall staff in Sheffield gave me assistance in answering detailed questions. Finally, I wish to thank Angela Johnson most warmly for her competence in turning a handwritten draft into a typescript prepared in the complex style required by the publisher. She also helped me by preparing lists of quotations: a particularly onerous task in a textbook such as this.

It only remains to make the usual disclaimer on behalf of all those who have helped me in any respect and for whose help I am really most sincerely grateful. None of them bears any responsibility for the use I have made of their help. I accept full responsibility for everything that follows.

WAH

ACKNOWLEDGEMENTS

We are grateful to the following for permission to reproduce copyright material:

The Controller, Her Majesty's Stationery Office for tables 2.1, 3.1, 3.2, 3.3, 3.4, 3.5, 6.1, 6.2, 6.3, 12.1; Longman Group Ltd for maps 2.1, 3.1, 3.2, 3.3 (Alexander 1982b) and fig 11.1 (Klein 1983).

Chapter one
INTRODUCTION

From a quiet, almost dull branch of public administration, local government has developed in recent years into both a matter of major public debate and one of the most vigorous specialisms within political science. A series of government reports and inquiries has introduced changes in every aspect of the practice of local authorities. Yet far from producing a settled system for the final decades of the twentieth century, the changes have been accompanied by continuing political controversy. Amid this controversy, the constitutional relationship between central and local government is changing as the conventional understandings upon which it is based are redefined. The academic study of the subject has also developed over the recent past. The public administration approach was first supplemented by political scientists who examined local authorities as political systems in their own right: the political scientists are now joined by social theorists who seek to penetrate the complex relationships underlying the provision of public services at a local level. Attempts are being made to locate general explanations within wider theories of the state. The purpose of the present book is to discuss these developments in both practice and theory so that students may gain an integrated approach to the study of local government and urban politics.

The book is divided into three parts entitled respectively: the administrative context; the political context; and the structural context. Such a framework is necessary for the orderly presentation of the material, but it suggests a clear-cut division that is misleading in many respects. Administrative description can only be understood properly if it is placed within its political context, and local government cannot be considered apart from the more general environment within which it exists. Other government agencies and private industry and commerce provide a structure for the local political process. There will, therefore, be constant cross-references to the various bodies of literature as the discussion proceeds.

1

THE NATURE OF LOCAL GOVERNMENT

Many authors have commented upon the lack of a theory to sustain the British system of local government (Sharpe 1970; Hill 1974). There is, however, a measure of consensus underlying the arguments both about definitions and about the values that need to be discussed in describing the purposes served by local government.

The definition of local government implies that it is both local and government. Neither term is simple in its content. First, considerable argument has taken place about the meaning of 'local'. For some people it implies an area consecrated by long history and tradition: the counties and urban settlements that structure our formal spatial awareness. For others, the appropriate locality for local government purposes is the socio-economic area governed by journeys to work and the scale needed to provide certain public services. From both perspectives 'local' is understood as wider in scope in Britain than in many other systems of local government. Some of our local authorities have budgets and populations equivalent to the smaller nation states, and our major cities are not fragmented into small local government units in the manner of those in the United States or many other countries (Bowman and Hampton 1983). 'Local' is accepted on all sides in Britain as being large enough to provide several major services such as education and housing in addition to the environmental amenities that are often the focus of local government elsewhere.

Second, there is the tricky problem of defining 'government' in this context. Local authorities are not sovereign bodies. Local government in the United Kingdom is a creature of the Westminster Parliament which retains a constitutional sovereignty enabling it to change or to revoke previously enacted legislation. Local government possesses no original powers despite the romantic titles and images retained from its Saxon or medieval antecedents. Modern local authorities depend upon statute and are subject to a strict interpretation of the legal rule of *ultra vires*. That is, they may only act – with certain limited exceptions – if they can find positive authority for their actions in a specific law. They have no general competence to act for the benefit of the people of the local area. Silence on the part of the law is not enough: specific authorisation must be given. The powers provided may, of course, be either mandatory – something *must* be done, or permissive – something *may* be done. If no legal authority exists then the actions of a local council will be overruled by the courts even though councillors may claim that their policies have been supported through the ballot box.

Although 'government' does not have the strength of meaning in local terms that it possesses when related to the nation state, it retains a stronger meaning than 'administration'. Local authorities are elected bodies and are expected to develop policies appropriate to their localities within the framework of national legislation. There has customarily been a relationship of creative tension rather than command and subordination between central departments and local authorities. This relationship, like many other aspects of constitutional practice in Britain, is subject to conventions and unwritten understandings; but few people maintain that local authorities are simply local functionaries of the national state. The elected status of councillors is one indicator of their putative independence. Another is their power to raise revenue by levying a rate – a form of local taxation. The whole question of the relationship between central and local government is discussed in detail in Chapter 10 as it forms a major source of controversy in local government at the present time.

Despite the disagreements that exist about the definition of local government, we may summarise the common understanding of its British meaning. First, local authorities have a clearly defined physical structure. That is, they have geographical boundaries that are contiguous but which do not overlap. No part of the country is either excluded from local government or is included in the territory of two local authorities of the same status. Second, local authorities are multi-purpose or compendious bodies responsible for many services. The term 'local government' does not usually include, as in some countries, elected bodies responsible for only one service. Third, local councils are directly elected on a similar, though not identical, franchise to that used for parliamentary elections. Fourth, local government has an independent power – albeit carefully circumscribed – of raising taxation. These four characteristics enable us to distinguish local government from other agencies that provide public services in localities. Some of which are discussed in Chapter 11.

Having defined local government we need to consider the purposes or functions[1] it serves within the broader political system. The necessity for administering some services close to the point at which they are delivered to the public is obvious, but there are many ways in which this might be done without creating local authorities. The Committee on the Management of Local Government put it concisely: 'The local administration of public services is essential, that the local organs of administration should be democratically elected bodies is not' (Maud 1967:Vol.1,68). Some services, such as supplementary benefit, are administered by local offices of central government departments; others, such as gas or electricity supply, are the responsibility of appointed boards; and some, such as water supply or the health service, are run by single-purpose bodies which contain indirect representation from local government. It is clear that we must go deeper if we are to justify local government in general terms.[1]

Local government has two advantages over other forms of local administration. These relate to the characteristics referred to earlier and may be summarised as follows. First, as compendious bodies, local authorities are able to co-ordinate the provision of several services within a corporate framework. Great emphasis has been placed on the benefits of corporate planning in recent years (see Ch. 5). The expectations have not been matched fully by reality, but the possibilities for co-operation are obviously better within a single local authority than between several government departments or special purpose agencies. Second, the independent element introduced by both local elections and a separate basis for taxation allows local authorities to develop policies which reflect the needs and aspirations of local populations. We know that they take advantage of these opportunities: the political disposition of a local authority undoubtedly affects its level of service provision (Boaden 1971:112; Sharpe and Newton 1984). Conservative governments under Mrs Thatcher's premiership opposed what they described as 'excesses' by some local authorities, but the degree of independence implied by this phrase can be construed as an advantage which would not be present in other forms of local administration.

Local government has also been justified in terms of wider political values. Among the foremost of these is the promotion of liberty by the dispersal of power from the centre to the localities. L J Sharpe has criticised the more extravagant versions of this view (Sharpe 1970:156–8) on the grounds that local authorities are not immune from arbitrary tendencies, but this criticism is not entirely satisfactory. No one would argue that local governments always act fairly, or that central government is always autocratic. The argument is simply that of pluralism: when there are several centres of power, disagreements are likely to come into the open, and open government is preferable to the coteries of centralism. Local government shares with institutions as diverse as the House of Lords and the trade unions the function of providing jagged edges to snag the smoothness of governmental power.

Sharpe discussed two further values which some writers have claimed are enhanced by local government. In addition to liberty, Paul Ylvisaker (1959) defines these as equality and welfare, but Sharpe prefers to substitute participation and efficiency. Equality, like most of the concepts being discussed, is capable of bearing many meanings. Local government certainly does not enhance equality by allowing for a level provision of services throughout the country. The case is quite the contrary. One of the advantages claimed for local government on the grounds of efficiency is precisely that services may be varied to suit conditions in different localities. But local government may enhance equality by providing access to political office and political activity for wider groups of people than are accommodated through national politics. This widening of the opportunities for participation in public life was one of the strongest reasons why John Stuart Mill celebrated local government in the nineteenth century. He 'justifies local government as political education. . . . As such it is the prime element in democracy, and has an intrinsic value regardless of the functions it may carry out' (Hill 1974:23). Participation in local services is still limited and ambiguous in its political impact (Boaden *et al.* 1982), but local government provides a better focus for public activity than anonymous central government departments or appointed boards which may conduct their affairs in private by excluding the press or public from their meetings.

Provision for the welfare needs of the population in an efficient manner remains, for Sharpe, the major justification for local government. He identifies several ways in which efficiency is enhanced by locally elected bodies. First, as we mentioned earlier, they perform a vital co-ordinating role. It may be convenient for central government to divide policy-making among several departments each responsible for a different range of services such as education, housing and welfare, but the delivery of these services takes place in localities where the needs are expressed as complex mixtures of these services. Central government is poorly placed to deliver services in a manner sensitive to local conditions. Sharpe considers that the role of local government in Britain is enhanced in this respect ' ... because alone among advanced industrial democracies it does not have an intermediate level of administration responsible for the bulk of public services within its area between central and local government proper. Federal systems have it by definition and most other comparable states follow with variations, the French prefectoral pattern' (Sharpe 1970:167; cf. Bowman and Hampton 1983).

Second, local government provides 'an alternative basis for responding to demand for public services that have no market' (Sharpe 1970:171). Sharpe's arguments in this respect are now less widely acceptable than they were in the conditions of an expanding economy. Conservative governments have tried to curtail local government expenditure by both introducing a private market element into some services and reducing expenditure on others. The public opposition to reductions in expenditure justifies to some extent Sharpe's view that the public will demand higher levels of service, if given local opportunities to express that demand, than central administrators will readily provide. The electorate will, of course, vote for lower taxation; just as they would vote against sin. There is not a similar measure of support for the cuts in local expenditure that may be necessary to achieve a reduction in taxes. For example, few schools are closed, however uneconomic in terms of the number of pupils on roll, without a public outcry; and an expensive cheap-fares policy has been widely supported in South Yorkshire. The educative effect, perceived by Mill, of balancing the desire for a service against its cost can be achieved by local government in a way that the remote scale of centrally controlled agencies makes impossible. The fact that the methods of financing local government make this process more difficult than it might be is rather an argument for reforming the methods of finance than a reason for abolishing local government.

Finally, local government provides an opportunity for containing the power of professional people working in the public service. Sharpe maintains that ' ... where there is a high degree of discretion involved and professional autonomy is essential, a potential threat to effective democratic government is posed. The service gradually comes to serve objectives set by the professional group or groups running the service rather than those of its recipients or society at large' (Sharpe 1970:174). Professional groups claim, and no doubt intend, to act in the interests of their clients; but by the exercise of their professionalism, they substitute their judgement of these interests for those of the public they purport to serve. War, we are told, is too important to be left to generals. The argument may be carried further: welfare is too important to be left to social workers; education is too important to be left to teachers; and the environment is too important to be left to planners. Such thoughts have profound implications for the public involvement in the provision of public services (Boaden *et al.* 1982). They also justify the control made possible, if not easily realised, by elected local councils. As compendious bodies, local authorities may also subject the various professions 'to the moderating influence of a face-to-face relationship with other comparable and competing professional groups' (Sharpe 1970:174)

THE ADMINISTRATION OF LOCAL GOVERNMENT

Having discussed some of the broader principles that lie behind the study of local government we may look in a little more detail at the organisation of the present book. The structure of local government should relate to the purposes for which it is established. As there is no agreement about these purposes then it follows that the structure of local government itself is controversial. The structure which is often considered appropriate for the purpose of enhancing democracy is small scale and parochial, whereas the structure deemed suitable for the purpose of providing efficient services is more likely to be large scale. Stanyer has attributed most of the difficulties underlying the British system to the competing needs of these two principles. He describes them as the *community* principle and the *technical efficiency* or *service* principle (Stanyer 1976:38). There is constant disagreement both about the size of settlement which can properly be described as a community and about the scale that is necessary in relation to different services. Opinions change with the prevailing climate of the era. For some people 'Small is beautiful'; but in other circumstances we asked 'Is big really so ugly?' (Newton 1982). Attempts to reconcile the two principles generally lead to some form of multi-layer structure which then creates further problems of the relative size of the different tiers and the relationship that should exist between them. Because of these difficulties, and others concerned with central government relations with local authorities, there is constant discussion of local government reorganisation as people press for a new structure that will embody their particular views.

Reorganisations when they occur are never universally acceptable, and between occasional major restructurings there is constant debate and elaboration.

Just as the structure of local government should relate to its purpose, so will it be affected by the particular services that local authorities are expected to provide. It is a matter of which services – and how many of them. Similarly, the internal administrative arrangements adopted by local authorities are part of the debate between efficiency and democracy. Few democrats would accept the full implications of the old adage 'whate'er is best administered is best'; but, equally, a system of democracy that precluded efficient decisions being made would not be effective in carrying out the will of the people. The resources available to local authorities and the way they are provided will also relate to questions of structure. Some forms of taxation, for example, may be practical in a system of large-scale local authorities but would be impossible for a system based on small local communities. These topics are considered further in the chapters comprising our first section.

THE POLITICS OF LOCAL GOVERNMENT

The traditional administrative description of local government upon which we draw in our first section was supplemented with a political perspective during the 1960s and 1970s following the pioneering work of Birch in *Small-town Politics* (1959). A great expansion of the literature followed, particularly after the newly formed Social Science Research Council sponsored several case-studies of local politics. The case-study areas varied widely and included Sheffield (Hampton 1970), Birmingham (Newton 1976a), rural Wales (Madgwick 1973) and small-town Scotland (Bealey and Sewel 1981). The new initiative in Britain was influenced to some extent by academic developments in the United States where a debate had occurred between those who believed local decision-making was confined within a small group – a 'power-élite', and those who thought power was dispersed – the 'pluralist' approach. The argument was scarcely relevant in Britain, at least in the terms on which it was conducted, as the local government systems in the two countries vary so considerably (Newton 1969, 1975). The intellectual excitement, however, and the methodologies used – particularly sample survey techniques – were conveyed across the Atlantic.

The city politics case-studies in Britain follow a common pattern. The early chapters in each book describe the socio-economic background to the area being studied and frequently include a potted local history. With the exception of Newton they emphasise the distinctiveness of each area and thus became open to the criticism that attaches itself to all case-studies: the material presented is not cumulative and does not generate more general theories. With varying degrees of emphasis the books include survey evidence describing the characteristics of councillors and electors – there is little attention paid to the officers of local authorities. The local political process is the focus of attention and this includes considerable discussion of local pressure groups. Finally, most of the books include accounts of local political controversies. These include among others: a rent rebate scheme in Sheffield; race in Birmingham; language in rural Wales; and the building of a swimming bath in small-town Scotland.

The case-studies provide a considerable amount of information about the working of individual local authorities and are a useful reminder of the diversity of local government practice in Britain. By concentrating on the *local* political process, however, the case-studies avoid the interaction of this process with either national political institutions or local organisations with a national base. The national local government system and the local government trade unions are important examples of these omissions. Even more significant is the whole question of intergovernmental relations between local authorities and central government. These matters are also referred to in part two which then leads into the even broader questions discussed in part three.

THE STRUCTURAL CONTEXT

During the 1970s there was a further change in the direction of interest of urban politics and urban sociology. The neo-Marxist theories of Castells, first published in French, became available in translation (Pickvance 1976; Castells 1977) and students of local government and local politics began to examine the urban basis for the economic structure of the state. From this perspective the study of individual localities was replaced by a consideration of the impact of national (or even international) political and economic structures on localities in general. Once again the discussion, conducted at a highly abstract level, is often difficult to relate to the British experience. Nevertheless, the stimulus it has given to the study of the subject has been considerable.

The subject-matter of the new urban politics is far wider than the traditional coverage of the study of local government. Economic forces, regional agencies for the administration of public services, and the complex interaction of governmental bodies at various levels are recognised as significant contributors to the process of urban policy-making. Urban in this context refers, of course, to the nature of the social and economic framework as a whole and does not exclude the study of rural communities within a predominantly urban society.

It is clear that urban politics implies more than a description of what goes on in cities. But why is it thought necessary to supersede the earlier description of the subject as 'local government' or 'local politics'? In part the answer lies in the problems faced by major urban areas throughout the world. These problems, occasionally erupting in dramatic riots, have focused attention since the 1960s on city politics and in particular on the needs of the 'inner city'. The other part of the answer lies in the growing academic interest in developing a theoretical approach to the nature of urbanism.

These practical policy-making and theoretical approaches have both found difficulties in confining themselves to narrow definitions of their problem. From the policy-making perspective, attempts to tackle the difficulties manifesting themselves in the inner cities in the localised areas in which they are most acute have only revealed the inadequacy of such approaches (Edwards and Batley 1978; Higgins *et al.* 1983). It is now understood that the problems of the inner cities are related to wider changes in the economic and social structure and cannot be tackled except in this context. Both the spatial and the institutional framework for developing inner-city policy must be wider than the limits of an individual local authority. Central government has, therefore, promoted the concept of 'partnership' by bringing together appropriate government departments, county councils and district (sometimes entitled city) councils in the areas worst affected. The partnerships seek to involve private industry as well as public agencies in the regeneration of run-down urban areas. They have not been an unqualified success either in promoting co-operation between the 'partners' or in improving the conditions of the areas in which they were established (Higgins *et al.* 1983:155–69; HC 1983), but they emphasise the broadening horizons for students of local government.

Theoretical approaches to urban politics face difficulties no less intractable, if less severe in personal terms, than those found in the urban areas themselves. Professor Banfield has indicated that ' ... the urban political scientist cannot satisfactorily specify the object he is investigating. What do we mean by "urban" political phenomena? Is urbanism a habitat, a state of mind, the outcome of an interaction between the two, or something else?' (Banfield 1975:viii). The problem is that although an urban area is different from a rural area in visual terms, the differences begin to disintegrate when the focus is turned to social or political matters. Many of the characteristics of village life, for example, have been discovered in urban neighbourhoods, for example in the classic study of Bethnal Green (Young and Willmott 1962). At the same time rural villages have frequently become residential adjuncts of urban areas (Pahl 1975). Industrial change has led to both the decline of traditional industries in older urban areas and the development of new high-technology industries in what Professor Massey has described as a 'swathe of tamed rurality' stretching from Bristol to the Wash (Massey 1983:24). Such considerations have led Dr Saunders to deny the significance of space for the development of urban sociology and to outline a theory with a 'focus on particular social processes which cannot be confined within particular spatial locations' (Saunders 1981:9). These social processes consist of 'social provisions in the context of the relationship between the state, the private sector and the population of consumers' (Saunders 1981:258). The emphasis on the state alerts us to the essentially political nature of this approach. Saunders is a political sociologist but political scientists have reached similar conclusions. Dr Dunleavy adopts a 'content definition of urban politics' that has a 'focus on the politics of collective consumption'. This phrase, taken from Castells, describes the provision of a number of public services. Some, but not all, of these are at present provided by local government. Dunleavy's analysis 'examines decision processes at any relevant institutional level' and takes urban politics away from a narrow concern with local government. Finally, he considers that the 'urban/rural dichotomy has no relevance to the field of urban political analysis' which is concerned with 'functions and activities within a society which is itself wholly urbanised' (Dunleavy 1980a:51–2).

These new approaches to urban politics, which are discussed in more detail in Part three, provide a content that shatters the previous confines of public administration. We find our thoughts directed into new directions in three different ways. First, the institutional focus of the subject is broadened to examine various governmental and non-governmental agencies that impinge on policy-making in localities. Second, the subject-matter takes account of topics that are the concern of other social scientists such as economists and sociologists as well as political scientists. Third, there is a theoretical concern to examine the role of local government and urban politics in the broader context of the economic, social and political structure of the state. These new dimensions give an added interest to the subject and help to explain why it is a growing specialism within political science, but they also provide difficulties for students seeking an introduction to the subject.

CONCLUSION

The literatures deriving from the traditions of public administration, local political studies and urban politics or urban sociology are seldom presented in a form that enables a student to make the necessary connections between the different approaches. It is to this task that the present text is devoted. The references in the text are intended to be a guide to further reading rather than a scholarly display of sources, and for this reason other books are often quoted rather than primary material. In such a broad sweep it becomes even more necessary than usual for students to be aware of the need to allow for the different perspectives of the various authors quoted. The literature varies greatly both in its theoretical perspective and in its claims to possess any such perspective. Whatever the extent of these claims, each item in the literature does, of course, incorporate a particular view of the world. The material presented is partial in both senses of the word: each author can only deal with a part of the total empirical reality; and the selection of that part is influenced by a general system of values. Students should take an author on his or her own merit, and it is in this eclectic spirit that the present book is written. Attempts to integrate all approaches to knowledge through a grand overarching theory are treated with caution. Such attempts are difficult to reconcile with human limitations even though the probability of failure does not necessarily invalidate the usefulness of the attempt. John Stuart Mill made this point eloquently in a book first published in 1843: 'The circumstances . . . which influence the condition and progress of society, are innumerable, and perpetually changing; and though they all change in obedience to causes, and therefore to laws, the multitude of the causes is so great as to defy our limited powers of calculation.' But, he goes on, ' . . . an amount of knowledge quite insufficient for prediction may be most valuable for guidance' (Mill 1900, Book VI: Ch. VI Section 2).

In the century since Mill wrote these words, politics and sociology have developed as major academic subjects, with distinctive theoretical approaches which themselves are the source of much academic controversy. For the present the student should be aware that this text is written both with an awareness that the presentation of 'facts' can never be 'objective', even though every effort is made to ensure accuracy, and with a deep scepticism of attempts to develop a theory to cover all eventualities, as opposed to appropriate theories to explain empirical data in particular circumstances.

NOTE

1. The services provided by local government are described in official reports and much of the literature as its 'functions'. We have preferred to refer to them as 'services' in Chapter 4, retaining the word 'function' to describe the purposes local government serves within the wider political system.

Part One

THE ADMINISTRATIVE CONTEXT

Chapter two

THE STRUCTURE OF LOCAL GOVERNMENT: ORIGINS TO 1970

The origins of local government in Britain are lost not so much in the mists of time as in a fog of detail. Bryan Keith-Lucas describes how Sidney and Beatrice Webb began an analysis of English local government with a preliminary chapter on pre-1835 arrangements. This chapter grew to eleven volumes totalling 4,212 pages. They never fulfilled their original intention (Keith-Lucas 1980:11). The difficulty was the lack of system: local government's lack; not the Webbs'! Every generalisation had to be accompanied by qualifications and exceptions. Every municipal corporation had a separate and different charter; various *ad hoc* bodies each had their own Acts of Parliament; parish councils arose from the operation of the common law without benefit of statute; and Quarter Sessions 'had developed a rich variety of practice' (Keith-Lucas 1980:154). In Scotland, local government services were provided by parishes, county commissioners of supply, and burghs which were 'governed according to their own different constitution'. In contrast with England, the magistrates played only a relatively minor role in local government (Page 1983:42).

Traditional local government arrangements came under increasing pressure from the continuing industrialisation that gathered momentum from the middle of the eighteenth century. People began to move from rural areas into the new industrial towns. Living conditions in the countryside had never approached the Arcadian well-being implied in romantic notions of sturdy peasants following the plough. The cottages were small and damp, with earth floors and none of the cooking or sanitary arrangements that make for domestic comfort. Nevertheless, these conditions did not produce the consequences that became apparent in the industrial towns. The reasons have been strikingly depicted by Cole and Postgate (1961:306):

> Now twelve insanitary houses on a hillside may be a picturesque village, but twelve hundred are a grave nuisance and twelve thousand a pest and a horror. . . . Picturesque courts in small towns become squalid and filthy slums in large cities. Dung, which was still regarded as a marketable

produce, when left to decay in the streets of Lancashire towns, led to results which it is not suitable to describe.

The appalling sanitary conditions were accompanied by an increase in destitution and pauperism as people left the countryside, or were forced to leave by the Enclosure Acts, and sought jobs in the manufacturing towns. Crime, and even sedition, festered in the crowded streets. These evils in the Webbs' view 'completely undermined the old principles of government inherited from time immemorial and embodied in local custom, the Common Law and the Tudor and Stuart legislation' (Webb and Webb 1963:91).

The immediate response was to establish new types of local authorities for specific purposes. These *ad hoc* bodies, as they are frequently described, were created by local or private Acts of Parliament, the scope of which is limited to the locality or interests concerned. This method avoids the full demands upon parliamentary time that is made by the better known procedure for considering general, or public, legislation. The private Acts of Parliament affecting local authorities were numbered in thousands. They included provisions to establish 'some 1,100 turnpike trusts, over 100 poor law boards, and some 300 boards of improvement commissioners' (Keith-Lucas 1980:108). The improvement commissioners were given powers which varied in every Act. In addition to paving, cleansing, lighting the streets and providing watchmen, they might be empowered to deal with a variety of nuisances. These included, in particular instances, the muzzling of bulldogs, the prevention of impropriety on public beaches and early attempts at smoke abatement (Keith-Lucas 1980:115).

Changes in the social environment were not the only consequences of the Industrial Revolution to have importance for the development of local government. There were also changes in the social and political structure that were not accommodated in existing local government institutions. The new manufacturing towns were growing around collections of villages in the north of England far removed from the privileges of the chartered municipal corporations. Growing cities were governed for some local government purposes by the county magistrates: an indignity that the prosperous entrepreneurs resented. The manufacturers found themselves 'excluded alike from the County Commission of the Peace and the Municipal Corporation', and from 'this essentially "caste" struggle between the Tory squires and the radical manufacturers' (Webb and Webb 1963:93) there emerged not only the widening of the parliamentary franchise but also the pressure for change in the urban areas.

One of the first decisions of the reformed Parliament elected in 1833 was to appoint a Royal Commission staffed 'by eager young intellectuals of Whig opinions' to inquire into the municipal corporations (Webb and Webb 1963:141). The consequent Municipal Corporations Act 1835, gave the existing boroughs a new constitution based upon an elected council (Redlich and Hirst 1958:116ff). The larger unincorporated industrial towns could petition for incorporation under this Act and many did so over the following years. Although the county areas remained unreformed until the end of the nineteenth century, the modern system of local government really begins with the creation of the municipal corporations in 1835. Local government is thus clearly intertwined with the growth of the towns.

The middle years of the nineteenth century witnessed a continued preoccupation with the consequencies of urbanisation. Measures concerned with the relief of destitution, public health, sanitation, housing, highways, public order and eventually education were provided through the reforming social legislation of the period. In some cases responsibility was entrusted to the municipal boroughs or the existing county institutions or parishes, but there was also a continuous proliferation of *ad hoc* bodies. Many of these bodies had the right to levy a tax. Their boundaries might overlap; or leave some areas in a curious limbo unattached to any part of the institutional structure. There were, for example, settlements claiming to be 'extra-parochial' and thus outside the jurisdiction of local Poor Law Boards of Guardians (Lipman 1949:69ff). Even after legislative efforts to remove some of the anomalies, the complexity of the system was apparent in the number of authorities existing at a local level. Lipman gives figures for each of the main classes of local government existing in England and Wales in 1870. They included some 3,000 authorities at town, district or county level, and nearly 25,000 smaller authorities such as parishes and school boards (Lipman 1949:72–3). It was no wonder that the position was described in the House of Commons in 1871 as 'a chaos as regards authorities, a chaos as regards rates, and a worse chaos than all as regards areas' (quoted in Thornhill 1971:49).

THE ACTS OF 1888 AND 1894

The confusion of local authorities provided the need for a reorganisation of the structure of local government: the occasion was once more the aftermath of parliamentary reform. The Great Reform Act of 1832 had been followed by the Municipal Corporations Act 1835; the extensions of the franchise in 1867 and 1884 were accompanied by further discussions of local government reform. The 1884 Act, which brought a wider suffrage to the countryside, was particularly significant as it was in the counties that local government retained its unreformed structure. The municipal corporations had 'shown such vigour and enterprise in the use of their new powers' (Redlich and Hirst 1958:201) that the benefits of representative democracy were to be brought to the rural areas. The political initiative was again taken by the radicals: on this occasion the Liberal Unionists led by Joseph Chamberlain, upon whose support the Conservative government of Lord Salisbury depended (Redlich and Hirst 1958; Dunbabin 1963).

The Local Government Bill when introduced to Parliament contained six principal features which may be summarised from Redlich and Hirst (1958:202–3) as follows:

1. The transfer of the administrative powers and duties of the Justices of the Peace to the county council;
2. The division of the county into electoral districts of equal size within which each ratepayer had one vote – voting to be by ballot;
3. London, with the exception of the City of London, to become an administrative county;
4. Within county areas, urban and rural districts to be created;
5. The transfer of certain functions of administrative control from central departments of government to the county councils – decentralisation;
6. A new method of licensing public houses.

The debates that accompanied the passage of this Bill through Parliament reflected two themes which constantly reoccur in discussions about local government reorganisation. First, the relationship between local democracy and central government; and second, the relationship between the larger towns and cities and the surrounding county areas.

The impetus for the Bill, as we have seen, came from two sources: first the need to deal with the growing mass of social legislation and the proliferation of agencies responsible for its administration; and second, the belief in popular democracy. Thus, the arguments from efficiency and democracy were joined in the proposals contained in the Bill; but they were not held by all the protagonists in equal measure. The intention of the government, as remembered in evidence to the Royal Commission on Local Government in 1925, was 'to set up in nearly every County a Local Authority which he called a provincial Parliament' (quoted in Hampton 1966:463). The provincial parliament would relieve the central government in Westminster and Whitehall of much of the detail associated with the growth of the interventionist state. This dream of decentralisation as a means to administrative efficiency continues to the present day, but it always wakes to the reality of political control.

The extension of the suffrage for parliamentary elections meant that working-class voters had to be accommodated within the 'pale of the constitution' in Gladstone's well-known phrase: the extension of this principle to local elections raised the possibility of working-class control in some councils. This was the real fear behind the arguments about the declining calibre of the new county councillors compared with that of the magistrates of Quarter Sessions (Dunbabin 1965; Dearlove 1979:Ch. 4): 'democratic alterations were widely believed to be dangerous, and expected to lead to extravagance, inefficiency, or even rapacity and disorder' (Dunbabin 1963:227). For similar reasons the House of Lords had insisted on the introduction of aldermen to the councils of the municipal boroughs established by the 1835 Act. Aldermen were indirectly elected by the councillors for a six-year term and comprised one-quarter of the total council membership. The intention was to add 'continuity or stability' to the council (Redlich and Hirst 1958:132). The aldermanic principle was carried into the new county councils, and there were other indications that power would not easily be dispersed: 'the provisions for decentralisation ... were whittled away, and in the end very little was left of the grand scheme of devolution' (Redlich and Hirst 1958:207). There was hesitation, too, in providing for decentralisation within the counties. The proposals for district councils within the counties 'seemed to be premature' (Redlich and Hirst 1958:207). They were withdrawn at that time but enacted in 1894 along with provisions 'to introduce local self-government into rural parishes' (Redlich and Hirst 1958:216).

The other major change which developed as the Bill passed through Parliament related to the position of the towns and cities within county areas. The government had recognised that the largest of these had a claim to continued autonomy and proposed to exclude ten of them from the jurisdiction of their surrounding counties. They were to become boroughs with the status of counties – or county boroughs. Following parliamentary pressure, the population which would attract this privileged status was reduced to 50,000 to allow for the claims both of the boroughs with ancient histories and the growing manufacturing towns. By the time the Bill was enacted sixty-one boroughs – including a number which had a population below 50,000 – had received county status. The exception had become the rule; nearly half the counties had lost their largest urban centres; the division between rural and urban local government had hardened in a form which caused controversy for nearly a century, and which is still reflected in the current structure (Hampton 1966:464–5).

The structure of local government existing immediately before the changes in the 1960s and 1970s was, therefore, largely settled by the end of the nineteenth century. The system was different in London from the rest of England and Wales, and differed again in Scotland and, of course, in Northern Ireland.

ENGLAND AND WALES

England and Wales were divided into counties each of which contained a number of districts variously known as municipal, or non-county, boroughs, urban districts or rural districts depending on a combination of size, type of area, and historical circumstances. The rural districts were further divided into parishes. The main services provided by local government were divided between the counties and the districts with the parish councils, where they existed, looking after footpaths, parish halls and similar 'parochial' matters. Completely outside this county structure were the county boroughs in cities and larger towns. The county boroughs were responsible for all local government services within their boundaries.

In London, the 1888 Act had created the London County Council (LCC) as an administrative county comprising parts of Middlesex, Surrey and Kent. The picture was completed in 1899 by the creation of twenty-eight London boroughs within the LCC area. The City of London itself, the square mile comprising the financial and commercial heart of the capital, retained its ancient privileges and independence.

SCOTLAND

Developments in Scotland followed a rather different pattern from that of England and Wales. The Royal Burghs (Scotland) Act 1833, established elected burgh councils, thus anticipating the 1835 Act in England and Wales. Not all Scottish burghs were covered by the 1833 Act, but 'it was open to any community of 2,000 or more inhabitants to apply for a charter' (Keating and Midwinter 1983:95). In 1889, the counties were given additional responsibilities and subsequently the four largest cities became counties of cities – the equivalent of the English county boroughs. There was no equivalent of the 1894 legislation that created the districts in England and Wales. Further major change awaited the Local Government (Scotland) Act 1929. This Act 'created a local government system that persisted for 45 years, until reorganisation in 1975' (Page 1983:43). There were 'five kinds of local authority, each with its elected council: counties of cities (4); large burghs (21); small burghs (176); counties (33); districts (196)' (Wheatley 1969:26). The large burghs retained more functions than the small which had given up 'most of their important functions to the surrounding county council' (Wheatley 1969:25). The districts existing in the rural areas following 1929 were not as powerful as their English counterparts. They were concerned with only limited amenity services unless the county council delegated something more substantial. The parishes, for local government purposes, were abolished in 1929.

IRELAND

The origins of Irish local government echo the history of the three other countries of the United Kingdom. Some elements may be traced to medieval times or even earlier, but in the main local government is a product of nineteenth-century urbanisation. In Ireland, however, the position has been complicated by the failure of the attempted union with

Britain. The structure of Irish local government, in common with all Irish politics, must be considered against the backcloth of continuous struggle between Unionists and Nationalists.

Municipal reform came later in Ireland than in either England or Scotland; and when the Act was passed in 1840, the new councils were given more restricted powers (Roche 1982:33–4). Similarly, major reforms were not enacted until the Local Government (Ireland) Act in 1898. The delay from the earlier English legislation was due to 'unionist fears of nationalist ambitions and spendthrift councils' (Roche 1982:45). The Act introduced county councils, county boroughs and county districts on the English pattern (Rowat 1980:289). Parish councils were not created.

When Ireland was divided under the government of Ireland Act 1920, control of local government in the six counties of the north was given to the Stormont government in Belfast. The Nationalists held majorities on some local bodies which led the Unionist majority in the province to disband several councils and to withdraw the system of voting by proportional representation that had been introduced in 1919. The systematic manipulation of the franchise and local authority boundaries continued as the Unionists used their control of local government as a source of patronage. One man, one vote, was not conceded in local government in Northern Ireland until 1969 (Arthur 1980:108).

THE EARLY YEARS OF THE MODERN SYSTEM

The division between counties and county boroughs established in England and Wales in 1888 did not provide a settled and agreed pattern for the future. The urban areas continued to grow in population and as they did so they claimed an improvement in their status within the local government structure. By 1922 the original sixty-one county boroughs 'had increased to 82 and, by new creations and extensions, about 350,000 acres, with a population of 3 million people, had been lopped off the counties and incorporated into the county boroughs' (Keith-Lucas and Richards 1978:199). The counties were always liable as they grew, therefore, to lose their most populous and most highly rated areas to new or expanded county boroughs. A similar, if less dramatic, process 'was taking place at a lower level; new urban districts were being carved out of the rural districts' (Keith-Lucas and Richards 1978:200). Dissatisfaction with this position led to the establishment of a Royal Commission in 1923 and after it reported in 1925 it was made more difficult to achieve county borough status. Doncaster, in 1927, became the last new creation until further measures of reorganisation in some major urban areas began in the late 1950s. In 1929 legislation provided for each county council to review the boundaries of its districts every ten years (Keith-Lucas and Richards 1978:202).

For thirty years the structure of local government in England and Wales remained untouched. There were significant changes in the services provided, but these are more properly discussed in Chapter 4. The lack of change in the structure did not imply satisfaction. The disputes between the counties and county boroughs continued as the population began to move out of the industrial cities into surrounding suburban estates or commuter villages in county areas. The ebbs and flows of population movement could not be matched by changes in a local government structure which had become fixed in the pattern established in the nineteenth century. There were constant discussions, and some attempts to produce new proposals, but all foundered upon the entrenched conservatism of the existing authorities with respect to their boundaries. There was also the underlying awareness of senior politicians that changes in local government boundaries might have unpredictable effects on parliamentary constituencies (Brand 1974:132; Alexander 1982b:19). Few felt the risk worth taking.

THE REORGANISATION YEARS

Every aspect of local government in Britain was placed under scrutiny, and many changes were made, in the two decades following 1960. The territorial structure, the distribution of responsibilities, the internal organisation and the system of finance were each examined. The proposals that emerged were different for London, the rest of England, Wales and Scotland: to say nothing of the difficult position which developed in Northern Ireland. The amount of detail facing the student is immense. We will continue to concentrate on the structure leaving the other matters to later chapters, but a few general remarks may help to clear the ground before the discussions over boundaries are outlined.

The general analysis of the need for local government reorganisation was presented in straightforward terms relating to changes in the socio-economic geography of the country. The growth of suburbia and the use of the motor car, it was argued, were making the old boundaries irrelevant for planning purposes and a cause of friction between existing local authorities. In addition, many of the authorities were considered too small for existing or possible future purposes. These inadequacies of structure in turn were thought to have a bad effect on the efficient delivery of local government services, and on the ability of citizens to understand the role of local democracy. This analysis was presented very clearly in the Report of the Royal Commission on Local Government in England (Redcliffe-Maud 1969:Ch. 3), but it is there to a greater or lesser extent in all the discussions of the period (cf. Wheatley 1969).

Beyond this analysis there were more complex considerations. There was a concern in many quarters that local authorities should be controlled by officers and councillors more in tune with the needs and methods of local industry and commerce. There was also an interest in integrating local authorities more closely with the developing machinery for economic management at both a regional and a national level. These aims required larger local authorities irrespective of the more usual arguments advanced in favour of reorganisation (Dearlove 1979). Support for these generalisations will be given as we proceed, but we should be aware that *descriptions* of institutional change need to be understood in the light of political and theoretical considerations.

LONDON

The restructuring of the British economy in the depression years between the two world wars was accompanied by a movement of population into the south-east of the country. The population of Greater London increased by about 2 million (Cullingworth 1972:23) and many were housed in new developments beyond the existing LCC area. As a result, Greater London extended into the surrounding counties and contained in total '117 separate organs, of which all but 4 are directly elected' (Robson 1948:165–6).

The Royal Commission on Local Government in Greater London was established in 1957 'to examine the present system and working of local government in the Greater London area; to recommend whether any, and if so what, changes in the local government structure and the distribution of local authority functions in the area, or in any part of it, would better secure effective and convenient local government ... ' (Herbert 1960:I). The reasons for the establishment of the Royal Commission lay in the continued growth of London and the confusion of local government institutions that had resulted. The occasion for its appointment was the coming to office as Minister of Housing and Local Government of Mr Henry Brooke in January 1957. Mr Brooke was a former leader of the Conservative opposition on the LCC and he was receptive to the advice given by his civil servants that an examination of London government was necessary. The decision was strongly opposed by the Labour Party who suspected the Conservative minister of being more concerned to destroy the Labour-controlled LCC than to reform local government. A later assessment of the decision found no evidence to support these suspicions (Rhodes 1970:233–5).

The Royal Commission recommended the creation of a Greater London authority extending over an area with a population of some 8.5 million – roughly double the population of the LCC area. Within this area they recommended fifty-two London boroughs with populations ranging from about 100,000 to 250,000. The exception was the City of London with a population of less than 5,000 (Herbert 1960:233–6).

The proposals of the Herbert Commission were opposed by groups other than the Labour Party. First, the existing local authorities argued for the retention of the status quo; second, some Conservative Members of Parliament sought to retain the existing system as far as possible in such areas as Surrey; third, groups concerned with some services – particularly education – pointed out weaknesses in the proposals as far as their service was concerned (Rhodes 1970:120). The government's response was to introduce changes with respect to both areas and services in the Bill based on the Royal Commission Report. First, some peripheral areas were excluded from the new Greater London area (see Map 2.1); second, the number of boroughs was reduced to thirty-two (plus the City of London which received the responsibilities of a

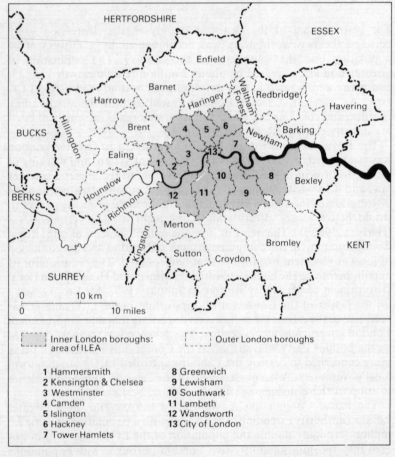

MAP 2.1 Greater London since 1965 (*Source*: Reproduced from Alexander 1982b:23)

TABLE 2.1   Local government in London (1981)

	Area (hectares)	Population
Greater London	157,944	6,713,165
Inner London		
City of London	274	5,864
London Boroughs		
Camden	2,171	172,014
Hackney	1,948	180,434
Hammersmith & Fulham	1,617	148,447
Haringey	3,031	203,553
Islington	1,489	160,890
Kensington & Chelsea	1,195	138,837
Lambeth	2,727	246,426
Lewisham	3,473	231,324
Newham	3,637	209,494
Southwark	2,880	211,858
Tower Hamlets	1,973	142,841
Wandsworth	3,492	254,898
Westminster, City of	2,158	191,098
Outer London		
London Boroughs		
Barking & Dagenham	3,419	149,786
Barnet	8,953	293,436
Bexley	6,065	215,233
Brent	4,421	253,275
Bromley	15,179	296,539
Croydon	8,658	317,980
Ealing	5,547	279,846
Enfield	8,115	258,770
Greenwich	4,744	211,840
Harrow	5,082	196,571
Havering	11,776	240,849
Hillingdon	11,036	229,913
Hounslow	5,852	200,829
Kingston upon Thames	3,756	132,957
Merton	3,796	166,100
Redbridge	5,647	226,280
Richmond upon Thames	5,525	159,693
Sutton	4,342	169,343
Waltham Forest	3,966	215,947

Source: Census 1981 County report Greater London (part 1) (HMSO 1982)

borough but retained its own status) (see Table 2.1); third, education became the responsibility of a new *ad hoc* body in Inner London and of the enlarged boroughs in Outer London. The Bill was enacted in 1963 and came into effect in April 1965. At the first elections, Labour gained a majority on the GLC and in twenty of the thirty-two London boroughs (Rhodes 1970:222). Subsequently, the GLC showed that it had indeed become more marginal than the previous LCC and control fluctuated between the Labour and Conservative parties.

The reorganisation of local government in London provided the forerunner of the reorganisations in other parts of the country in the 1970s. The nettle had been grasped: the sting had not proved unbearable. But had the reorganisation in London achieved its objectives? In a careful review of the first few years after reorganisation, a group of academics from the London School of Economics assessed the performance of the new London local authorities (Rhodes 1972). In a final chapter the editor evaluated the experience against the objectives identified by the Herbert Royal Commission: 'administrative efficiency and the health of representative government' (Rhodes 1972:457-8). Rhodes suggested that the two-tier structure had been related to these two objectives. The new strategic authority, the GLC, had been created to improve the efficiency of strategic planning whereas the boroughs were to maintain closer links between local government and citizens in the provision of more personal services. Rhodes considered that there had been an improved performance in services which were the sole responsibility of either the GLC or the boroughs: but of those services which were shared 'only the group of transportation functions seems to show any marked advantages; over both housing and planning there hang certain question marks' (Rhodes 1972:468). As far as local democracy was concerned, no evidence was clearly discernible either for an improvement or for a deterioration. The councillors were drawn heavily from people who had served on the previous local authorities: and most of the public remained ignorant and apathetic towards local government (Rhodes 1972:420-1).

ENGLAND

The Royal Commission on Local Government in England established in 1966 was restricted in its terms of reference to provincial England. London, as we have just seen, had recently been reorganised. Scotland, Wales and Northern Ireland were also treated separately. Scotland had its own Royal Commission established in the same year; in Wales consultations had already begun leading to the appointment of a working party (Wood 1976:119; Alexander 1928b:29); and Northern Ireland was still governed in these matters from Stormont.

Bruce Wood has written of the long- and short-term factors coinciding in 1966 which caused a Royal Commission to be appointed in this controversial area. The long-term reasons were the perceived weaknesses of the existing structure of local government in relation to socio-economic geography, size of authorities, and complex division of powers. The short-term factors included the election in 1964 of a Labour government committed to an administrative reform of the institutions of government; the appointment of a reforming minister – R H S Crossman – to the Ministry of Housing and Local Government; and the support for the idea of reform that he received from his senior civil servants (Wood 1976:176–7). At first this support was for a cautious continuation of the patching of the existing system. This had begun in 1958 when a Boundary Commission had been appointed to consider piecemeal structural reform in various parts of the country. Crossman eventually became convinced of the need for more radical action: the Boundary Commission was dissolved and the Royal Commission appointed (Alexander 1982b:18–19).

The Royal Commission was chaired by Sir John Maud (he became Lord Redcliffe-Maud in 1967) who was already chairing a departmental committee on management in local government. Of the other members, only two were completely new to the problems of local government structure. The rest included such experienced practitioners as Dr A H Marshall, a former treasurer of the city of Coventry, and T Dan Smith, a former leader of the city council of Newcastle upon Tyne – as well as Dame Evelyn (Baroness from 1966) Sharp who had been Permanent Secretary at the Ministry of Housing and Local Government when Crossman arrived in 1964 (Wood 1976:40–1). The membership also included Derek Senior, who had for many years been advocating a fundamental reorganisation of local government. Lord Redcliffe-Maud considered that Senior was the only one of the eleven commissioners who had made his mind up before the first meeting of the Royal Commission (Wood 1976:8). Certainly he was not convinced of the soundness of the Royal Commission's eventual recommendations and submitted a Memorandum of Dissent as long as the majority Report.

The Royal Commission began by analysing the need for change and the challenges that local authorities would face in the future (Redcliffe-Maud 1969:Vol.1 Ch. III). Given the existing climate of optimism in Britain in the mid-1960s the challenges foreseen were those of growth. The demographic trends indicated a growth in population of 30 per cent by the end of the century with a consequent substantial increase in the proportion of children. Car ownership was expected to increase 'at a very much faster rate than population' (Redcliffe-Maud 1969:Vol.1 14). Finally, the Royal Commission foresaw a general demand for higher standards in local government services. The expectations of growth were not fully realised. The number of births soon began to fall dramatically – by the early 1980s it was only two-thirds of the figure reached twenty years earlier; car ownership did not increase at the expected rate – due in part to the sharp increase in petrol prices in the early 1970s; the demand for higher standards conflicted from the mid-1970s with central government's belief that local government expenditure needed to be curtailed in line with a monetarist approach to economic policy. Such mistaken prognostications do not necessarily invalidate the Royal

Commission's conclusions, but they warn of the difficulties facing any attempt to order human affairs for the future.

The Royal Commission did not believe that the existing local authorities were in a position to meet the challenges they had identified. There were weaknesses in respect of boundaries, the administration of certain services, and the workings of local democracy (Redcliffe-Maud 1969: Vol.1 25–31). Each of these factors had two aspects (see Fig. 2.1). First, they deplored the separation of town and country which was reflected in the distinction between county boroughs and county councils, and in the existence of urban and rural districts in the county areas. The resulting conflicts between county boroughs and county councils had 'dominated the work of local government for many years past' (Redcliffe-Maud 1969: Vol.1 26). Second, the division of responsibility within the county areas was seen as a weakness; and many local authorities were seen as too small to accept the responsibilities appropriate to the needs of their areas. There was also a great variation in the size of local authorities of the same status. Counties ranged in population from about 2 million (Lancashire) to less that 30,000 (Rutland); county boroughs ranged from over 1 million (Birmingham) to 33,000 (Canterbury) – less than the minimum population stipulated in 1888. Districts varied in population from over 120,000 to under 2,000, with one-third failing in the range between 10,000 and 20,000 (all figures from Redcliffe-Maud 1969:Vol 1 Annex 4). Third, there was the question of local democracy. The Royal Commission considered that the 'relationship between local authorities and the public is not satisfactory' (Redcliffe-Maud 1969:Vol.1 28). They drew attention to the difficulties of knowing which local authority was responsible for a

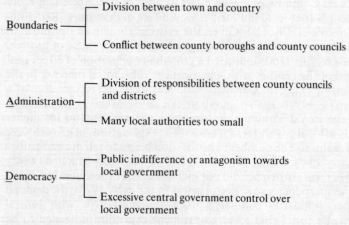

FIG. 2.1 The Royal Commission's criticisms of the existing local government structure in England

particular service – especially in the county areas. The inadequacies in the existing structure of local government also meant that central government needed to keep too close a watch on the provision of local services, thus reducing the scope for local decision-making.

The recommendations of the Royal Commission were based upon three premises. First, local authorities should be bigger and more uniform in size. Second, they should be all-purpose (unitary) in character. Third, they should be based wherever possible on existing boundaries in order to maintain continuity and build upon traditional loyalties. The proposals accepted by the majority as flowing from these principles provided for fifty-eight unitary authorities with populations increasing in a steady progression from 195,000 (Halifax) to 1,081,000 (Sheffield and South Yorkshire). In three areas of the country the unitary principle was considered impractical because of the heavy concentrations of population within a continuous built-up area. These were designated as metropolitan areas and were given a two-tier structure of metropolitan counties and districts. The three areas comprised SELNEC (south-east Lancashire and north-east Cheshire) with a population of 3,232,000; the West Midlands (3,014,000); and Merseyside (2,063,000). The smallest metropolitan county had, therefore, a population approximately double that of the largest unitary authority. The twenty metropolitan districts ranged in population from 176,000 (Warrington) to 1,314,000 (Birmingham) (see Fig. 2.2).

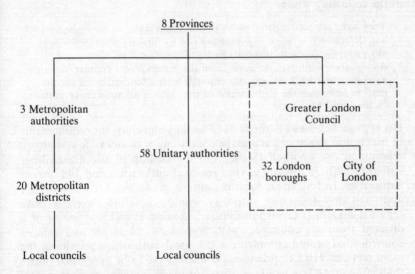

Note: London had been reorganized in 1965

FIG. 2.2 Structure proposed by the Royal Commission on Local Government in England 1966–69

In addition to these main units of local government, the Royal Commission proposed both provincial and local councils. The eight provincial councils were required to 'settle the broad economic land use and investment framework for the planning and development policies of operational authorities' (Redcliffe-Maud 1969:Vol 1 74). They were to be indirectly elected from the main local authorities. In this instance Greater London would have been included within a provincial area. Finally, local councils were to be formed for each former borough, urban district or parish council area in the new unitary authorities, and where wanted in the metropolitan areas. They were to have parish council responsibilities. The variation in size would have been enormous as the existing parish councils would have been joined by such cities as Sheffield as 'local councils'. Neither the proposals for provinces nor for local councils were accepted by either the Labour or Conservative governments. The proposals for provinces were referred to the newly established Royal Commission on the Constitution, while the proposals for local councils were thought to add too much extra work to the already formidable task of local government reorganisation.

Senior
Derek Senior accepted the analysis of the problems facing local government, indeed in some ways he could count it as his own, but he did not accept the possibility of effective unitary authorities. He explained the difference in approach between himself and his colleagues in the following words:

> They have adopted a principle of organisation – the unitary principle – and determined a range of *population* size for unitary authorities by analysing the theoretical requirements of functional efficiency and democratic viability in isolation from the geographical context in which local government must operate – though with a tender regard for the need to 'maintain the momentum' of the existing administrative pattern (Senior 1969:5).

His approach, based on 'the facts of social geography, the requirements of functional effectiveness and the conditions of democratic viability in relation to one another' (Senior 1969:5) led him to adopt a two-tier structure with 35 directly elected regional authorities and 148 district authorities. In four areas local conditions made him favour a unitary approach and the same authority would, therefore, 'exercise both regional and district responsibilities' (Senior 1969:159). Senior also differed from his colleagues with respect to the larger and smaller councils that would complement the local authorities providing the main services. His five provincial councils were to be appointed rather than indirectly elected and concerned primarily with intergovernmental relations. At a 'grass-roots' level he proposed a series of common councils without statutory duties that were similar in conception to those later established in Scotland.

WALES

Discussions of local government reorganisation in Wales were not conducted in an atmosphere of concern over population growth – quite the contrary. The population was distributed in a very uneven pattern with the concentration in four county boroughs of the south providing a contrast to the scattered and declining population of north and mid-Wales: 'six of the thirteen counties were experiencing falling populations and most of the others were only just holding their own' (Wood 1976:117). These circumstances led the Boundary Commission established in 1958 to recommend radical changes for Wales in 1962. These would have extended the county boroughs of Cardiff and Newport; made minor adjustments to the boundaries of Swansea; demoted Merthyr Tydfil to a non-county borough; and reduced the number of counties to seven. Ministerial caution and the General Election of 1964 ensured that these proposals were not implemented.

The incoming Labour government created a separate Welsh Office with a Cabinet minister at its head in line with the long-standing Scottish Office. One of the first actions of the new department was to begin consultations about local government reorganisation. A working party consisting of senior civil servants and an academic political scientist was appointed. These consultations resulted in a White Paper (Welsh Office 1967) completely at variance with the views developing in the English Royal Commission. The three main county boroughs were to be retained and five counties were to replace the existing thirteen. Within the counties 36 districts instead of 164 would form a second tier. The White Paper thus retained both the separation of town and countryside and the two-tier system – both of which were criticised by Redcliffe-Maud. Crossman 'regarded the Welsh proposals as reactionary, inadequate and miserable' (Keith-Lucas and Richards 1978:218) and the Labour government began a fresh search for a solution more in keeping with the principles being adopted in England. The outcome was a proposal to create three unitary authorities in Glamorgan and Monmouthshire which would replace the proposed system of counties and county boroughs in those areas (Wood 1976:124–5). Another General Election in 1970 intervened before these proposals could be implemented.

SCOTLAND

The Royal Commission on Local Government in Scotland (Wheatley 1969) followed the same broad analysis of the ills of the system as their English counterparts, but their prescriptions were different and in some ways more radical. Wheatley was heavily influenced by evidence given by the departments of the Scottish Office and particularly by the planners of the Scottish Development Department (Keating and

Midwinter 1983:97; Page 1983:44). The Royal Commission recommended a two-tier structure based on the concept of the enlarged city region. The arguments were similar to those Senior had used in criticising the English unitary authorities: all-purpose authorities would reflect neither the administrative needs of the services, nor the boundaries of community feeling (Wheatley 1969:164–5). They recommended, therefore, seven regional authorities which would be responsible for most of the major local authority services and thirty-seven district authorities. In addition they recommended the creation of community councils 'to express the voice of a neighbourhood' (Wheatley 1969:206). Community councils would have no statutory functions. Once again the correspondence with Senior's views is clear.

NORTHERN IRELAND

The population of Northern Ireland is about 1.5 million which is less than the larger units of local government in England or the Strathclyde region in Scotland. Together with the political background in the province, this smallness of scale has complicated discussions of local government reorganisation. First, there has always been the option of providing local services directly from Stormont or some other provincial agency. Second, any change in the existing structure might affect the distribution of power between the two rival communities.

When discussions on reorganisation began in the mid-1960s both these considerations were present. The proposals for 'a simplified, single-tier, strong local government system with a wide range of powers based on twelve to eighteen "area councils"' (Arthur 1980:97) were strongly opposed by local interests who wished to retain their sectarian control in the existing small local authorities. When the disturbances began with a fresh fury in 1969, the Unionist domination of local government was a focal point for discontent. The allocation of public authority housing produced a 'patently sectarian decision' which 'ignited the powder-keg' (Roche 1982:290). As part of the government's response to these disturbances, all housing responsibilities were removed from local authorities and a review body was established 'with three Protestant and three Catholic members under the Chairmanship of Patrick Macrory' (Rowat 1980:296).

The Macrory review considered the existing proposals for reshaping local government in Northern Ireland but they were not limited to these in making their recommendations. They looked at both the Redcliffe-Maud and Wheatley approaches and concluded that the principles of the latter 'were more appropriate to the circumstances of Northern Ireland' (Macrory 1970:24). When the review was completed in 1970, Macrory recommended the creation of twenty-six district councils to provide mainly environmental health, cleansing, recreational and other services able to operate on a similar small scale. The major services of local government, including child care, education, planning and roads, were to become the responsibility of the appropriate departments of the Stormont government. In effect this produced a two-tier structure based on the Wheatley approach of regions and districts with Stormont acting as a 'region'. Of course, only the district councils would normally be thought of as 'local government'. The Macrory proposals also received 'a rough ride' (Arthur 1980:98) but they nevertheless formed the basis of the Local Government (NI) Act 1972.

CONCLUSION

By 1970 proposals for reorganising the structure of local government had been suggested for every part of the United Kingdom; but only in London had the changes been introduced. It is a good year, therefore, at which to take stock of the various proposals and identify a number of common themes. First, there was a movement towards larger units of local government. The small units based upon traditional settlements or rural areas were to be replaced by wider areas with larger populations. Second, there was a general acceptance of the need for a multi-tier structure if the demands of democracy were to be reconciled with the administrative or functional need for larger units. The recommendations of the Redcliffe-Maud Commission were the major exception to this generalisation. They favoured unitary authorities for most of England though, as we shall explain in the next chapter, this recommendation was never implemented. Even in this case, Redcliffe-Maud recommended a two-tier structure in the three major conurbations outside London. The population of these three conurbations was over 8 million which when added to a similar population in London meant that approximately one-third of the population of England would have been within areas covered by a two-tier structure of local government. The special pressures and problems of the major urban areas form the third common theme to emerge. London was the subject of a separate Royal Commission. In the other areas the larger cities and conurbations proved difficult to incorporate in a wider uniform pattern. The three metropolitan areas in England and the county boroughs of South Wales were exceptions to the general recommendations for those two countries. In Scotland the size of the recommended region centred on Glasgow caused considerable controversy. These three themes of scale, single versus multi-tier, and the special problems of the conurbations will reoccur both in the following chapter and when we discuss the services provided by local government in more detail in Chapter 4.

Chapter three

THE STRUCTURE OF LOCAL GOVERNMENT: 1970 TO THE PRESENT

The previous chapter illustrated both the complexity of the development of the present structures of local government in the United Kingdom and the common trends which emerged during the reorganisation years. In this chapter we shall outline the present position in each country and consider the response to the reorganisation of the early 1970s. First, however, we need to consider further the principles which informed the debates about local government structure.

The government White Paper issued as a prelude to the reorganisation of local government in England outlined the aims which a new system should incorporate:

> A vigorous local democracy means that authorities must be given real functions – with powers of decision and the ability to take action without being subjected to excessive regulation by central government through financial or other controls. Local authority areas should be related to areas within which people have a common interest – through living in a recognisable community, through the links of employment, shopping or social activities, or through history and tradition. Local boundaries, the allocation of responsibilities and the system as a whole should be understood and accepted as sensible by electors, by members and by officers. And, above all else, a genuine local democracy implies that decisions should be taken – and should be seen to be taken – as locally as possible (DOE 1971:6).

At the start of the next paragraph the White Paper summed up the problems inherent in this approach with a statement of the classic political dilemma: 'Practical realities prevent all these aims being fully achieved together' (DOE 1971:6). The boundaries suggested by history and tradition, for example, while appearing sensible to the electors, might bear little relationship to the patterns of employment or shopping that were appropriate to officers preparing a transportation system. Nor is the phrase 'recognisable community' capable of a precise meaning. Research conducted for both the Redcliffe-Maud and Wheatley Commissions indicated that people recognised extremely localised communities as a basis for their social life. Such communities might provide a basis for a neighbourhood approach to management, or for some development of the parish council concept (Boaden *et al.* 1982:Ch.3), but there was no possibility of using them as the basis for a reorganised local government structure.

The conflicting demands of efficient service provision, democratic involvement, and local historical or community traditions led to different proposals for dealing with the perceived shortcomings of the existing local government system. In part these various proposals reflected the circumstances of the areas concerned, whether they were densely or sparsely populated for instance; but in part they represented the different emphasis in the proposals on the objectives being pursued. Senior, for example, was primarily concerned with the socio-geographical areas that would provide the best focus for the services needed by city regions. The Redcliffe-Maud Commission on the other hand – and later the Conservative government – placed more weight on the importance of established boundaries.

After the reorganisations had been completed there were six main local government systems in the United Kingdom: three in England, together with separate approaches in Wales, Scotland and Northern Ireland. The structure adopted in London in 1965 has been described in the previous chapter. The changes introduced in other areas will be discussed below.

ENGLAND

The Labour ministers who received the Redcliffe-Maud Report were willing to accept the recommendations in principle and issued a White Paper in February 1970 outlining their proposals. The most important variation from Redcliffe-Maud as far as the structure of local government was concerned was the addition of two further metro-politan areas. These comprised the West Yorkshire area and an area based on South Hampshire and the Isle of Wight. In both cases the reasons advanced were concerned with the need for co-ordinating planning policies in these urbanised areas (MLG 1970:12–13). The government was defeated in the General Election of June 1970 before further progress could be made on proposals which would have added another 3.3 million people to those already to be covered by two-tier local government. With these additions the unitary principle, sup-posedly at the heart of the Redcliffe-Maud recommendations, had been rejected for nearly 20 million people out of England's population of approximately 45 million.

The incoming Conservative government announced a reopening of consultations on local government reorganisation. The proposals in the

Labour White Paper were rejected as the Conservatives intended to 'provide for the existence of a two-tier structure' (Conservative election manifesto quoted in Wood 1976:100). A White Paper outlined their proposals in February 1971 and legislation followed in the parliamentary session of 1971-72; but before looking in detail at the consequent Local Government Act 1972, a few general considerations need to be discussed.

First, there is the question of how far the Conservative proposals which form the basis of the present structure were consistent with the Redcliffe-Maud analysis. The central concept of the unitary authority had been rejected, but in other respects Wood suggests that there was more consistency (Wood 1976:104–5). The general diagnosis of the weaknesses of the existing structure followed the usual pattern of a criticism of small outdated local authorities: 'There are too many authorities and many of them are too small . . . ' (DOE 1971:6). The size of population accepted as necessary to fulfil the functions of the new major authorities was within the range 250,000 to 1 million. Also the necessity for a separate structure for local government in some of the conurbations was accepted, and the Conservative White Paper criticised 'the artificial separation of big towns from their surrounding hinterlands' (DOE 1971:6). Even allowing for the similarities in language in these respects, however, the Conservative proposals sometimes had a different content from the Redcliffe-Maud approach. The Conservatives 'were unwilling to interfere any more than was absolutely necessary with existing county boundaries' (Alexander 1982b:38). This attachment to the historical counties led to tighter boundaries for the metropolitan areas and to the maintenance of some boundaries which separated major urban centres from their surrounding region. In these cases Wood concluded that 'the "shire county" principle overrode that of the ending of the urban–rural dichotomy' (Wood 1976:106; cf. Brand 1974:80). There were also important differences in the allocation of services to the different tiers but these will be considered in Chapter 4.

Second, there is the question of the parliamentary process through which the Bill became an Act. In his careful assessment of this process, Wood shows how the existing authorities kept up their pressure for local interests – essentially for as much of the existing structure as they could maintain intact – until the last possible moment for amendments (Wood 1976:Ch. VI). The government responded to this pressure: the Bill differed in some respects from the White Paper, and the Bill itself was constantly amended as it went through Parliament. A major amendment was accepted by the government even at the report stage in the House of Lords' consideration of the Bill: the Isle of Wight was separated from Hampshire and retained a separate county council (Wood 1976:151). The government showed itself willing to accept a large number of amendments of detail and a few of substance affecting boundaries as long as they could maintain the principle of a two-tier structure.

Third, it is instructive to consider how far the final form of local government reorganisation in England was affected by party politics. There are several aspects to this question. In the first place, there was undoubtedly a major difference of approach between the Labour and Conservative governments. Labour favoured a unitary system based on the experience of the county boroughs while the Conservatives preferred a two-tier structure based on the existing counties. The result of the parliamentary election of 1970 was, therefore, crucial to the final outcome. We need to consider, however, whether the different approaches of the two parties were based on a rational assessment of party advantage. Here the evidence is less conclusive. The Labour proposals to extend urban boundaries to take in surrounding suburban and rural areas in a pattern of unitary authorities threatened the traditional Labour dominance in the major cities in the non-metropolitan areas. On the other hand, the Conservative proposals, while abolishing the Labour strongholds in the county boroughs, retained districts based on towns and cities that Labour could be expected to control – and created large metropolitan counties which Labour could dominate in favourable years. Thus the proportion of the population, as opposed to the number of local authorities, under Labour control might be substantial. Following the elections in the early 1980s Labour controlled all six metropolitan counties together with the GLC. The party considerations, in this as in so many other aspects of local government reorganisation, seemed to have been based more on an assessment of the past rather than on considerations for the future. The Labour Party was influenced by the county boroughs and the Conservatives by the counties because that was where their current political strength rested in local government. The prospect for the future authorities was less carefully examined. Local government reorganisation was also extremely unpopular among people concerned with the smaller local authorities which would be abolished. Many of these people were conservative by either party or inclination – or both. The Conservatives faced strong opposition within their own ranks to any major changes in boundaries: they could only contain this opposition by their readiness to accept detailed amendments throughout the process.

THE 1972 ACT

The Local Government Act 1972 provides for a two-tier structure throughout England with the addition in some places of a third tier of parish councils. The two-tier principle has been strictly adhered to even when there seemed little justification for it in particular circumstances. In the most extreme case, the county of the Isle of Wight is divided into two districts even though this creates three local authorities for a population of 100,000 (Alexander 1982a:26–7). The two tiers are not intended to exist in a hierarchical relationship to each other. Each tier

37

has its separate responsibilities. There is no provision for a regional or provincial level of local government.

The distinction between the metropolitan and non-metropolitan areas lies in the distribution of services between the counties and their districts. In metropolitan areas the districts are responsible for education, social services and libraries. In non-metropolitan areas these responsibilities are retained by the county. This distinction is linked to the different population size of the various units of local government and it will be discussed further in Chapter 4. For the present we may note the importance of the distinction for the status of local authorities. The tier of local government which accepts responsibility for the major spending departments of education and social services becomes dominant in financial terms and consequently in status. As early as 1976, the Layfield Committee was distinguishing not between counties and districts, but between 'major spending authorities' and the rest in their discussions of the possible introduction of a local income tax (Layfield 1976:196). The 1972 Act created, therefore, four rather than two types of local authority in England. These can be thought of as two separate systems with the non-metropolitan counties and metropolitan districts forming the core authorities (see Fig. 3.1) The first local councils under the 1972 Act were elected in 1973 and after a year of preparation, took office formally on the first day of April 1974.

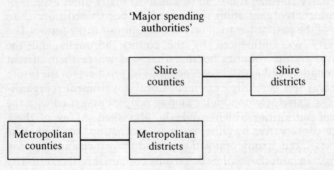

FIG. 3.1   Relationship between local authorities in England after 1974

Metropolitan counties
Six metropolitan counties were created, comprising Tyne and Wear, Merseyside, Greater Manchester, West Yorkshire, South Yorkshire and the West Midlands (Table 3.1). The six counties varied considerably in character: four were based almost exclusively on continuous urban areas – the original meaning of *conurbation* – but the two in Yorkshire included stretches of rural countryside. South Yorkshire in particular did not conform to the normal definition of a conurbation. The county comprised four districts based on city regions surrounding the former county boroughs of Sheffield, Barnsley, Doncaster and Rotherham.

TABLE 3.1 Metropolitan counties and districts (1981)

	Area (hectares)	*Population*
Greater Manchester	128,674	2,595,753
Bolton	13,973	260,654
Bury	9,918	176,112
Manchester	11,621	448,674
Oldham	14,112	220,017
Rochdale	15,976	207,480
Salford	9,687	243,865
Stockport	12,605	290,422
Tameside	10,323	217,708
Trafford	10,565	221,788
Wigan	19,895	309,083
Merseyside	65,202	1,511,915
Knowsley	9,739	172,957
Liverpool	11,291	509,987
St Helens	13,347	189,759
Sefton	15,054	299,724
Wirral	15,772	339,494
South Yorkshire	156,049	1,303,948
Barnsley	32,863	225,084
Doncaster	58,153	289,532
Rotherham	28,278	251,775
Sheffield	36,756	537,557
Tyne and Wear	54,006	1,142,675
Gateshead	14,317	211,333
Newcastle upon Tyne	11,187	277,829
North Tyneside	8,377	198,209
South Tyneside	6,357	160,410
Sunderland	13,768	294,894
West Midlands	89,943	2,648,939
Birmingham	26,430	1,006,527
Coventry	9,654	313,875
Dudley	9,794	299,741
Sandiwell	8,559	307,992
Solihull	18,007	199,261
Walsall	10,606	267,042
Wolverhampton	6,892	254,561
West Yorkshire	203,912	2,037,165
Bradford	37,010	457,423
Calderdale	36,377	191,122
Kirklees	40,992	371,955
Leeds	56,215	704,885
Wakefield	33,317	311,780

Source: Census 1981 County reports (part 1) (HMSO 1982)

Only the urban areas of Sheffield and Rotherham have contiguous boundaries and Doncaster is separate in many ways from the Sheffield urban influence.

'Shire' counties

The non-metropolitan counties, or 'shire' counties as they have come to be called, are substantial local authorities in terms of both area and population (see Map 3.1 and Table 3.2). They comprise most of the traditional names from English history though there are three newcomers: Humberside, Avon and Cleveland. In the early 1970s the new counties of Humberside and Avon were expected to grow rapidly as the population of the country expanded. Feasibility studies which examined the possibilities of growth, including the development of large new cities in the two areas, were published by the Central Unit for Environmental Planning in 1969 (Humberside) and 1971 (Severnside) (Cherry 1974:197). The decline in the birth-rate from the mid-1960s and the developing economic recession made many of these plans redundant, but the counties of Humberside and Avon remain. The other new county, Cleveland, was also created to deal with large-scale planning developments, though in this case there was no thought of a major population expansion. The area had already been reorganised in 1968 following a report from the Local Government Boundary Commission (LGBC). Middlesbrough had been joined with five neighbouring local authorities to form the county borough of Teesside. The new county borough proved to be one of the shortest-lived local authorities in local government history. Six years after its creation it was transformed into the county of Cleveland by the addition of Hartlepool and other parts of south-east Durham and a small area of north-east Yorkshire

Metropolitan districts

The metropolitan counties were divided into metropolitan districts. The number varied according to the population size and nature of the area (see Table 3.1), from four in South Yorkshire to ten in Greater Manchester. The typical population of a metropolitan district is about 250,000 though some based on the larger cities reach 500,000. Outside these limits, Birmingham is exceptional in having a population of about 1 million and a few districts have populations below 200,000. These smaller districts have populations well below those thought necessary by Redcliffe-Maud for the effective provision of some of the services allocated to them.

Only three of the thirty-six metropolitan districts do not include a former county borough within their boundaries. The former county boroughs had preferred the unitary approach which would have made them the core of enlarged areas, but when a two-tier system was adopted it was obviously preferable from their point of view to obtain metropolitan district status and thus retain as many services as possible.

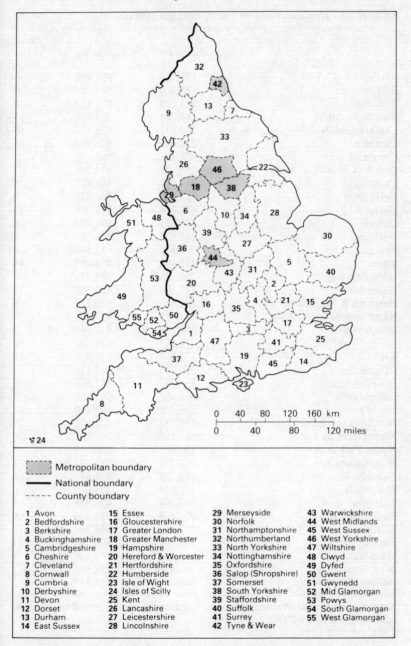

MAP 3.1 England and Wales: metropolitan and non-metropolitan counties
(*Source*: Reproduced from Alexander 1982b:40)

TABLE 3.2   Non-metropolitan (shire) counties (1981)

	Area (hectares)	Population	No of districts
Avon	134,614	909,408	6
Bedfordshire	123,460	504,986	4
Berkshire	125,890	675,153	6
Buckinghamshire	188,284	565,992	5
Cambridgeshire	340,892	575,177	6
Cheshire	232,846	926,293	8
Cleveland	58,308	565,775	4
Cornwall & Isles of Scilly	356,428	430,506	7
Cumbria	681,012	483,427	6
Derbyshire	263,094	906,929	9
Devon	671,088	952,000	10
Dorset	265,375	591,990	8
Durham	243,592	604,728	8
East Sussex	179,513	652,568	7
Essex	367,192	1,469,065	14
Gloucestershire	264,266	499,351	6
Hampshire	377,698	1,456,367	13
Hereford & Worcester	392,650	630,218	9
Hertfordshire	163,415	954,535	10
Humberside	351,212	847,666	9
Isle of Wight	38,067	118,192	2
Kent	373,060	1,463,055	14
Lancashire	306,346	1,372,118	14
Leicestershire	255,293	842,577	9
Lincolnshire	591,485	547,560	7
Norfolk	536,776	693,490	7
Northamptonshire	236,737	527,532	7
Northumberland	503,165	299,905	6
North Yorkshire	830,865	666,610	8
Nottinghamshire	216,365	982,631	8
Oxfordshire	260,782	515,079	5
Shropshire	349,014	375,610	6
Somerset	345,094	424,988	5
Staffordshire	271,615	1,012,320	9
Suffolk	379,663	596,354	7
Surrey	167,924	999,393	11
Warwickshire	198,054	473,620	5
West Sussex	198,935	658,562	7
Wiltshire	348,070	518,167	5

Source: Census 1981 Preliminary report for towns, England and Wales (second edition) (HMSO 1982)

Each former county borough also preferred if possible to retain its independence from neighbouring county boroughs (Wood 1976:76) unless it was large enough to dominate the merger. These considerations affected the boundaries of the new districts. There was also the undoubted administrative convenience of having the experience and structure of the former county boroughs to draw on when establishing departments in the new authorities: a district without this advantage would need to create departments from scratch amid the other upheavals of reorganisation.

'Shire' districts

The detailed arrangements for the non-metropolitan districts were not included in the 1972 Act but determined subsequently by the LGBC. The original intention was to produce authorities within a population range of 75,000 to 100,000 with 40,000 as an absolute minimum (LGBC 1972:2). In the event, 'the effect of local pressure was to reduce the amount of change and produce rather more authorities' (Keith-Lucas and Richards 1978:229). Of the 296 districts, 111 had a population below 75,000 and 14 were below 40,000 (LGBC 1972:9). The new districts were very largely based on amalgamations of existing district authorities which in turn derived from the sanitary districts created in the mid-nineteenth century.

Parishes

For local government purposes the parish had only existed within the boundaries of the former rural district councils. The 1972 Act enabled these parishes to continue into the new system and also made provision for some small former boroughs or urban districts to continue with parish status. They could adopt the title of a town if they wished (LGBC 1973). As town councils may elect a mayor there is the curious anomaly of local town mayors existing within shire districts headed by a chairperson. There are no parish or town councils within London or the major urban centres of other large cities though some exist within the more rural parts of metropolitan districts.

Titles and dignities

In legal terms local government in England outside London is divided into areas known as counties and districts with parishes existing in certain circumstances. None of the other titles such as 'borough', 'city' or 'town' convey any additional powers or responsibilities. The Act allowed the retention of adoption of such titles simply as a further concession to local sentiment. Similarly, the title of mayor or lord mayor where retained adds to the social status but not to the legal position of the person holding the chair of the council. Such questions of status and local dignity are not unimportant. When Liverpool City Council abolished the title of lord mayor in 1983 there was a 'public outcry' (*The Times* 18.5.83), thus demonstrating once again a point made 100 years earlier in 1888: 'that a sentimental grievance is by no means the least difficult to overcome' when considering changes in local government (quoted in Hampton 1966:463).

WALES

The 1972 Act that legislated for England also accomplished the reorganisation of local government in Wales. The principles established in England were followed in the smaller country. A two-tier structure of counties and districts was established: 8 counties were created from the existing 13 and 37 districts from the existing 164 (see Map 3.1). There are, however, no metropolitan areas in Wales and three other differences from the position in England deserve some comment: the small population of many of the Welsh authorities; the exceptional dominance of Cardiff in South Glamorgan; and the role of community councils.

Much of Wales is sparsely populated. Some of the counties, therefore, have very low populations despite covering a wide area. Powys is the extreme example: with an area comparable to the larger English counties, it has a population smaller even than the Isle of Wight (Table 3.3).

TABLE 3.3   Welsh counties (1981)

	Area (hectares)	Population	No of districts
Clwyd	242,650	390,173	6
Dyfed	576,781	329,977	6
Gwent	137,632	439,684	5
Gwynedd	386,911	230,468	5
Mid Glamorgan	101,833	537,866	6
Powys	507,741	110,467	3
South Glamorgan	41,630	384.633	2
West Glamorgan	81,658	367,194	4

Source: Census 1981 Preliminary report for towns, England and Wales (second edition) (HMSO, 1982)

The division of Glamorgan allowed each of the former county boroughs to be placed in a separate county though in terms of total area or population a unified Glamorgan would not be unusual in an English context. The separation of South Glamorgan proved particularly controversial. Introduced by the government for the first time in the Local Government Bill, the county consists of only two districts and is dominated by Cardiff which at the time contained 'just about the only pocket of Conservative Party strength in south Wales' (Wood 1976:127). As a result of this circumstance, the creation of the separate county was described as a 'gerrymander' and was a source of bitterness in south Wales (Alexander 1982a:27).

Community councils

Community councils provide the Welsh equivalent of the English parish councils. Richards suggests that 'since the Anglican Church in Wales was disestablished in 1919, it is not fitting that a name associated with church organisation should be linked to a secular unit of local administration' (Richards 1983:39). The variation in name appears to be the major difference between the two types of minor authorities: the functions allocated to them are the same. As the population of Wales is smaller and more dispersed than in England, the creation of community councils as successors to former boroughs and urban district councils was more widespread than the creation of successor parishes in England. In neither country were these created in the larger urban areas, but in the principality this only meant a few heavily populated areas in south Wales. The Welsh community councils should not be confused with the Scottish community councils (see below) which are quite different in character.

SCOTLAND

The proposals of the Wheatley Commission were substantially accepted by the government, but this did not ensure an easy passage into law. Page considers: 'There was little enthusiasm for the legislation among Members of Parliament, and substantial opposition from local councillors' (Page 1983:44). In part this reflected the usual vested interests of existing local authorities, but there were also the special difficulties caused by an uneven distribution of population. This uneven distribution produces anomalies far more obvious than those in England or even Wales (Alexander 1982a:125–131). The Bill contained some departures from the Wheatley proposals and there were further amendments as it passed through Parliament. The main effect of these changes was to create a number of new authorities and thus reduce their average size. Two new regions were created in the Borders and Fife; sixteen new districts were formed; and three islands authorities were separated from the regional structure to become unitary authorities. The government also allocated housing to the districts rather than to the regions.

THE 1973 ACT

The Local Government (Scotland) Act 1973 created nine regional councils, fifty-three district councils, and three islands councils (Map 3.2). The Act also provided for the introduction of community councils

45

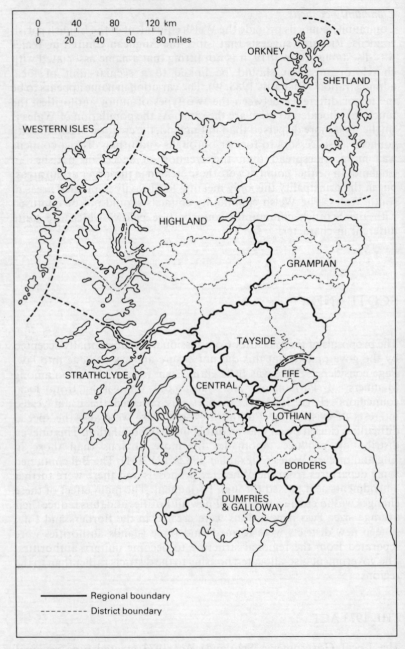

MAP 3.2 Scotland: regions, districts and islands (*Source*: Reproduced from Alexander 1982b:45)

as a vehicle for the expression of local opinion. The Act took effect from May 1975.

Regions

The nine regions have widely differing populations and areas (Table 3.4). The Wheatley Commission was concerned to establish regions that would conform to four criteria: they should be large enough to carry out their functions effectively; they should correspond with genuine communities; they should form distinctive parts of Scotland; and finally, there should be a 'certain balance' between the various regions (Wheatley 1969:176). Geography and the distribution of population made the achievement of these aims difficult.

For the purpose of examination, Wheatley divided Scotland into five major parts: the Highlands, the North-east, the East (or Tayside), the South-east and the West. Three main questions were then identified:

1. Should the Highlands be treated as a single region, or divided?
2. Should the Borders be treated as a region distinct from the rest of the South-east?
3. Should the West be treated as a single region, or divided? (Wheatley 1969:176).

The answers Wheatley gave to the first two questions were in favour of retaining the larger unit, but in both cases the government reversed this recommendation in the final legislation. The recommendation for the West was to divide it into three regions: South-west (Dumfries and Galloway); Central – based on the Falkirk–Stirling area; and the West

TABLE 3.4   Regions and islands authorities in Scotland (1981)

	Area (hectares)	Population	No of districts
Regions			
Borders	467,158	99,784	4
Central	263,147	273,391	3
Dumfries & Galloway	637,006	145,139	4
Fife	130,708	327,362	3
Grampian	870,389	471,942	5
Highland	2,539,122	200,150	8
Lothian	175,518	738,372	4
Strathclyde	1,353,698	2,404,532	19
Tayside	749,297	391,846	3
Islands			
Orkney	97,581	19,056	—
Shetland	143,268	27,277	—
Western Isles	289,798	31,884	—

Source: Census of population, 1981.

or Clyde Valley (Strathclyde). These recommendations were accepted by the government with only relatively small boundary changes.

The Wheatley Commission was not unanimous in recommending a single region for the Highlands and Islands. Three commissioners entered notes of reservation recommending separate all-purpose island authorities. They drew attention to the distances involved and the communication problem for islanders visiting the mainland. The Shetlands, for example, are 338 kilometres (210 miles) north of Aberdeen and attendance at a mid-week meeting on the mainland could involve five days away from home for a councillor from the northern isles (Wheatley 1969:292). The Orkneys and the Shetlands also have a long history of independence in local government terms and pride themselves on their Scandinavian roots and their distinctiveness from Scotland. The 1973 Act followed the notes of reservation and the three island authorities were the only unitary local authorities created in Britain during the reorganisations of the 1970s.

The separation of the Borders and Fife from the proposed South-east region was more controversial. The Borders form a region with a population no larger than many English and some Scottish districts. The removal of the south Fife coalfield from a Lothian region based on Edinburgh has been criticised on similar political grounds to the slicing of Glamorgan into three counties: it appears to derive from considerations of Conservative Party advantage. But if political calculations did enter the minds of the Conservatives (Alexander 1982b:46) then they have been disappointed. Labour controlled Lothian Regional Council until 1982 and engaged in substantial disagreements with Conservative governments. The Borders have also resisted Conservative attempts to gain control and Independent councillors retain their power (Keating and Midwinter 1983:109).

The size of the Strathclyde region has been a constant source of argument. The Wheatley Commission was convinced 'that the lack of a single unit for the entire Clyde Valley area is one of the greatest impediments to the economic and social regeneration of the west of Scotland' (Wheatley 1969:186). They refused, therefore, to consider separating the Glasgow conurbation from the more distant parts of the region and the government accepted their opinion. The result is a region that dwarfs all the others, containing about half the population of Scotland and bringing remote rural areas into association with the urban problems of Glasgow. The region is often criticised for being bureaucratic and remote without too careful an analysis of these concepts (Page and Midwinter 1979); but one criticism must surely be accepted – the 'certain balance' that Wheatley advocated is scarcely obtained when one region outweighs the rest.

Districts

The districts are even more varied in size than the regions. The largest, Glasgow, has a population of 765,951 (1981): several of the smaller districts have populations below 10,000. The district of Glasgow therefore is larger than each of the regions other than Strathclyde. Of the fifty-three districts, 70 per cent have populations below 100,000 and over a quarter are below 40,000 – many very much below.

Community councils

Parish councils for local government purposes were abolished in Scotland in 1929. The 1973 Act provided for community councils to operate at a similar 'grass-roots' level, and in so doing introduced a new concept into British local government – a statutory body without statutory functions. The Act states ' ... the general purpose of a community council shall be to ascertain, co-ordinate and express to the local authorities for its area, and to public authorities, the views of the community which it represents ... and to take such action in the interests of that community as appears to it to be expedient and practicable' (Section 51(2)). The councils are established in accordance with schemes drawn up by the district or island authorities and are partly funded by them, but the procedures are only operated where there is a clear local demand. The schemes provide for 1,343 community councils to be established (McQueen, Freeman 1978:2) of which approximately nine out of ten had been formed by mid-1978 (Masterson 1979:106). The councils have 'tackled a great variety of jobs: commenting on local plans, clearing up their area, dealing with traffic problems, organising carol services and other social events, protesting about bus routes and becoming involved in the many other neighbourhood activities so typical of residents' groups and parish pump politics' (Boaden *et al.* 1982:47).

NORTHERN IRELAND

The Local Government (NI) Act 1972 closely followed the recommendations of the Macrory Report, but this did not imply a consensus about the merit of the proposals. Like everything else in Northern Ireland, local government is evaluated in the context of a wider political controversy. 'Among Catholics the response ranged from mild support to disinterest. Local councils were to be made more democratic but less important' (Carroll and Carroll 1980:297). Some Protestants opposed the weakening of the dominance that they had exercised in local government since partition. The legislation was introduced in Stormont by the Unionist majority, but the provincial parliament was suspended in favour of direct rule before the process could be completed. The British government then continued with the reorganisation. Elections took place in May 1973 under a system of proportional representation and the new local authorities came into being.

Local Government and Urban Politics

Districts

In a formal sense, local government in Northern Ireland consists of twenty-six unitary district councils. (Map 3. 3). Each of these is centred round a town and includes the adjacent rural areas. The populations range from 14,372 to 297,862 (Belfast), but only the latter exceeds 100,000. The rest of the districts have populations between 20,000 and 80,000 (Table 3.5). They are, therefore, very similar in size to many of the Scottish districts, but they are not responsible for as many services: housing, for example, a district function in the whole of Britain, is administered centrally in Northern Ireland.

Regional boards

The small size of the population of Northern Ireland, together with the political difficulties experienced by the province, have led to many services being administered at a provincial level. These include education, personal health, welfare and child care, housing, libraries, planning, roads, water and sewage. Since the suspension of Stormont

MAP 3.3 Northern Ireland: the district councils (*Source*: Reproduced from Alexander 1982b:51)

TABLE 3.5   Districts in Northern Ireland (1981)

	Area (hectares)	Population
Antrim	56,289	45,303
Ards	36,949	57,598
Armagh	67,249	48,169
Ballymena	63,837	54,696
Ballymoney	41,871	22,932
Banbridge	44,423	29,831
Belfast	13,979	297,862
Carrickfergus	8,687	28,388
Castlereagh	8,479	61,107
Coleraine	48,493	47,524
Cookstown	62,311	26,323
Craigavon	38,164	71,049
Down	64,639	52,984
Dungannon	77,906	41,087
Fermanagh	187,557	51,973
Larne	33,821	29,475
Limavady	58,698	26,451
Lisburn	44,376	83,188
Londonderry	38,249	82,862
Magherafelt	57,328	30,781
Moyle	49,543	14,372
Newry and Mourne	89,483	72,615
Newtownabbey	15,163	71,917
North Down	7,316	65,692
Omagh	112,874	41,137
Strabane	86,969	34,912

Source: Census of population, 1981.

these services are administered by the appropriate department of the Northern Ireland government. Local government is associated with some of these services through a system of regional boards. There are four regional Health and Social Services Boards, and five Education and Libraries Boards. These are 'largely nominated but ... about one-third of the members are district councillors' (Roche 1982:290).

DISCUSSION – SINGLE-TIER OR TWO-TIER?

With the exception of the three islands' authorities in Scotland, the system of local government in Britain in the 1970s consisted of a two-tier system. Even in Northern Ireland, the districts are best thought of as the lower tier in a system that simply lacks a democratically elected higher level of local government. In this respect the United Kingdom was not

51

unique. Throughout the world, local government has been moving increasingly towards two-tier systems in recent years – often under pressure from the needs of major metropolitan areas for overall planning agencies (Rowat 1980:1–3). The moves towards a two-tier structure are accompanied by considerable and continuing controversy as the advantages and disadvantages of the single- and two-tier systems are discussed in the context of political advantage. These questions will be elaborated as a prelude to a discussion of local government services in Chapter 4.

The advantages of a single-tier system are considerable. They were put most clearly by the Redcliffe-Maud Commission which recommended, as we have seen, a system of unitary local authorities. They based their case on grounds of both efficiency and democracy:

> A single authority has the great advantage that, through allocation of priorities and co-ordinated use of resources, it can relate its programmes for all services to coherent objectives for the future progress of its area considered as a whole. Being responsible for the total span of local government activity, it can see the full extent of the relationships between different services, what developments in each are necessary to meet people's needs and what gaps between services ought to be filled. It is *the* local government of its area. There is no doubt where responsibility lies, no confusion over which authority does what. This is local government in its simplist, most understandable and potentially most efficient form (Redcliffe-Maud 1969:Vol 1 68).

These advantages were obtained by many of the former county boroughs which Redcliffe-Maud considered to have 'been the most effective local government unit we have known' (Redcliffe-Maud 1969:Vol 1 68).

The difficulty with a single-tier system is to arrive at areas large enough to obtain the benefits of unifying the provision of services requiring an extensive area for their efficient operation, yet small enough to form a basis for local democratic involvement. This problem is compounded in metropolitan areas where socio-geographic boundaries may spread far beyond any normal understanding of 'community'. A further difficulty arises when considering the catchment areas required for different services. Some, such as strategic planning or transportation, require far wider areas than others, such as housing or the personal social services. For these reasons, Senior opted for a two-tier system, and the Conservative government in the early 1970s also sought to marry the advantages of a quite different two-tier structure for the benefit of both efficiency (top tier) and democracy (lower tier).

The controversies that have since arisen are of threefold origin. They are concerned, first, with the demoting of the former county boroughs and the consequent loss of the strengths that Redcliffe-Maud identified; second, with more general questions of relations between the two tiers; and third, with the party political considerations that cast shadows behind the curtain of official reports.

First, there is the problem of the former county boroughs. Cities the size of Glasgow, Bristol and Hull are no longer responsible for education or social services. They have the same responsibilities as the smallest district councils. The large cities have not been happy with this position and various proposals have been made to meet their objections. In Scotland the possibility of devolution has kept alive the thoughts of further changes in local government. Both the Scottish Nationalists and the Liberals favour the transfer of some strategic local government functions 'to a devolved Assembly, and the creation of a single-tier system of multi-purpose authorities' (Keating and Midwinter 1983:101). In England, the nine largest former county boroughs, all with populations above 200,000, began 'a campaign within two months of the new authorities taking over, to win back some of the powers they had lost to the counties' (Alexander 1982b:64). The nine are: Bristol, Derby, Hull, Leicester, Nottingham, Plymouth, Portsmouth, Southampton and Stoke-on-Trent. They expressed their 'dissatisfaction ... with the restricted powers available to them as a result of local government reorganisation. These powers have been found to be completely inadequate to deal with the challenges and problems presented in complex urban situations' (quoted in Alexander 1982b:64). The 'big nine' seek to regain some of the major services they have lost to the counties, but they are not the only districts dissatisfied with the present position. A further group of medium-sized districts seek less extensive changes in the allocation of responsibilities (Alexander 1982a:44).

Professor Stewart and his colleagues at the University of Birmingham identified a number of difficulties with these proposed changes, although with academic care they added the proviso: 'to identify problems is not to draw a conclusion' (Stewart *et al.* 1978:1). The study, commissioned by the Association of County Councils (ACC), discussed the implications of an allocation of responsibilities within a county that varies from district to district depending on its size. For example, education or social services might, under such a system, be a district responsibility in some places and a county responsibility in others. Though admirably flexible, this would lead to confusion in the financing, management and constitutional arrangements of the system as a whole. The constitutional questions include the tricky decision as to which councillors could vote on which issues at county council meetings. If they were restricted to those matters for which the county was responsible in their areas then this could lead to differing party majorities for different services. On the other hand, to allow county councillors from the larger districts to vote in the county council on matters which were a district responsibility in their own areas would be deeply resented by the smaller districts. Stewart *et al.* concluded, 'proposals for organic change cannot be regarded as a limited change ... it introduced a fundamental change within the existing structure of local government' (Stewart *et al.* 1978:58).

The difficulties of co-ordinating the work of counties and districts, or regions and districts, has not been confined to questions of status relating to the former county boroughs. The division of responsibilities between the two tiers means that some co-ordination is necessary if an effective service is to be provided. There are also provisions in the legislation for one local authority to perform a service on behalf of another in order to prevent wasteful overlap in provision. These 'agency' arrangements have proved a constant source of disagreement between local authorities. There are, no doubt, many examples of harmonious relationships between the two tiers, but the tensions have been significant in both England and Scotland since reorganisation (Alexander 1982a:Ch. 3 passim; 132–3). Nor are the disputes confined to those instances where the two tiers are controlled by different party majorities, though such differences may add to the bitterness of the disputes.

The implications of local government reorganisation for party political control is an important consideration in many of the debates between advocates of single- and two-tier systems. The Royal Commissions and official committees of inquiry have maintained a reticence on such matters that has at times made their recommendations appear naïve – as if one could consider the reorganisation of political institutions in isolation from politics! Governments, too, have adopted a suitably objective approach in public, basing their arguments on considerations of administrative efficiency and democratic improvement. In practice the actions of governments have been less high-minded: a fact the opposition is always quick to point out. Traditionally, the Labour Party has derived its strength from the urban areas while the Conservative Party is based in the suburbs and rural areas. Labour has, therefore, perceived its interests to lie in the protection of the urban authorities whether the former county boroughs or the present metropolitan areas. It was a Labour government that proposed to implement a process of 'organic change' to accommodate the demands of the former county boroughs (DOE 1979). The Conservatives, on the other hand, protect the counties and suspect the great urban authorities of being extravagant. The Conservative government rejected the proposals for 'organic change'. The perceptions of their interests by the two parties may not always be entirely accurate, or they may change over time, but there can be no doubt of the importance they hold for local government structure.

The 1980s saw another twist in the controversy surrounding the structure of local government. The Conservatives, who introduced the country-wide two-tier system, came to believe that 'in the case of Greater London and the six metropolitan counties ... the hopes of the last reorganisation have been disappointed' (DOE 1983b:2). They abolished both the metropolitan counties and the GLC. The ending of the metropolitan top-tier authorities destroyed one of the advantages that led Redcliffe-Maud to support the Conservative reorganisation in the early 1970s. As 'an unrepentant believer in the Commission's unitary plan' he came to accept as an advance on the existing system the Conservative proposals for 'two tiers everywhere' and in particular the establishment of 'the principle of metropolitan counties for great conurbations' (foreword to Wood 1976:8). In the further reorganisation in the 1980s some former GLC and metropolitan county services were allocated to the London boroughs and metropolitan districts which became single-tier authorities, and some services became the responsibility of joint boards or new *ad hoc* bodies. The political motive for these proposals is clear. They were accompanied by frequent attacks by Conservative ministers on Labour controlled councils in the urban areas who were alleged to pay little regard to central government economic policies. These issues are discussed at greater length in Chapter 11.

The debates between advocates of single-tier and two-tier local government are, therefore, conducted within an atmosphere in which the relative merits of the two different systems for the values of efficiency and democracy are infused with the expectations of party or local advantage. The result is often a series of complex compromises that obtains the theoretical advantages of neither system and forms the basis for further argument. Neither the reforms at the end of the nineteenth century, nor the reorganisations of the 1970s, stopped the debate. In both cases the legislation was followed almost immediately by suggestions of further change.

Chapter four

THE SERVICES PROVIDED BY LOCAL GOVERNMENT

When considering the services provided by local government there are two major questions to be discussed. First, what services are to be allocated to local government as a whole; second, how are these services to be distributed among the agencies of local government itself. The second question is, of course, a more specific version of the first if we consider local government within the broader context of public administration and attitudes to the state provision of goods and services. After a brief discussion of the first question, we shall go on to consider the present distribution of services within local government in the United Kingdom. We shall look in turn at the background to the allocation of the present services, the criteria adopted for the distribution of services during the reorganisation years in the early 1970s, the present position, and the problems that have arisen since reorganisation. Finally, we shall discuss the special position relating to the control of the police and the current controversy that surrounds their relationship with local government.

There is no universally accepted pattern for the distribution of governmental services between the various agencies of the state, or even of the appropriate services to be performed collectively through government rather than by private initiative. There are variations in the public services deemed necessary, desirable or possible in the circumstances obtaining in different countries at different times. For example, the governmental services provided in a modern industrial country differ from those provided in a country with fewer resources, and the services provided vary in any country over the years.

Disputes over the role of the state and the extent of state provision of public services are at the heart of many political controversies, but there are other considerations affecting the special role of local government. First, there are factors related to the size of the country and its internal organisation: whether it is a federal or a unitary state for example. A small country, either in terms of area or population, or one with a federal structure consisting of relatively small units, will retain more responsibilities at federal or state (that is, second-tier) government levels. Local government will correspondingly be denuded of services accepted by local authorities in other systems. Second, the allocation of services to local government will be affected not only by attitudes towards state provision and the concept of the Welfare State, but also by attitudes towards decentralisation in any provision being made. In some services, for example the making of monetary payments through social security in Britain, the necessity for equal treatment throughout the country is considered to override any benefits to be gained from local government involvement and discretion. Finally, the structure of local government itself will affect the services to be provided. Recent reorganisations have been strongly influenced by discussions about the appropriate size that would enable a local authority to accept particular responsibilities.

The effect of these considerations on a specific service can be illustrated by education. This service is provided by a central government department in New Zealand, by the state governments in Australia, by local government in Britain, and by local *ad hoc* bodies in many parts of the United States and Canada (Bowman and Hampton 1983). Even in Britain, the position varies considerably. Education is a top-tier service in Scotland and in the shire counties, a district service in the metropolitan areas, and the subject of special arrangements in London. In Northern Ireland, of course, education is a provincial service now administered by a special authority.

When considering local government services, therefore, we must be careful to avoid the assumption that these refer to a settled collection. The correct interpretation is to regard local government services as simply those services provided by local government in particular circumstances. Which services these are to be is always a matter of dispute and may be a crucial factor in relations between central and local government. There is, after all, no surer way of influencing the power of local government than by varying the range of services for which it is responsible. Some of these questions will reoccur in later chapters on both intergovernmental relations and the services provided regionally, but for the present we will remain with those services provided by local government in the United Kingdom.

THE DEVELOPMENT OF LOCAL GOVERNMENT SERVICES

Local government has its origins, as we noted in Chapter 2, in the growing urbanisation of the nineteenth century. The services provided were related to the social conditions associated with that growth: the need to regulate health and sanitary conditions, and to maintain public order. At first these services were administered by *ad hoc* bodies but legislation covering England and Wales in 1888 and 1894 began to draw them together into modern units of local government. The timing of these changes and the details of the structures adopted varied between the countries comprising the United Kingdom, but 'as a service provider, local government in Scotland developed at broadly the same pace as local government in England and Wales' (Page 1983:43; cf. Foster *et al.* 1980:102-7). In Ireland a similar but slower growth reflected both the political circumstances of the country and the slower rate of economic growth and urbanisation (Roche 1982:Ch. 4).

The Acts of 1888 and 1894 did not bring all local services under the control of the new local authorities. Some *ad hoc* bodies remained. The most significant of these were concerned with education and Poor Law relief. The Education Act of 1902 finally brought education under local authority control in England and Wales and abolished the school boards; similar legislation produced the same effect in Scotland in 1918. The 1902 Act, in the words of Maureen Schulz,

> marked the decisive turning point which divides the nineteenth century local authority which administered services such as lighting, paving, drainage, sewerage, police and public utilities, mainly directed towards the benefit of the neighbourhood and protecting and maintaining property, from the twentieth century authority which is in addition the agent for numerous personal social services initiated and controlled on a national level (Wilson 1948:69).

Following the Local Government Act of 1929 the last of the great nineteenth-century *ad hoc* bodies was laid to rest. The Poor Law Boards of Guardians were abolished in 1930 and their responsibilities distributed among the appropriate committees of the county councils and county boroughs.

The responsibilities of local authorities are not limited to those conveyed in general legislation. The promotion of private Acts of Parliament continued throughout the nineteenth century, and indeed beyond, bringing a bewildering and sometimes surprising range of services within the power of particular local authorities. By 1900 'Doncaster had a racecourse, Wolverhampton a cold store, Glasgow and Tunbridge Wells had telephone services; a few years later, Birmingham was to get powers to establish its "penny bank"' (Keith-Lucas and Richards 1978:36). Some of these powers remain with individual authorities. Doncaster racecourse, for example, is still controlled by municipal enterprise – to the great joy of the councillors who have special privileges during St. Leger week. There are numerous responsibilities of greater or lesser significance scattered among local authorities throughout the country.

After 1900 there was a dual development with regard to the services provided by local government. First, there was the accretion of new powers and the growth in scale of those that continued to rest with local authorities. Second, there was the loss of certain responsibilities either to central government departments or to the regional structure of nationalised industries or services.

The new powers were concerned, as Schulz pointed out, very largely with the development of the broadly defined personal social services. Education after 1902 immediately became the largest and most important service provided by local government and has remained so ever since (Regan 1979). Approximately half the total current expenditure on goods and services provided by local authorities goes on education. In addition to schools for children of compulsory school age, local authorities provide nurseries, colleges of further education, polytechnics and a general adult education and youth service.

Housing is another local authority service that grew rapidly from the beginning of the present century, particularly after the First World War (Cullingworth 1966). Housing represents most of the capital assets of local government. The proportion of the housing stock owned by local authorities in England and Wales was '13 per cent in 1947. This had risen to 25 per cent by 1961 and 30 per cent by 1976. In Scotland the proportion is higher: 54 per cent in 1976' (Darke and Darke 1979: 43). After 1979, the Conservative government adopted a policy for the sale of council houses. By 1984, over 600,000 had been sold (HC Debates 18.12.84). This policy halted the previously continuous growth of local authority tenancies and contributed to the overall increase in owner occupancy. In the early 1980s the proportion of owner occupiers was already well over 60 per cent and the Building Societies' Association estimated it would rise to 76 per cent by the end of the decade.

The personal social services in their modern form developed from the late 1940s. The earlier transfer to local authorities of responsibilities previously exercised by the Poor Law Guardians had not led to any rapid improvement in the services (Wilson 1948:76–7). Indeed, local government lost some of its recently gained powers to central agencies soon after the transfer. In 1934 an Unemployment Assistance Board was established to administer all unemployment relief (Bruce 1968:259). This board dropped 'Unemployment' from its title in 1940 when it also took responsibility for supplementary pensions from local authorities (Wilson 1948:97–8). As part of the post-war creation of the Welfare State, the Children Act 1948, introduced local authority departments responsible for the welfare of children. This Act laid the basis for the growth of a new professional approach in social work. Subsequently, the Local Authority Social Services Act 1970 provided for the combination of the children's department with other local authority social work services into new social service departments (Sainsbury 1977:27–33). These departments have become a major force in local government and are among the main spending departments after education.

The other responsibility we need to mention at this stage is planning. This, of course, is an exception to the generalisation that the growth of local government services in the twentieth century has been concentrated in the social services. Planning as a local authority responsibility has its origins in the public health and housing policies of the nineteenth century, but from the outset the objectives were broader than a simple emphasis on the efficient use of land. John Burns, President of the Local Government Board, when introducing the first legislation with 'town planning' in its title in 1909 declared:

> The objective of the Bill is to provide a domestic condition for the people in which their physical health, their morals, their character and their whole social condition can be improved by what we hope to secure in this Bill. The Bill aims in broad outline at, and hopes to secure, the home healthy, the house beautiful, the town pleasant, the city dignified and the suburbs salubrious (quoted in Cullingworth 1972:18).

These objectives may seem happily optimistic when contrasted with subsequent achievements, but they serve to remind us of the tension that always exists in town planning between the engineers and the sociologists (Goldsmith 1980:Ch. 7). The present powers of local authorities in respect of town planning derive from the Town and Country Planning Act 1968 and the equivalent Scottish Act of 1969. These provide for local authorities to prepare both structure (that is, strategic) plans and local plans for the implementation of the strategy in smaller areas or for specific purposes. The legislation includes provision for the involvement of the general public in the planning process, but we shall come back to this point in Chapter 7.

The possibility of transfer of responsibility to central government agencies for some services previously provided by local authorities has already been mentioned. Such losses of services occurred in the 1930s and 1940s. 'The Ministry of Transport became the highway authority for 4459 miles of main roads, by the Trunk Roads Act of 1936, and for another 3685 by that of 1946' (Lipman 1949:210). The Minister of Agriculture assumed direct responsibility for a number of services between 1937 and 1944, and in the post-war years local authorities lost their hospitals to the National Health Service (NHS) and their gas and electricity undertakings to nationalised boards. The process was continued by the Local Government Act 1972 which transferred the remaining local authority health responsibilities to the NHS and their water and sewage responsibilities to new regional authorities.

THE DISTRIBUTION OF SERVICES

There are several ways of analysing the services provided by local government. The choice between these ways will depend upon the purpose for which the analysis is being made. From a legal point of view all services must derive their existence from statute or else fall foul of the *ultra vires* rule (see Ch. 1). This gives a threefold division. First, those services which are *mandatory* upon a local authority such as the education of children between the compulsory school ages or the preparation of a structure plan in appropriate circumstances. In these cases the local authority *must* provide the service. Second, those services which are *permissive* such as the provision of adult education or numerous recreational and cultural facilities. In these cases the local authority *may* provide the service. Third, there is a small but important category of provision deriving authority from Section 137 in the Local Government Act 1972 which allows local authorities to spend the product of a rate of 2p in the pound on anything 'which in their opinion is in the interests of their area or any part of it or all or some of its inhabitants'. A local authority shall not spend money under this clause on any purpose authorised by other legislation. A number of initiatives have developed from the use of this 'free 2p'. Among the most notable of these are the economic and employment departments referred to in Chapter 12.

Another way of distinguishing the services provided by local government is to group them according to certain shared characteristics. Thus Byrne (1981:70–84) creates five categories: (1) protective services, such as police and fire, that seek to protect the citizen from various dangers; (2) environmental services to control and improve the physical environment such as highways, transport and planning; (3) personal services, such as education, housing and social work, that seek to enhance personal welfare; (4) amenity services, such as museums, theatres and sports facilities, that provide for citizens' leisure time; and (5) trading services for which local authorities make commercial charges. This last category includes markets, crematoria, and more controversially, public transport. Some local authorities have at times defined transport as a personal service, or as an adjunct to their planning policies, and consequently they have heavily subsidised the fares.

There can be considerable overlap between Byrne's categories. Some people, indeed, would not wish to distinguish at all between the personal and amenity services, regarding them all as essentially people-based. The major drawback with the Byrne approach, however, is that it provides only an incidental guide to the way in which the services might be allocated between different types of local authority. This is a problem that greatly exercised the Royal Commissions and the Northern Ireland review body on local government. In Northern Ireland, as we have seen, the matter was solved by allocating all the services of major significance to the provincial level, but in London, England and Wales, and Scotland a local government solution had to be found.

The solution advocated in general had two aspects. First, an effort was made to give to each local authority 'functions and powers which are separate and distinct' (Herbert 1960:197). This would, it was thought, avoid difficulties which might otherwise arise through local authorities failing to co-ordinate their activities, and it would also make the system more intelligible to the general public. Second, services were grouped together with respect to the scale upon which they needed to be provided. This second principle proved difficult to implement. There is more than one criterion of scale. It can refer to geographical area as in planning or other land-based services, or to the administrative needs of personal services such as education. Housing in particular is hard to allocate: house construction is firmly linked to planning and land-use while housing management needs to co-operate with the social services.

The Royal Commission on Local Government in England preferred a unitary approach but recognised that this solution would not be appropriate throughout the country. They distinguished, therefore, between an 'environmental' group of services – planning, transportation and development – and a 'personal' group of services – education, personal social services and housing. Where two tiers of local government were necessary, the services should be divided in this manner and 'related services kept together' (Redcliffe-Maud 1969, Vol I:68). Because, no doubt, of the different structure of the population in Scotland, the Wheatley Commission took a different view. They divided local government services in such a way that most of the major services including education, major planning, personal social services and housing would have gone to the regional authorities while the districts would have been left with minor aspects of these services and certain amenity services. The government did not accept all these proposals: housing in particular was treated differently in the legislation from the recommendations of both the English and Scottish Commissions.

POPULATION SIZE AND LOCAL GOVERNMENT SERVICES

The basis for the allocation of services both in the various reports and in the subsequent legislation was the size of population accepted as necessary for effective administration. The Redcliffe-Maud and the Wheatley Commissions were persuaded by the evidence from government departments that education, housing and the personal social services required catchment areas with populations of at least 200,000 to 250,000. The reasons were to be found in the strong links between housing and planning, and in the large populations required to justify certain special services and residential accommodation in education and the personal social services. This evidence is frequently interpreted as suggesting that larger local authorities are likely to be more efficient than smaller ones, but no statistical evidence has been produced to support this claim. The only evidence to link size with quality of performance was contained in the subjective opinions of the inspectors for education and child care (Redcliffe-Maud 1969, Vol III: Chs 11 and 12).

The statistical evidence was particularly disappointing for Redcliffe-

Maud who commissioned several research studies with a bearing on the issue: none could offer a definite answer. In a wide range of services including housing, education, personal social services, highways and even ambulances, the results did not support the suggestion that size could be linked with efficiency. Such phrases as 'no consistent pattern', 'no strong relationship' and 'difficult to draw any conclusion' are typical of the language of the reports. In some cases a tendency to diseconomies of scale was even observed (Redcliffe-Maud, Research Study 3:6 and 19). Redcliffe-Maud summed up: 'Size cannot statistically be proved to have a very important effect on performance' (Redcliffe-Maud 1969, Vol I:58); and then went on to point to the difficulties faced by such statistical studies. First, they were necessarily related to the existing structure – they could not predict the performance of a new structure based on different principles. Second, and more fundamentally, they drew attention to the difficulties of finding a satisfactory measure of performance in statistical terms. The quality of a service has to be related to the environment in which it is provided; and it is difficult to quantify the various facets of each service (Redcliffe-Maud 1969, Vol I:58).

The failure of the Royal Commission's own research to support their advocacy of large-scale units of local government led to scepticism in the 1970s as opinion swung away from a belief in bigness as a correlate of efficiency and progress. Dearlove considers the whole pressure for increased scale simply as a cover for regaining or maintaining the influential position of business interests in local government (Dearlove 1979). From another point of view, Newton has reconsidered the whole debate in an attempt to assess the impact of size both on functional effectiveness and democracy. He maintains that the 'classical conundrum' of the incompatibility of functional effectiveness (depending on large-scale units) and democracy (depending on small-scale units) is a false one. After a thorough summary of the evidence he reaches the following conclusions:

1. The democratic merits of small units of government have often been exaggerated and romanticised, while their democratic deficiencies have been overlooked;
2. Large units are as economically efficient as small ones, and have a greater functional capacity;
3. Large units do not seem to be deficient in democratic qualities and may even be more democratic in some respects;
4. Hence there is no necessary incompatibility between the size necessary for functional effectiveness and that required for democracy (Newton 1982:191).

Thus the approach of the Royal Commissions would appear to have been justified, but no doubt the 'classical conundrum' will continue to cause controversy despite Newton's attempt to shift the discussion to firmer ground.

THE PRESENT POSITION

Local services are not distributed in the same manner throughout Britain. Table 4.1 gives the general distribution following the reorganisations of the 1970s. The position in Wales is almost the same as in the non-metropolitan areas in England. The principal differences are that Welsh district councils are responsible for refuse disposal as well as collection, and may exceptionally be designated to provide libraries and certain other services. The districts are also able to provide both on-street and off-street car parks, subject to the consent of the county council; and share the provision of allotments with the community councils (Department of the Environment/Welsh Office 1974:10).

In addition to the variations in the distribution of responsibilities between the two tiers in different parts of the United Kingdom, there are two other points to note from the table. First, the two tiers exercise concurrent powers in a wide range of services. Second, some services are divided between the two tiers. For example, refuse collection is the responsibility of the English districts while refuse disposal rests with the counties. Planning is also divided: responsibility for local plans is with the districts and for structure plans with the counties and regions. The effects of the division of planning have been particularly disturbing. Relations between county and district planners have frequently been strained. The planning process has been delayed and made more expensive by the need for constant negotiations between authorities responsible for two separate parts of a process which was intended in the Town and County Planning Acts of 1968 and 1971 to be fully integrated. In 1980 the Local Government, Planning and Land Act specified that all planning applications would be received by district councils. The Act made several other changes in the hope of reducing the friction between counties and districts, but the difficulties remain – especially between the counties and the districts based on former county boroughs (Alexander 1982a:55–7; 1982b:67–8).

The current distribution of responsibilities goes against the principle endorsed by the Herbert Commission of giving each local authority 'functions and powers which are separate and distinct' (Herbert 1960:197). The present system is no more comprehensible to the public in this respect than was its predecessor. Moreover, the recommendations of the Redcliffe-Maud and Wheatley Commissions that the personal services of education, social services (social work in Scotland) and housing should be allocated to the same local authority were not followed outside London and the English metropolitan areas. In non-metropolitan England and Wales and in Scotland, housing is allocated to the districts, thus separating it from the personal social services. This separation has caused considerable difficulties and again fresh legislation was needed in 1977 to provide adequate procedures for housing the homeless (Alexander 1982a:53; 1982b:69).

In Scotland, the problems caused by the distribution of services between the two tiers of local government have been considered by a Committee of Inquiry (Stodart 1981). The terms of reference of the committee were limited. It could only make recommendations that did not challenge the basic structure of the system. As a result, Stodart 'concentrated on tidying up overlapping and concurrent functions in planning, leisure, tourism, environmental health and industrial development' (Keating and Midwinter 1983:102). Most of the recommendations have been implemented, but they too have failed to end the controversies that the reorganisations of the 1970s provoked.

The complexity of the British local government system is increased by two further features: first, the possibility of co-operation between different local authorities; and second, the more formal agency arrangements. In his study of the problems of implementing the Local Government Act 1972 in England and Wales, Richards describes the various means that 'exist to facilitate county/district co-operation, some of which depend on the 1972 Act and some of which do not' (Richards 1975b:76). These means include the appointment of joint committees for a particular purpose, the ability of one authority to place its staff at the disposal of another, and the possibility of local authorities entering into agreements to provide each other with goods and services. Alexander considers that 'the inherent need for liaison in a two-tier system became a major practical disadvantage of the new local government structure from the moment the legislation was passed' (Alexander 1982b:63). At first many counties established county-wide committees, but these either degenerated into battlegrounds for county/district rivalries or else atrophied through lack of business (Alexander 1982a:37–8; 58–9). Liaison is now conducted mainly at officer level. In some cases the districts alone have established joint committees within the area covered by a top-tier authority. The most notable example is the London Boroughs' Association (LBA) which acts both as a representative of the boroughs to outside bodies, and as a forum 'to advise and assist the constituent councils in the administration of their powers and duties' (Rhodes 1972:446). In more recent years the LBA was supplemented by a separate association representing the interests of Labour-controlled boroughs.

Agency

The concept of agency – though not the word – was introduced in England and Wales by Section 101 of the Local Government Act 1972. The former arrangements by which district councils over a certain size could receive or claim delegated powers from counties in respect of certain services were repealed and replaced by a 'provision under which local authorities can agree between themselves for one to carry out functions on behalf of another' (Department of the Environment/ Welsh Office 1974:2). Such arrangements are specifically excluded from education and the social services. Agency arrangements have been

TABLE 4.1 Allocation of principal services provided by local government in Great Britain following reorganisation in the 1970s

Top tier					Second tier			
England					England			
GLC	Met. counties	Non-met. counties	Scottish regions	Service or responsibility	London boroughs	Met. districts	Non-met. districts	Scottish districts
				Allotments*	x	x	x	x
				Arts and recreation:				
x	x	x	x	Art galleries	x	x	x	x
	x		x	Libraries	x	x		x†
x	x	x	x	Museums	x	x	x	x
x	x	x	x	Recreation	x	x	x	x
x	x	x	x	Tourism	x	x	x	x
				Cemeteries and crematoria	x	x	x	x
	x	x	x	Consumer protection	x			x
		x	x	Education	x	x		
				Environmental health:				
				Building regulations, rodent control, street cleansing, clean air	x	x	x	x
				Refuse collection	x	x	x	x
x	x	x		Refuse disposal				x
x	x	x	x‡	Fire service				
				Footpaths and bridleways:				
	x	x	x	Creation and protection	x	x	x	
	x	x	x	Maintenance and signposting	x			
				Housing	x	x	x	x
				Local licence duties	x	x	x	x
				Markets and fairs	x	x	x	x
				Planning:				
x	x	x	x‡	Building preservation, conservation, derelict land	x	x	x	x†
			x	Development control	x	x	x	x†
x	x	x	x	Development plan schemes				
			x	Listed building control	x	x	x	x†
			x	Local plans	x	x	x	x
x	x	x	x	Structure plans				
	x	x		National parks				
	x	x	x‡	Police				
			x	Rate collection	x	x	x	
x	x	x		Smallholdings				
		x	x	Social services	x	x		
				Traffic, transport & highways:				

TABLE 4.1 (Continued)

Top tier					Second tier			
England					England			
GLC	Met. counties	Non-met. counties	Scottish regions	Service or responsibility	London boroughs	Met. districts	Non-met. districts	Scottish districts
x	x	x	x	Highways	x	x	x	
				Lighting:				
x	x	x	x	Footway	x	x	x	x
x	x	x	x	Highway	x			
				Parking:				
x	x	x	x	Off-street	x	x	x	
x	x	x	x	On-street				
x	x	x	x	Public transport				
x	x	x	x	Transportation planning				
			x§	Water & sewage				

Sources: Department of the Environment/Welsh Office 1974; Local Government (Scotland) Act 1973.

*In England parishes, where they exist, are the allotment authorities. In Wales community councils hold allotment powers.

†In the three regions of Dumfries & Galloway, Highlands and Borders, the regions only are responsible for these services.

‡For these services the islands authorities are combined with the Highland Region.

§The islands authorities also have these responsibilities. In England and Wales they are no longer local government services (see Ch. 11).

fraught with controversy. The government did not intend them to be used in order to restore to the districts responsibilities they had lost to the counties, but many districts hoped this would be possible. During the preparations for the reorganisation in 1974 no fewer than 127 applications were made to government departments for decisions in disputes over agency (Richards 1975b:84). Since the early days of the transition from the old to the new system of local government, agency arrangements have continued to be disputed between counties and districts, and in some cases counties have withdrawn or altered agency arrangements into which they had previously entered (Alexander 1982a:60–5).

SUMMING UP

The services provided by local government originate in two ways. First, local government is part of the overall organisation of public administration within the state. As such, the central government will allocate responsibilities to local government in accordance with criteria that meet the political and administrative objectives of the centre at any particular time. Of course, no government operates with a clean sheet: the allocation of responsibilities between the various agencies of the state cannot always be changed easily or quickly. Nevertheless, changes constantly occur as is shown by a cursory glance at the development of local government services in Britain.

Second, local government is part of the overall democratic structure of the state. As such, local people expect to exercise power to initiate the provision of services desired in the locality. This power is secured through permissive or private legislation and is, therefore, granted at the discretion of central government. Although the services provided by local government originate in these different ways, aspects of the same service may be considered from both points of view. Education again provides a good example: central government has a strong interest in the provision of an education service which meets its perception of national priorities; local people, especially parents, expect to have considerable influence over the education provided for their children. There is, therefore, no settled agreement either about the services to be provided by local government or about the discretion local authorities can exercise over the services they provide. The allocation of services within a multi-tiered system of local government adds another dimension to the complexity.

DISCUSSION – WHO SHOULD CONTROL THE POLICE?

The police in Britain, outside London, have traditionally been the responsibility of local government. The degree of control that local police committees can exercise over police activities is limited, however, by special provisions that separate the police from the rest of the services provided by local authorities.

The modern police services in Britain originated in the needs of the growing urban areas at the beginning of the nineteenth century. These needs were twofold: the control of both 'the burglars, footpads and cut-throats who were the pest of London', and 'political malcontents as well' (Cole and Postgate 1961:260). The 'political malcontents' included the members of the developing trade union movement as well as the stage armies of the perennial fantasies of armed insurrection that were entertained by both the government and small sections of the working class in the aftermath of the Napoleonic Wars. The police were needed, therefore, not only to combat crime, but also to provide an alternative to the army in suppressing serious public disorder. In most European countries these two functions are the responsibility of separate police forces. The 'normal' police work is under local control while a paramilitary force operates either regionally or on a national basis. The combination of these two functions in Britain is seen as a safeguard against the development of authoritarian police methods, but it brings other problems as the methods of public control necessary to one function may not always be acceptable for the second.

Following the reorganisation of local government in the early 1970s, the police became the responsibility of the counties in England and Wales and of the regions in Scotland. In London, the metropolitan police – established in 1829 – continue to be under the direct control of the Home Secretary. Although the area covered by the metropolitan police is roughly equivalent to that of the former GLC, there is no local government involvement in the police service. In Northern Ireland, the police, in common with the other security services, are controlled directly by central government.

Local authority control of the police is complicated by three organisational factors. In addition there is the complex constitutional position of the constable to which we shall return later. First, in England and Wales the police authority is the police committee itself rather than the full council (Loveday 1983). The council receives reports from its police committee, but its control is possibly more tenuous than where its legal responsibility is clear (Elcock 1982:166). Care must be taken not to exaggerate the effect of the special position of the police committee in England and Wales. In Scotland, the full council is the police authority but one commentator has concluded that 'the difference is difficult to discern' (Gordon 1980:77). Second, police committees in England and Wales – though not in Scotland – must include magistrates as one-third of their membership. These magistrates are present as full members in their own right and are not co-opted as non-council members may be to the education or certain other committees. Third, some counties and regions are combined for police purposes. In England and Wales outside London, there are forty-one police forces of which ten cover areas comprising more than one county. In Scotland, there are eight police authorities. Two of these cover more than one local authority: the Islands authorities are joined to the Highlands region for police purposes, and Lothian and Borders are combined (Gordon 1980: 30–32). Joint committees develop attitudes and policies of their own which, again, are more tenuously linked to their parent councils than is the case where a committee reports directly to one authority.

The constitutional position of the police has been explained clearly and concisely by David Regan in his pamphlet, *Are the Police under Control?*:

> Before the creation of modern police forces, law and order was the responsibility of borough watchmen and parish constables. The latter is an ancient common law office. Policemen today are also constables and thus inherit the status of that office. This means that a policeman's

responsibilities to enforce the law and maintain the peace are original, not delegated. Consequently he cannot be subjected to the orders of any political superior in the exercise of these duties. Decisions about operational policing can only be taken by policemen. Constabulary independence applies not only to England and Wales but, despite its different legal tradition, to Scotland too (Regan 1983:4).

Police committees, therefore, are precluded from either directing or even questioning the chief constable on operational matters (Loveday 1983). They are confined to discussions of a very general nature and to providing the resources necessary for an efficient service.

Central government retains some direct powers in relation to the police. Local police authorities receive a 50 per cent grant in respect of police services and Her Majesty's Inspectorate of Constabulary checks the efficiency with which the service is provided. The police authority appoints the chief constable, his deputy and assistants, but the short list must be acceptable to the Home Office, who thus control the type of person appointed even if not the specific individual. The chief constable is responsible for other appointments and promotions. The various police forces also keep some links with the metropolitan police especially with respect to the special branches established to counteract 'subversive' activity (Gordon 1980:Ch. 4).

In recent years, controversies about the police have centred on three issues: the role of the police in investigating complaints against their own officers; their role in England and Wales as prosecutors – in Scotland there is an independent prosecuting service; and the development of paramilitary wings of local police forces through the creation of Special Patrol Groups or similar formations. Often these issues become linked as complaints about political or racial harassment or brutality on the part of the Special Patrol Groups are investigated by their own superiors; or allegations are made about discriminatory use of prosecuting powers. Unless the cause for such complaints arises in London, the matter cannot be raised in Parliament as no minister will accept responsibility for a local government service. On the other hand, local police committees cannot question the chief constable's operational judgement. The position is far from satisfactory and several well-publicised scandals involving police corruption or incompetence have not enhanced public confidence.

The solution to these problems is a matter of considerable debate. Michael Wheaton, an academic who has served on a police committee, believes 'police accountability to local authorities is now so ineffective that it would probably be preferable to make police forces throughout the country accountable to the Home Secretary, who in turn would have to answer to the House of Commons for police activities' (Elcock 1982:170). The Labour members of the former GLC took the opposite point of view and would have liked the metropolitan police to become the responsibility of local government in their area as well as in the rest of the country. Several police committees throughout the country are seeking more involvement with the service they supposedly control. David Regan, after a survey of current practice, thinks there may be room 'for police committees to adopt a more active and involved stance but *within* the existing system' before there is a need for new legislation (Regan 1983:13). He instances a greater use of subcommittees and more frequent reports as possible improvements which could be introduced.

Agreement on these issues is unlikely to be reached in the near future. Meanwhile the government is proposing two new measures that will keep the controversies alive. First, an independent prosecuting service is to be introduced in England and Wales in 1986, thus aligning the procedure with that of Scotland. There has been opposition to this proposal both from the Home Office and from the police, but finally the view has prevailed that 'those with an interest in solving crime should not have to be responsible for deciding whom to prosecute and for what' (Fairbairn 1983). Second, the abolition of the metropolitan counties places responsibility for the police in those areas with a joint board consisting of district council representatives and magistrates (Local Government Act 1985). Such joint boards are likely to become even more remote than existing police committees from direct popular influence.

Chapter five

INTERNAL ORGANISATION

Local authorities are large-scale organisations providing a multiplicity of services and as such present a number of managerial problems. Some of these are similar to the problems found in any large organisation. They are concerned with the procedures through which policies are implemented: communications, co-ordination and control; and with the monitoring of the effectiveness of institutional actions. Local authorities have distinctive features, however, that complicate the application of managerial theories. They are public bodies having a duty of accountability both to central government and to the electorate in their area. They employ large numbers of professional people such as teachers and social workers who practise their skills in providing a direct service to the public. Finally, and most significantly, the responsibility for providing local services is shared between appointed officials and elected councillors in a way that corresponds neither to the practices found in private organisations, nor to those obtaining in other branches of public administration. Each of these matters will be taken up later but first we need to outline the growth in awareness of the organisational needs of local authorities.

The origins of modern local government in the many single-purpose authorities created in the nineteenth century continued to be reflected in the strength of departmental organisation in the newly created compendious authorities. Greenwood and Stewart refer to 'the *traditional* conception [which] emphasises the provision of limited, statutorily defined services each of which has a distinct and separate influence upon the environment of the local authority' (Greenwood and Stewart 1974:1). Each of these services had a separate department with its own chief officer. The departmental structure was paralleled by a committee system for councillors. The chief officer and the chairperson of the committee would often work closely together for years, if not decades, to run 'their' particular service. The clerk to the local authority was the principle legal adviser and, therefore, invariably a lawyer. In smaller local authorities a local solicitor sometimes accepted this as a part-time position. The clerk was regarded as 'first among equals' by the other chief officers, but the co-ordination of services was at a minimum and sometimes non-existent.

In addition to the 'traditional' approach, Greenwood and Stewart identify two other possible conceptions of the role of the local authority in relation to its environment that have implications for internal management structure. The 'federal' approach recognises the advantages to be gained if the separate local authority services are provided within a framework that allows for economies in the use of resources and recognises departmental interdependencies. The 'governmental' approach moves away from a preoccupation with individual services altogether to a concern for the well-being of the entire local area (Greenwood and Stewart 1974:1–2). These two approaches correspond to the main movements for organisational change that dominated the 1960s and 1970s: the pressure for improvements in administrative efficiency and the encouragement of corporate planning (Stewart 1974:28–9). These movements found expression in the Reports of the Maud Committee and the Bains Committee respectively.

THE MAUD REPORT

The Committee on the Management of Local Government was appointed, 'to consider in the light of modern conditions how local government might best continue to attract and retain people (both elected representatives and principal officers) of the calibre necessary to ensure its maximum effectiveness' (Maud 1967 Vol I:iii). A parallel Committee on the Staffing of Local Government was established at the same time 'to consider the existing methods of recruiting local government officers and of using them; and what changes might help local authorities to get the best possible service and help their officers to give it' (Mallaby 1967:iii). Both committees, therefore, were concerned with similar questions and they were serviced by the same secretariat. The Mallaby Committee concentrated on the problems presented for local government recruitment in a time of full employment and a declining number of eighteen-year-olds entering the labour market. They also made recommendations concerning training, including the establishment of a Local Government Training Board. Where their interests overlapped with the Maud Committee they reached similar conclusions, and we may concentrate on the latter as dealing in greater detail with the concerns of this chapter.

The Maud Committee interpreted its terms of reference in a specific and at first sight unexpected manner. They identified the internal management of local authorities as an important factor in attracting and retaining councillors and officers of sufficient calibre and went on to be very critical of the existing system. Most of their criticisms were related to the survival 'of a nineteenth century tradition that council members must themselves be concerned with actual details of day-to-day administration' (Maud 1967, Vol I:IX). This led to a reliance on an elaborate system of committees and subcommittees and a failure to trust officers sufficiently in the taking of routine decisions. The work of local authorities was 'fragmented between too many separate departments, and these [were] seldom coherently organised or led by the Clerk. The result [was] often both inefficient and undemocratic' (Maud 1967, Vol I:IX). They found council members swamped with paper: several hundred, or in extreme cases a thousand sheets of paper being distributed to each councillor each month. Much of this paper was filled with lists of the precise car allowances paid to individual officers, details of minor repairs to council property and similar routine matters (Maud 1967, Vol I:34 and 32). At the same time as this appearance of detailed control was being given, there was little opportunity for councillors to exercise a co-ordinated leadership for strategic policy-making.

The major recommendations following from this analysis may be summarised as follows (Maud 1967, Vol I:X). First, there should be a clearer division between council member and officer. Committees should cease to be executive or administrative bodies and should concentrate on policy determination. There should be an increase in the amount of delegation from committees to both their chairmen and officers. Second, there should be a reduction in the number of committees appointed by a local authority. The Maud Committee thought half a dozen should be enough and it followed that each committee would be concerned with a wider range of matters than the existing committees. Third, all but the smallest local authorities should appoint a management board of between five and nine members. This board would receive wide delegated powers and be the sole channel through which business done in committees reached the full council. It would formulate and present proposals requiring council approval and serve as the focal point for managing and supervising the work of the local authority. Members of this management board might be paid a small part-time salary in addition to their normal council allowances. Fourth, a chief executive officer should be appointed as the undisputed head of the paid officers of the local authority. He or she would not necessarily be a lawyer.

The response to the Maud Report was mixed. In a devastating criticism Jeffrey Stanyer concluded 'that the Maud Committee must be regarded as one of the most disastrous uses of an advisory committee that can be envisaged, if one asks and expects that an advisory committee will provide an authoritative analysis of the problems set by its terms of reference, and by rigorous reasoning propose defensible solutions which have a practical use' (Stanyer 1970:66–7). Stanyer sets a high standard, but the response from practitioners was scarcely more enthusiastic. Councillors rejected completely the proposal for a management board with its implied differentiation of councillors into board members and the rest. The drastic reduction in the number of committees was felt to be impracticable.

Despite the response to some of the Maud Committee proposals, many local authorities were already re-examining their management structures. Indeed, the Maud Committee in some of its less contentious proposals simply represented an encouragement to practices already being developed in larger local authorities (Greenwood *et al*. 1969). The number of full committees were being reduced from the two or three dozen common in the early 1960s to a more manageable fifteen or sixteen, and chief executive officers were being appointed in many parts of the country. There were even some moves towards a central co-ordinating committee, though none of these shared the characteristics of Maud's management board (Hampton 1970:54-61).

THE BAINS REPORT

Following the decision to reorganise the structure of local government in the 1970s, further consideration was given to matters of internal organisation. A study group was appointed jointly by the Secretary of State for the Environment and the local authority associations under the chairmanship of M A Bains, Clerk of the Kent County Council. The membership consisted of five other local authority officers and a company secretary from Imperial Chemical Industries Ltd. A similar working group was appointed in Scotland under the chairmanship of I V Paterson but as its recommendations differed from its English counterpart only in matters of detail we need not treat it separately (Keating and Midwinter 1983:119-23).

The central theme of the Bains Report (1972) is reflected in the following quotation ' ... the traditional departmental attitude within much of local government must give way to a wider-ranging corporate outlook' (Bains 1972:6). The committee did not engage in a research programme in the manner of the earlier Maud Committee, but contented itself with receiving evidence and visiting a number of local authorities in the early months of 1972. The report was seen, therefore, as essentially practical though it was heavily influenced by the corporate planning theories advocated through the Institute of Local Government Studies and elsewhere.

The main recommendations of the Bains Committee centred around the respective responsibilities of members and officers. They took a very different attitude from Maud to this relationship believing 'that if local government is to have any chance of achieving a corporate approach to its affairs members and officers must both recognise that neither can regard any area of the authority's work and administration as exclusively theirs' (Bains 1972:8). While members must make the major policy decisions, Bains recognised that officers contribute to the stimulation and formulation of policy: ' ... the skilled professional officer is not just a servant who is paid to do as he is told' (Bains 1972:8). On the other hand, members must have an interest in matters of day-to-day administration when these affect their constituents.

The implications of this approach were outlined for both members and officers. The members should receive full information on matters affecting their electoral area and be provided with basic secretarial assistance in carrying out their duties. At the policy-making level, decisions should be taken within an administrative context that allowed policy objectives to be examined against the financial constraints imposed by finite resources. The officers should receive fuller delegated powers and then accept responsibility for decisions taken under such powers. Their advice should be available to party groups if that was where effective decisions were being taken: this is a point we shall return to later.

The committee also believed that while corporate management had implications for both councillors and officers, the structure applicable to one side was not applicable for the other. The identification of one committee with one department should be ended. It only encouraged the departmentalism that corporate management was intended to avoid. They recommended that the committee structure should be linked to the objectives of the local authority rather than to the provision of particular services. At the heart of the system there should be a policy and resources committee. This committee would include opposition members and would work through subcommittees that might include members who were not on the full committee. The officers should be led by a chief executive assisted by a principal chief officers management team consisting of about six members. These principal chief officers should in appropriate cases be responsible for more than one department. The report included structure diagrams for each type of local authority based on the outlines shown in Figs 5.1 and 5.2.

Finally, the report suggested the adoption of a 'community' approach that would include joint committees 'of county and district members for each district within the county to co-ordinate the interaction of all county and district functions and policies for the locality' (Bains 1972:93).

Most of the new local authorities based their management structure on the Bains recommendations (Alexander 1982a:69–72), usually with modifications affecting the number of committees: local authorities did not follow Bains any more than Maud in the creation of programme committees. The number of committees in most authorities is now smaller than before the 1974 reorganisation but larger than Bains suggested. Departmentalism is still strong, and has recovered some of its ground in recent years. Nevertheless, most local authorities appointed a chief executive officer, a management team of principal chief officers, and some form of policy and resources committee.

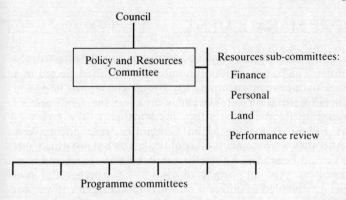

FIG. 5.1   Bains's outline committee structure (*Source*: Based on Bains 1972:99)

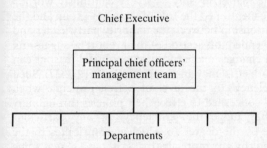

FIG. 5.2 Bains's outline departmental structure (*Source*: Based on Bains 1972:99)

The correspondence of these measures with the Bains recommendations gave, perhaps, a false impression of the commitment of the new local authorities to the principles involved. In an assessment of the years following reorganisation, Alan Alexander examined each of the three major innovations in turn. He found first, that the chief executives did not play as strong a leadership role as Bains recommended; second, that professionalism and departmentalism had prevented the development of a corporate management team; and third, that the policy committees were frequently not supported by the full range of subcommittees suggested by Bains. In particular there were few examples of a successful performance review subcommittee. Alexander concludes 'that the influence of Bains ... may be more apparent than real, more form that substance' (Alexander 1982a:76). He also notes the tendency for the various county–district joint committees 'to decline very substantially in significance and effectiveness' as the new system became established (Alexander 1982a:37). The community planning approach fell foul of the extensive county–district rivalries referred to in Chapter 3.

POLITICAL MANAGEMENT

Most local authorities are now contested by the major political parties at local elections. The parties produce manifestos and when elected in a majority seek to implement their policies. The official reports into local government administration were extremely coy about the significance of such partisanship for the matters they investigated. In the survey of councillors conducted for the Maud Committee, respondents were asked whether they were members of a political party but not which one. The results could be analysed, therefore, only between party and non-party councillors. The important dimension of whether different political perspectives led to different attitudes to management was not explored.

The Bains Committee received evidence on this question (Hampton 1972) but dealt with the matter in only two very cautiously worded paragraphs. One of these mentioned the role of the party group and the other dealt with the relationship between the majority party leader and the chief executive. They ended this section of their report by suggesting that 'frequent structural changes made for purely political reasons can only result in a loss of both efficiency and morale' (Bains 1972:37). Such a comment raises 'efficiency' to the level of a first principle when politicians are naturally concerned to effect their policies through any appropriate means. They judge the 'efficiency' of any particular administrative structure by the degree to which it contributes to the success of the policies, not by any more abstract criteria. There is some reason to suppose that different types of political policies require different approaches to administrative questions (Hampton 1972; Gyford 1976:84–5), but it is not a matter that has been examined at any depth. There is more evidence available on the internal organisation of party groups on local authorities, and a growing literature on the complex relationship of councillors and officers in politically controlled councils, and it is to these matters that we may now turn.

Formal authority in local government rests in the full council. Responsibility may be delegated to committees or to individuals occupying the chair at such committees, or indeed to officers, but the legal power to act remains with the council. Local government is different in this respect from central government where ministers derive their constitutional authority from the Crown and their political power from control of the majority of the House of Commons. Back-bench Members of Parliament whether of government or opposition parties are far more removed from questions of policy and administration than are councillors who discuss these matters through a series of committees and subcommittees.

In the councils where the members are not organised along party lines or where no party has a clear majority the debates and votes in committee and full council retain their significance. In such circumstances decision-making may become more difficult, or simply more prolonged, and forward planning may be inhibited (Haywood 1977; Wendt 1983). The councils where one political party has control, however, develop a parallel structure of policy-making alongside the formal machinery of committees and council. When fully developed the party organisation can transform the decision-making procedures of local authorities.

The organisation of party groups on the council varies between parties and within parties in different areas (Gyford 1976:77). There may be a loose arrangement which does not preclude a councillor accepting a committee chair even if in a minority party. On the other hand there are strongly organised groups that expect all members to vote in accordance with group decisions. This more disciplined approach is becoming normal procedure, particularly in the larger local authorities and in the urban areas (RIPA/PSI 1980:16–22). The group will meet once or twice a month to discuss business coming before the council and to decide on a collective attitude. Similarly, party factions will meet before major committee meetings. The leader of the group will represent the group in policy debates.

The growth in partisan organisation on local authorities presents problems of integrating the political reality of decision-taking with the formal administrative structure. There are three political levels to be considered: individual leaders, group leadership and full group membership. First, the leader of the majority group now becomes the leader of the council – a position many officers were reluctant to recognise even a few years ago – and acts as a political 'chief executive'. As such he or she establishes a close working relationship with the chief executive officer. The Bains Report referred to the need for this relationship to be 'informal' (Bains 1972:37), but other commentators would emphasise the necessity for formality if both councillor and officer are to maintain their proper roles: 'friendly but not familiar' is a frequent description of the correct attitude for a councillor to adopt towards officers, either as leader or in the chair of a committee. The increasing prominence of political groups has enhanced the role of the leader but at the same time it has reduced the power of councillors occupying committee chairs. At one time these positions gave the power to affect policy in a particular area of local authority endeavour almost irrespective of the rest of council policy. In a politically organised council, however, the minutes of all committees will be discussed in the party groups who may decide that they shall either be altered at the full council meeting or withdrawn for further consideration in committee.

The position of the policy and resources committee is the second level to be considered. The leader of the council will usually occupy the chair of this committee or its equivalent. Thus the administrative changes since the mid-1960s have given the leader a formal co-ordinating position that was not previously available. The other members of this committee may be drawn exclusively from the majority group leadership or include representatives of the opposition. Both arrangements have their supporters. If the committee comprises only majority group members then it can develop as a local 'cabinet'. On the other hand, the participation of councillors from minority groups can lead to more informed decisions and avoid mistrust (Bains 1972:28). Some councils compromise by having minority representation on the full committee while reserving membership of a key subcommittee, such as that dealing with finance or the budget, for the majority group.

The chief executive officer will be the principal officer servicing the policy and resources committee and through him or her the committee will have access to advice from all the officers of the local authority. In a politically organised council, however, the true centre of policy decision-taking may be the party group and this is the third level we need to consider. Bains believed 'that the advice of officers must be available wherever the effective decisions are taken and if it is the party group which makes these decisions then a way must be found of making the officers' advice available' (Bains 1972:18–19). Several methods of achieving this aim have in practice been adopted. Some councils have designated the party groups as official committees of the council. The majority group may form Policy Advisory Committee 'A' and the opposition groups Policy Advisory Committee 'B' or some such device. Officers can then attend to offer advice and withdraw as the group sheds its formal title and proceeds to a political decision. Less formal methods include the extension of the briefing which an officer usually gives the chairperson before a meeting to include other senior councillors (RIPA/PSI 1980:5–6).

RELATIONSHIPS BETWEEN COUNCILLORS AND OFFICERS

The presence of officers at groups of councillors organised on political lines raises in an acute form the question of the correct relationship that should exist between them. We have already noted that local government operates in a different way from central government where ministers draw their executive power from the Crown. The statutory location of decision-making power in a local authority rests in the full council. This means that models of councillor–officer relationships based on comparisons between ministers and civil servants are likely to be misleading. An officer need not accept instructions from an individual councillor, however exalted his status, unless clear delegated authority exists: officers owe their allegiance to the full council and hence to *all* councillors so assembled irrespective of party. Of course, in practice when a particular political party has a clear majority then both councillors and officers will accept the realities of the position and act accordingly; but the difference in the constitutional position is not simply one of form – it undoubtedly affects attitudes throughout local authorities.

The position is complicated by two further factors: the statutory responsibilities placed directly upon certain officers, and the professional qualifications held by many people in local government service. There is, of course, a responsibility upon everyone to comply with the law. Officers cannot avoid that responsibility by relying upon the instructions given by councillors even if the unlawful decision is made in full council. The operation of the rule of *ultra vires* (see Ch. 1) makes this a particularly onerous responsibility for local government officers. If the officers believe that a council is considering a decision for which they have no statutory authority then the council must be advised of the legal position. If they persist then the officers may be placed in an invidious position: either they disobey their immediate employers and face possible dismissal, or they comply with council policy and risk various legal penalties if the action is later held to be unlawful.

In addition to these general responsibilities, some officers have specific duties placed upon them by statute. The special position of the chief constable has been discussed in Chapter 4, but there are other officers whose position grants them a degree of independent authority. The clerk to the council must ensure that they receive any necessary legal advice before they act; the treasurer is responsible for financial rectitude; and the various Transport Acts make the officers responsible for day-to-day commercial control of public transport in the metropolitan areas. The special position of transport is described in Chapter 11. Other officers whose position is defined in statute claim a less specific but still important independent locus of authority. The chief education officer is the usual example quoted. A local education authority must by law appoint a chief education officer (Regan 1979:28): the people appointed assume responsibilities within the major spending service provided by local government. Most of them exercise, and a few have claimed, considerable personal power as a consequence (Kogan and Eyken 1973; Neve 1977). It is, perhaps, one of the reasons why the education service has been so resistant to the integration demanded by corporate management (Regan 1979:206–8).

The chief education officer also provides an illustration of the second factor we wish to mention. Local authorities are directly responsible for providing services in a way that central government frequently avoids by the allocation of responsibility to other governmental agencies. Hence local government employs teachers, social workers, housing managers, architects, engineers and so on to carry out their professional duties. Appointment and subsequent promotion depend upon the possession or acquisition of appropriate qualifications (see Ch. 9). The professional officer relies upon professional expertise when tendering advice and may be bound by formal or informal codes of ethics or professional practice. A social worker, for example, may refuse to divulge confidential information relating to a case coming before a committee, or an architect may decline to sign the necessary documents if a professional judgement is not satisfied. Councillors need to be very strong-minded, and in some circumstances foolhardy, if they are to go against strongly offered professional opinions.

This is not to say, of course, that professional opinions are always correct. There are fashions among professionals that may lead to decisions lay people would justifiably avoid. The high-rise buildings of the 1960s are local government monuments to the fallibility of professional opinion (Dunleavy 1981). On other occasions there appear to be almost as many opinions as there are professionals. We referred in Chapter 1, also, to the possibility that professional people may develop attitudes which place the interests of the profession before those of the public they are intended to serve. For all these reasons, the lay control exercised by councillors is a necessary safeguard for the public in a democratic society, but it is a safeguard not easily exercised. For instance, councillors usually rely on their officers as the sole source of professional advice. They need to be aware of the tactics officers may use to get the decision they want. When he interviewed councillors in Birmingham, Kenneth Newton was told of many such techniques including the presentation of reports so long that nobody could read them, or so short that they contained inadequate information (Newton 1976a:156). To contain such possibilities one committee chairman sought to set one expert against another (Newton 1976a:150), but this is not always very easy in hierarchically controlled departments. Some of the larger local authorities are now appointing specialist advisers to the chief executive's office, or even to the leader of the council, who can give advice divorced from the service-providing departments, but such posts are few and regarded with some suspicion by mainstream local government officers. Some local political parties are also appointing working groups to develop election policies. These groups may draw on the professional skills of individual party members who can act as an independent source of advice to the party groups on the council. In a few areas a detailed election manifesto has been adopted at the first meeting of a newly elected council as a basis for council policies (Fudge 1981).

We return, therefore, to the relationship between the officers, particularly the chief executive officer, and the party groups on the council. At a symposium organised by the Royal Institute of Public Administration (RIPA) and the Policy Studies Institute (PSI) in 1979, there 'was general agreement that the role of the Chief Executive was very different from that of a traditional clerk to the Authority. The development of corporate management and the growth of politicisation had made the position of Chief Executive both more important and more exposed to criticism than his predecessors as senior advisor to the council' (RIPA/PSI 1980:43). His advice is increasingly needed where the political decisions are being made and this involves attendance at party group meetings in some guise or other. During the discussion at the symposium several questions arose from these considerations. It was asked whether the chief executive should be expected to work closely with any majority party. The answer was undoubtedly yes. There was rather more discussion about the relations a chief executive might have with minority parties. Councillors belonging to such parties may obviously be excluded from crucial policy decisions, but they still have legitimate claims on the chief executive. He is the servant of the whole council and any councillor can expect advice and help in obtaining available information. The chief executive should behave in an open manner and not allow his political neutrality or integrity to become a matter of doubt. At the end of the symposium Sir John Boynton, at that time Chief Executive of Cheshire County Council, presented a set of guidelines incorporating this approach (RIPA/PSI 1980:48–50). The need, and the possibility, of such guidelines only emphasises the complexity of the relationship between councillors and officers in local government.

DISCUSSION – SCIENTIFIC MANAGEMENT IN LOCAL GOVERNMENT

The basic principles of scientific decision-making produce a model with the following characteristics: 'identification of needs/problems; setting of objectives; identification of alternative choices; evaluation of alternatives; choice of preferred alternatives; implementation; and monitoring feedback and review' (Leach and Stewart 1982:6). At a simple level, some elements of this process enter all decisions – from day-to-day domestic choices to major questions of public policy. When approached more rigorously, however, difficulties and disagreements soon appear from both political and practical perspectives.

Politics and scientific management
The principles of scientific management expressed through the adoption of corporate planning in local authorities are sometimes criticised for placing too much power in the hands of the full-time officers, and hence reducing the importance of the role of the elected councillors in policy-making. Scientific management systems are complex and the absorption of the mass of material generated is time-consuming. The professional officers, particularly when organised through a chief officers' team, as advocated by the Bains Committee, and led by a chief executive officer can provide a formidable obstacle to councillors intent on policy innovation that goes against conventional assumptions. This was the essence of the arguments over management structure in Sheffield and elsewhere in the late 1960s (Hampton 1972). The Conservative Party were willing to accept a corporate structure based upon the chief

83

officers' team: the Labour Party wanted the locus of corporate power to rest in a strong policy committee emphasising the practical as well as formal power of the councillors.

The corporate approach demands, as Bains outlined, a central focus in both departmental and committee structures, and John Stewart has argued that this does not lead necessarily to domination by officers or to policies favourable to any particular groups in society. The corporate approach favours 'those less committed to service departments ... groups interested more in policy analysis than in professional standards, and ... those who tend to emphasise local circumstances rather than national standards. It cannot be assumed, however, that such organisational interests necessarily serve particular external interests. ... The corporate approach is a management instrument that can be used to serve or to oppose any particular external interests' (Stewart J 1983:172–3).

The critics of corporate approaches will not be satisfied by Stewart's arguments. They point first, to the political implications inherent in centralised policy systems irrespective of the policies decided. John Dearlove argues 'that they emphasise leadership and hierarchy and centralise and concentrate power into the hands of a small group of leading councillors and officers' (Dearlove 1979:183). The emphasis is thus on the command structures found in private industry or commerce, where corporate techniques developed, rather than on the popular involvement and bargaining that should accompany democratic processes of public policy-making. The very notion of public partici-pation becomes a means of incorporating local opinion into a centralised system (Cockburn 1977).

Second, political objectives cannot be as clearly specified as the scientific or rational model seems to demand. This leads to the adoption of objectives of such generality – 'to provide for the recreational needs of every section of the population' – that they are of little practical use. It can even be argued that 'overall objectives' are inappropriate in 'practical politics' (Haynes 1980:100). The practical politician will not be tied by a commitment to rigid policy objectives, but will search for a high level of consensus around a policy generally favourable to the viewpoint of his or her political party. The politics of the corporate planner are the politics of the rationalist for whom 'The conduct of affairs ... is a matter of solving problems' (Oakeshott 1962:4), rather than a process of maintaining our common heritage. Such arguments serve to remind us that scientific management has right-wing as well as left-wing critics.

Practicalities and scientific management

There is a long-standing debate among theorists of management and administration about the possibility of rational approaches. The rationalist model has been outlined above: it is matched at the other extreme by an approach emphasising the incremental nature of most actual decisions. The practical critics of scientific management point to the impossibility of meeting the strict demands of the rational model of decision-making. The collection and evaluation of the data necessary to make a full comparison of all the 'alternative choices' available in any policy process are beyond human capabilities, even when aided by computers. The difficulties are not simply concerned with the quantity of data, but with qualitative differences as well. If a new road is being considered, how does one judge between reduced lead pollution in one area and increased noise levels in another? Or between such environmental health factors and the demolition of a Saxon church? Attempts to reduce all the factors to a common denominator through placing a monetary value upon them are riddled with uncertainty. What is the monetary value of a Saxon church or a life saved from a preventable road accident? Cost–benefit analysis attempts an answer to such questions, and can provide a helpful stimulus in comparing alternative courses of action, but it is costly and ultimately based upon value assumptions that are not always made clear to those who read the reports (Self 1972:288–9).

Many of the techniques of scientific management have been developed in private industry and commerce. They do not always transfer easily to the public sector. Simon argues, 'In one respect the decision problem in private organisations is much simpler than in public agencies. The private organisation is expected to take into consideration only those consequencies of the decision which affect *it*, while the public agency must weigh the decision in terms of some comprehensive system of public or community values' (Simon 1957:69). These values may not be agreed between the political parties and may be subject to emotional fluctuations among the general public. A well-made television programme – 'Cathy Come Home' is often quoted – may have more effect on policy-making than a scientific assessment of alternative ways of utilising limited resources. A public body is also accountable both politically and administratively: the politicians consider the effect of a given decision on the electorate at the next election; and the administrators are anxious to avoid any risk of criticism. The procedures of public decision-making, therefore, may be more cautious than in the private sector, and more prone to the excesses of paper record-keeping in case the decision needs to be defended at a later date. The consequence may well be the forms of bureaucracy that so occupy the attention of administrative reformers. As W S Steer pointed out, ' ... the department which prides itself on never making a mistake is almost certainly grossly overstaffed' (Wiseman 1970:87).

Conclusion

The difficulties inherent in the 'rational' approach to public policy-making and administration have led to a renewed interest in 'incrementalism' in local authorities. There is less emphasis on corporate planning, and on 'structure plans' that would provide a policy framework within a county over a fifteen- or twenty-year period. In place of these grand documents are 'rolling programmes' that are revised each year, and the even more prosaic procedures of periodic adjustments in response to perceived needs and anomalies when resources become available – the classic 'incremental' approach of local government. These procedures are not without academic credentials (Haynes 1980:102–7), and describe the way most organisations have always behaved for most of the time. They are now conducted, however, within a very different administrative framework following the changes introduced in the wake of the Maud and Bains Reports. Stewart argues that 'the corporate approach has led to important structural changes that have created new roles for actors in local authorities' (Stewart J 1983:172). These changes provide an opportunity for the 'mode of thought' of the rational model to act 'as a countervailing force to the well-documented tendencies within organisations and departments to perpetuate existing policies and resist innovation and change' (Leach 1982:7). The high tide of corporate planning and its associated techniques may have receded, but it has left a pattern into which traditional practices flow in new directions.

Chapter six

LOCAL GOVERNMENT FINANCE

Many of the major controversies concerning local government in recent years have been related to finance. Ratepayers have objected to rates as a form of local taxation, and governments have sought to contain the overall level of local expenditure. The subject is so complex, however, that attempts to move beyond the shallows of generalities into the deeper water of detail frequently leave the reader floundering. The present chapter is written for students of urban politics rather than for accountants, but even so there will be a need for some technical discussion. We shall be concerned in the main with the amount spent by local government, the services upon which it is spent, and the ways in which the expenditure is financed. There is also a short section on the special role of the audit in local government. We conclude by considering alternatives to the present rating system. Some aspects of the methods of containing local government expenditure introduced by the Conservative government in the early 1980s have been left for the later chapter on intergovernmental relations. They have much more to do with the politics of the relations between central and local government than with financial procedures.

LOCAL GOVERNMENT EXPENDITURE

Local government expenditure is divided between current expenditure and capital expenditure. Current expenditure consists of those items that recur regularly: expenditure on wages and salaries is the most typical example. Capital expenditure creates an asset that provides a lasting benefit such as a school or a house. Naturally, the distinction is not as clear-cut as these simple definitions imply: current items do not all disappear on the initial day of consumption; and neither do all capital items last for generations. We may define capital expenditure as that expenditure which provides benefits lasting more than one year, adds to the permanent assets of the local authority and would qualify for loan sanction (see below). All other expenditure may then be be allocated to the current account. There are exceptions even to this practical approach but it serves our present purpose. In addition to current and capital accounts, appropriate local authorities must by law maintain separate accounts dealing with such services as housing and transport.

The difficulties of assessing total local government expenditure are of two kinds. First, what items should be included – or excluded; second, what comparative measure of expenditure should be used. Money spent on goods and services is sometimes the only expenditure included, on other occasions interest charges and transfer payments to companies and individuals are added to arrive at total current expenditure. To this figure capital expenditure is added to obtain an overall total. Some of the distinctions being made will be discussed further below, but the way in which different figures for local authority expenditure may be obtained should already be clear. Differences will also arise depending on whether the figures refer to England and Wales, Great Britain (including Scotland) or the United Kingdom (including Northern Ireland). As always with statistics, one needs to ask what exactly is being counted, and for what purpose.

Having arrived at a suitable total for local authority expenditure, the next problem is how to express it in a way that allows comparisons to be made either with other contemporary expenditures or with local authority expenditure over time. When we learn from National Income and Expenditure Statistics that local authority current expenditure in 1983 was £33,692 million our first inclination may be to gasp! Our second should be to search for appropriate measures for comparison. Obviously we cannot simply rely on the raw figures if we wish to consider whether local authority expenditure had grown since the £9,230 million spent in 1974 – the year of reorganisation. The considerable price inflation between these two dates, for example, had an effect on the figures. This effect can be removed by expressing the expenditure in constant prices by statistical manipulation with an appropriate price index – the choice of which is itself a sensitive issue – but even such sophistication does not allow comparisons with what is happening in the rest of the economy. The usual solution to this problem is to express local authority expenditure as a proportion of the gross national product (GNP), that is, the total value of the output of goods and services produced within the country, together with the net property income from abroad. Again, there are different ways of calculating GNP. The various outputs may be added at market prices, or the effect of subsidies and taxes on expenditure may be excluded to arrive at GNP at factor cost. The latter method will produce a lower total of which local authority expenditure will consequently form a higher proportion unless appropriate adjustments are made. Even with such adjustments the proportion may vary between the two approaches if local authority expenditure contains a different proportion of taxes than the GNP as a whole.

The previous two paragraphs may cause the non-mathematically minded to mutter the old adage about there being lies, damned lies, and statistics. Such a conclusion would be a pity. Statistics are a convenience and if properly used allow a mobility between one set of numerical data and another that is not otherwise possible. But, to pursue an analogy from the motor trade, the small print should be examined, and one should be careful of the person from whom one buys a second-hand statistic. The student should look underneath to check that the basic framework is sound, but not be surprised if the framework varies from one source to another. After all, the construction of one motor car may differ from another without affecting its performance.

However the statistics are compiled, an examination of local government expenditure shows a steady increase over the years. It now forms a significant part of the country's output. Christopher Foster and his colleagues estimate that total local expenditure in Great Britain, both current and capital, 'increased from about 3 per cent of GNP in 1870 to about 18 per cent in 1975' (Foster *et al.* 1980:78). Within the overall upward trend there have naturally been fluctuations and current and capital expenditure have not always behaved in the same manner. For example, between 1965 and 1975 current expenditure rose quite rapidly as a proportion of GNP, while capital expenditure remained 'reasonably constant at around 5 per cent' (Foster *et al.* 1980:78). Great Britain is not alone in witnessing a growth in local government expenditure. By 1975 local expenditure represented over 20 per cent of GNP in Scandinavian countries and had been increasing substantially in other parts of Europe (Newton 1980:8–9).

After 1975 the position changed in response to both economic and political pressures. Current expenditure continued to grow in real terms, that is allowing for the effect of general inflation, but capital expenditure fell sharply (DOE/Welsh Office 1983a;5–6). Between 1975 and 1981 'total local authority expenditure declined by more than 16 per cent in real terms, with a further sharp fall in 1981–2' (Wright 1982:17).

The reasons for the growth in local authority expenditure during the 1960s and early 1970s may be summarised as follows. First, an increase in the general wealth of a country is usually associated with a greater proportionate increase in expenditure on services of the kind provided by local government. Foster *et al* show a long-run tendency for 'a 1 per cent increase in real income per head ... to be associated with a 3 per cent increase in local current expenditure per head' (Foster *et al.* 1980:90). As the economy grows, basic living needs are met more easily and extra resources are available for travel, recreation, education, social care and other services that affect local authority budgets. The growth in such services will often stem from government legislation providing for higher standards as the following examples make clear. The establishment of polytechnics in the 1960s and the general growth of further education, followed by the raising of the school-leaving age to sixteen in 1972, caused a rapid growth in educational spending on both capital and current account. New schools and colleges had to be built and more teachers had to be trained and employed. At the same time there was a rapid growth in the provision of social services. This growth was again encouraged by government legislation such as the Local Authority Social Services Act 1970. This period also saw expansion of motor-car ownership which led to both the provision of more and better roads and other traffic-related expenditure. Finally, dissatisfaction with housing conditions produced schemes for slum clearance or improvement and substantial house-building programmes.

Second, an increase in demand will sometimes occur as a consequence of maintaining existing standards as other circumstances change. An increase in the number of children born, for example, will create an additional demand for education. Improvements in social conditions and health care will extend the life-span of many elderly people thus increasing the demand for welfare services. Social changes, such as an increase in the number of divorces, may lead to a growth in the demand for more, but smaller, houses or flats, and place extra demands upon child-care services. These changing circumstances, which are outside the control of governments either national or local, are often of considerable significance. The number of children born in a year, for example, reached a peak of about 900,000 in the early 1960s and fell to about 600,000 twenty years later. This circumstance placed extra demands on the education service during the 1960s and 1970s and made possible a reduction in expenditure in the 1980s, in both cases without any change in the level of service provided (Bailey 1982).

Finally, there are a number of factors leading to an increase in expenditure that may affect local authorities at particular times. In a period of inflation, for example, when wages and salaries are increasing rapidly, local government may be disproportionately affected. The services provided by local government are labour intensive and have fewer opportunities than other branches of the economy for introducing labour-saving equipment. The reorganisation of local government in 1974 was another event which undoubtedly accentuated the general tendency for local expenditure to grow. There was a natural pressure for the newly created local authorities to adopt the highest standards provided for particular services in any of the former smaller authorities within their boundaries. These higher standards were then generalised throughout the larger area. The two-tier structure introduced for the first time in some urban areas was another source of increased costs (Alexander 1982a:Ch.3). The abolition of some second-tier authorities in the mid-1980s will not, however, necessarily lead to corresponding savings. The transitional costs of any reorganisation can be high.

So far we have considered reasons for the general increase in local government expenditure over the years. Local government expenditure also differs between local authorities: some spend more than others per head of population on particular services (Foster *et al.* 1980:261–3). The reasons for these variations are difficult to disentangle. So many factors may be statistically linked that causality is hard to establish. In his pioneering study, Noel Boaden 'suggests that activity in any service will depend on the incidence of *need* for that service, on the *disposition* of the authority to provide the service and on the availability of *resources* with which to provide the service' (Boaden 1971:21). These three factors are central to any discussion about urban politics, and 'needs' and 'resources' are terms that recur in every consideration of central government grants.

The 'need' for a service may appear obvious. We might expect a clear relationship, for example, between the number of school children and the amount of spending on education. The policies pursued by one local authority may, however, differ from those of others with apparently identical 'needs'. After a study for the Layfield Committee, Diane Dawson concluded: 'we do not at present have any way of finding out *why* particular policies are adopted by local education authorities. Why do some authorities make greater provision for pupils with special needs than other authorities faced with the same problems?' (Dawson 1976:14; Hoggart 1983) 'Needs' other than education may be even more open to interpretation. How do we measure the 'need' for public parks, for an art gallery or for a pedestrian precinct?

When we turn from 'needs' to 'resources' we find that these vary with the general wealth of an area. One of the objectives of central government grants, however, is to reduce the importance of this factor for individual local authorities. Boaden found no evidence that the availability of resources was a *cause* of spending by local authorities though the lack of them may obviously 'limit how far any authority can go' (Boaden 1971:116).

We are left with the importance of 'disposition' which encompasses the political factors involved. Boaden found that Labour councillors have a tendency to favour higher standards, and hence to support larger expenditures by local authorities, even when allowance is made for other contributory factors (Boaden 1971:112). Foster *et al.* confirm this finding (Foster *et al.* 1980:302–3), while Dawson draws attention to the probable importance of parent demand (a political factor) in determining 'differences in expenditure per pupil' (Dawson 1976:14). The technicalities of local government finance obviously cannot avoid the political nature of the decisions being taken (Sharpe and Newton 1984).

DISTRIBUTION OF EXPENDITURE

The broad distribution of local authority expenditure in the United Kingdom is given in Table 6.1. The amount against current expenditure final consumption includes all the goods and services provided by local government. Nearly half of this amount goes on education. Other big

TABLE 6.1   Local authority current and capital expenditure (selected years)

	1973		1978		1983		(1983)*
	(£m)	*(%)*	*(£m)*	*(%)*	*(£m)*	*(%)*	*(%)*
Current expenditure							
Final consumption	5,557	68.0	13,265	69.3	25,236	69.6	(73.1)
Subsidies	108	1.4	532	2.8	1,467	4.0	(4.2)
Grants to personal sector	273	3.3	822	4.3	3,035	8.4	(3.7)
Debt interest	1,444	17.7	2,910	15.2	3,954	10.8	(11.4)
Total expenditure	7,382	90.4	17,529	91.5	33,692	92.9	(92.5)
Current surplus	788	9.6	1,623	8.5	2,589	7.1	(7.5)
Total	8,170	100.0	19,152	100.0	36,281	100.0	(100.0)
Capital expenditure	3,047		3,573		3,951		

Source: National Income and Expenditure (HMSO 1984), Summary Tables.
*From November 1982, the figures are affected by the introduction of the housing benefit scheme. This has the effect of transferring some £1,750 million from central to local expenditure. This expenditure is met by a grant from central government. The figures for (1983) remove this element to give a comparison with earlier years.

spenders include personal social services and the police, each of which takes about a tenth. No other service takes more than 3 or 4 per cent. The subsidies mentioned in the table are mainly directed to housing and passenger transport. The grants include scholarships and maintenance awards for students as well as rent rebates and allowances. Debt interest forms a substantial proportion of local authority expenditure: this burden was reduced as both capital expenditure and interest rates fell in the early 1980s. The table shows a surplus provided by local authorities to allow for contingencies such as salary and wage increases. The estimates of these contingencies tend to consider the worst outcome from the point of view of the local authorities. This avoids the embarrassment – or worse – of overspending. A substantial surplus usually remains, therefore, at the end of each financial year.

CAPITAL EXPENDITURE AND INCOME

Capital expenditure by local authorities is subject to close central government control. Each local authority submits requests for permission to spend on various capital projects. The expenditure is largely needed for roads, housing and educational buildings with smaller amounts spread over other services. The expenditure is financed to some extent by capital grants from central government or from current income (see Table 6.2), but often a local authority raises a loan. These loans, for which 'loan sanction' is required from central government, may be obtained from the Public Works Loan Board (a government-financed institution), from the issue of bonds and mortgages, or from internal sources such as superannuation funds. Short-term loans may be obtained from banks or the money market. It is usual for a local authority to operate a 'loans pool' that aggregates the capital requirements and resources of all its departments. This procedure minimises the net borrowing requirements of the local authority. In the 1980s the receipts from council-house sales produced a considerable capital income that became available for other purposes subject to central government control of the amount spent in any particular year. The amount received from sales in 1982 actually exceeded the capital expenditure on housing.

LOCAL GOVERNMENT CURRENT INCOME

Current expenditure is supported by income from three broad sources: grants from central government, rates and a residual mixture referred to as 'other income'. Details are given in Table 6.2. We will consider these three sources in the ascending order of their importance in supporting current expenditure.

OTHER INCOME

Local authorities obtain income from various rents, fees and charges for the services provided. Housing rents are the largest source of income under this heading, but many other services show some income. There are fees for further education courses and charges for school meals; people pay something towards the cost of home helps and residential care for children or the elderly; commercial customers pay for refuse collection; and so on. There is also an income, usually a small or even negative net figure when costs are taken into account, for such trading services as markets, slaughterhouses, aerodromes, cemeteries and crematoria, and passenger transport. Although these various sources of other income provide substantial sums of money, they only occasionally provoke political controversy. The charge for school meals is one sensitive issue. Another is the fares paid on passenger transport. In this latter case a major controversy arose in the early 1980s between a Conservative government committed to a reduction in public expenditure and several local authorities controlled by the Labour Party. The Labour councils sought to use low fares as both a part of their overall

TABLE 6.2   Local authority current and capital receipts (selected years)

	1973		1978		1983		(1983)*
	(£m)	*(%)*	*(£m)*	*(%)*	*(£m)*	*(%)*	*(%)*
Current receipts							
Grants from central government	3,985	48.8	9,963	52.0	18,495	51.0	(48.5)
Rates	2,647	32.4	5,658	29.5	12,456	34.3	(36.1)
Other	1,538	18.8	3,531	18.4	5,330	14.7	(15.4)
Total	8,170	100.0	19,152	100.0	36,281	100.0	(100.0)
Capital receipts							
Grants from central government	241	23.6	235	12.3	381	12.7	
Current surplus	788	76.4	1,623	86.3	2,589	86.0	
Miscellaneous	—	—	27	1.4	40	1.3	
Total	1,029	100.0	1,885	100.0	3,010	100.0	

Source: National Income and Expenditure (HMSO 1984), Summary Tables.
*From November 1982, the figures are affected by the introduction of the housing benefit scheme. This has the effect of transferring some £1,750 million from central to local expenditure. This expenditure is met by a grant from central government. The figures for (1983) remove this element to give a comparison with earlier years.
The difference between capital receipts and the capital expenditure shown in Table 6.1 is met by borrowing.
Note: Percentages may not exactly total 100 owing to rounding.

planning policies and a means of redistributing income in favour of lower income groups. This conflict resulted in legislation that will be considered in Chapter 11.

Conservative governments and local authorities have recently taken a renewed interest in charges. They are considered a useful source of income and an efficient method of measuring or allocating demand. For the latter purpose proposals are sometimes made for charges to be linked with the distribution of vouchers that can be 'spent' on the appropriate service. An education voucher, for example, could be used to obtain a place at a state school, or as part payment of private school fees. This would provide, in some people's view, a fairer competition between state and private education, and lead to a reduction in the need for the state to provide such a large proportion of the service. Such proposals are naturally a major source of controversy between the political parties but some local authorities have undoubtedly been looking at charges with a fresh eye in recent years.

RATES

Rates are a particularly unpopular tax. Occasionally, as in 1974, a sharp increase in rate demands can lead to substantial national and local protests that find expression in the formation of organisations to contest local elections (Grant 1977; Lowe 1986). Mrs Thatcher once promised to abolish the rates; and several inquiries have looked at alternatives. Yet rates remain. In 1983 the government concluded ' ... they do have advantages. They are highly perceptible to ratepayers and they promote accountability. They are well understood, cheap to collect and very difficult to evade ... rates should remain for the foreseeable future the main source of local revenue for local government' (DOE/Welsh Office 1983a:14). A description of the basis of rates followed by a discussion of the incidence of this tax will help explain both the antagonism they arouse and also the reasons for their retention. The alternatives will be discussed at the end of the chapter.

Rates have their origin in attempts to share responsibility fairly among local residents for services provided in common. They pre-date modern income taxes and have developed in their present form since the Poor Relief Act 1601 (Foster *et al.* 1980:157–9). In formal terms, rates are a local tax levied on the occupiers of land and buildings. Like all taxes they consist of two elements: the tax base, or what is to be taxed; and the tax rate, or the amount to be levied on the tax base. The tax base, or rateable value, is the net annual value of the property occupied. This is defined as the rent which it might reasonably be expected to command if let from year to year, with the tenant bearing the rates and the cost of insurance and repairs. The rate is then expressed as a poundage on the rateable value. The rates actually paid, therefore, may be calculated,

$$\text{Rateable value} \times \text{Rate poundage} = \text{Rates paid}$$

It will be clear that the rates paid may vary with a change in either the rateable value or the rate poundage. This is true of any tax. For example, the income tax we pay may vary with changes either in our income or in the rate of tax charged.

Rateable value
Since 1950, the Inland Revenue has assessed rateable values in England and Wales thus removing this sensitive matter from local authority influence. The assessments, however, are fraught with difficulties. They are supposed to be related to rental values, but little property is now rented on a year-to-year basis. Commercial and industrial property is usually subject to longer agreements while domestic property is either owner-occupied or rented from a local authority or other public agency. Privately rented housing declined 'from around 90 per cent in the early years of this century, to 61 per cent in 1947 and 15 per cent in 1976' (Darke and Darke 1979:57). The calculation of rateable values, therefore, has become more and more removed from the base upon

95

which it is supposed to rest. The amount deducted from the estimated gross value in respect of repairs and maintenance in order to arrive at the net annual value is also an arbitrary figure that bears little relationship to reality (Foster *et al.* 1980:398).

These difficulties are compounded by the infrequency of revaluations. They are supposed to take place every five years but they have been postponed by successive governments and in practice only three have occurred in England and Wales since the Second World War: in 1956, 1963 and 1973. During the long gaps between revaluations, distortions in the relative valuations of different properties can occur and, of course, new property has to be valued at the notional figure that would have obtained at the date of the last previous revaluation. A revaluation of non-domestic property is promised for the near future, but a domestic revaluation is not expected until the late 1980s: a revaluation in Scotland in 1985 caused a political furore and the government will proceed cautiously. In the meantime the rateable value of the two classes of property will be adjusted in England and Wales at the time of the non-domestic revaluation 'to preserve the present ratio between the aggregate values of the two sectors' (DOE/Welsh Office 1983a: 22).

The difficulties of the present valuation system are widely recognised and alternative proposals have been made. These proposals would make either the site value or the capital value the basis for valuation. Site value rating would tax 'the market rental of each site on the assumption that it was available for the most profitable permissible development' (Layfield 1976:170). The difficulties associated with this approach include the assumption that comprehensive and detailed development plans exist for every property. These neither exist nor are necessarily desirable on planning grounds.

Capital value rating has received more substantial support. The Layfield Committee recommended its adoption for domestic property (Layfield 1976:171) and the government appeared to accept the point (DOE 1977e). But once again the prospective change was lost in further postponements of a general revaluation. The use of capital value 'that is the price which a property would realise if sold on the open market' (Layfield 1976:170) would not be neutral in its effects on ratepayers. This is one reason, perhaps, for the caution of successive governments. The caution is the more justified as there seems little agreement on the precise consequences that would flow from capital valuation except that the geographical effects would be uneven. Layfield, for example, thought capital valuation would be likely to increase the assessments on more expensive houses (Layfield 1976:172) while Foster *et al.* seem to suggest the assessments on such property would decline (Foster *et al.* 1980:409). There are also other difficulties. Some properties, for example, may not be sold at the proper market values: the price may be reduced for a sale to relatives or to obtain a quick completion; or the price may be increased by an idiosyncratic bid by a particular purchaser. Attempts to avoid these difficulties may end up with a notional capital value as far removed from reality as the present rental values (Foster *et al*. 1980:401–11). Nevertheless, some form of capital valuation would appear to be an improvement on the existing system.

Rate poundage

Financial management is a continuous process in local government. Howard Elcock, an academic who is a former councillor, has given a detailed account of this process from which the following few lines are adopted (Elcock 1982:179–83). During the summer each year the various committees consider their financial needs for the coming year, or in some cases for a rolling three-year programme. In the autumn proposals from the committees are co-ordinated by the policy and resources or finance committee and if necessary sent back for revision. At the same time the co-ordinating committee will be making a preliminary assessment of the resources available. Just before Christmas, the government announces the grant settlement for the coming year. The rest of the winter is occupied with discussions of the needs expressed by the committees, the overall policies of the council, and the resources available from grants, reserves or elsewhere. The gap between total estimated expenditure for the coming year and expected revenue from all other sources is filled by the income from the rates. A rate poundage to achieve the amount necessary is set in early spring at a formal meeting of the full council and takes effect in April. The amount levied may be restricted by central government direction thus forcing particular local authorities to curtail their expenditure.

Incidence of rates

The incidence of a tax describes the distribution of the burden it places on different individuals or groups within society. A *proportionate* tax distributes these burdens as a ratio of income: each taxpayer contributes the same proportion of income in tax. A *progressive* system increases the proportion of tax as income increases. The justification given is that richer people are better able than poorer people to carry a relatively larger share of the tax burden. A *regressive* system reverses this process. The proportion of tax paid decreases with increases in income: or to put it the other way round – the proportion of tax paid increases at lower levels of income compared with higher levels. Rates are essentially a regressive tax: the value of the house or other property occupied by a taxpayer tends to decline in relation to increased income. In other words, if one person has double the income of another, the property occupied will not necessarily have twice the rateable value. The regressive nature of rates is alleviated for domestic ratepayers by both the domestic element of the government grant (discussed later in the chapter) and the rate rebates that are available for ratepayers with incomes judged to be inadequate relative to their responsibilities and rateable value. The effect of rate rebates is to turn rates into a proportionate tax over the broad range of middle incomes, into a progressive tax at lower income levels, and to leave them as a regressive tax at higher income levels (Layfield 1976:430). Until the mid-1970s there was a tendency for the total of domestic rates to remain at 2–2.5 per cent of personal disposable incomes (income after taxes) despite wide fluctuations in other economic factors (Foster *et al.* 1980:136–8). Non-domestic rates are also regressive and there are no rebates available in England and Wales to soften the effect on industry. Agricultural land and buildings, however, have been completely free of rates since 1929. Scottish industry has been half-rated since 1958 (Foster *et al.* 1980:316–17; 413). Industry in Northern Ireland is not subject to rates. Rates are a deductible expense for tax purposes from company or partnership profits.

GOVERNMENT GRANTS

Government grants to local authorities may be justified for two reasons. First, as a support for services that have a national or general significance as opposed to being of simply local concern. The government places a statutory responsibility on local authorities to provide certain services and is not indifferent to the general level of service in localities. Second, grants may be justified as a method of redistributing the burden of providing an equal level of services among local authorities that differ in both their needs and their available resources.

Grants may be paid to local authorities in either a specific or general form. Specific grants provide a set proportion of approved expenditure on particular services. The proportion may vary: 50 per cent for one service; 75 per cent for another; 90 per cent for yet another. A specific grant allows central government to encourage local authorities to pursue particular policies by making money available only for programmes of which they approve. Specific grants have increased in importance since 1974 and now account for approximately one-fifth of current grants (excluding the housing benefit scheme) from central government to local authorities. The police account for over a third of these specific grants. General grants, on the other hand, provide a lump sum in support of local authority expenditure: the amount is not allocated to specific services. From this very complex subject two topics concerning government grants to local authorities have been selected for discussion in this section: the overall relationship between rates and grants as sources of local authority income and the methods used to distribute the general grant.

Rates and grants
The proportion of local authority income deriving from central government grants grew steadily from the middle of the nineteenth century. At that time grant was minimal but by the 1930s it matched the

rates as a source of current income (Bennett 1982:44). This rough equivalence continued until the 1960s after which the rapid growth in local authority expenditure placed such pressure on the rates – with predictable political controversy – that central government steadily increased its contribution to local finances. This contribution reached a peak of around two-thirds of the combined income from rates and grants in 1976. Thereafter the grant contribution fell. The pattern of these recent movements is shown in Table 6.3. The consequences of the declining importance of grants after the mid-1970s were obviously the opposite of the consequences of their former growth. A greater burden was placed on the rates which could only be met either by cuts in services or increases in rate demands.

The reduction in the proportional importance of government grants to local authorities accompanied a general attempt by governments in the 1970s and 1980s to reduce public expenditure. The reduction was intended not only to save central government expenditure but also to put pressure on local authorities to curb their own spending by increasing the cost to the rates thus making the expenditure more 'visible' to both councillors and the electorate. In the government's view the relationship between the decision to spend and the financial discipline of meeting the cost had been weakened as the proportion of local expenditure covered by grant had increased. Ratepayers were insulated from the costs of local decisions as central government paid a large proportion of the bill. Nor was this the full extent of the growing division between political and financial responsibility. Over half the rates are paid by commercial and industrial concerns that have no voting rights in an electoral system based on an individual franchise. These considerations led to further government legislation to limit the level of rates a local authority could levy (see Ch. 10 below).

Central government in the 1980s restricted, therefore, both the grant payable to local authorities and their ability to make good the whole of the deficit by increasing rates. The government's concern was with the level of public expenditure rather that with the relationship between grant and rate income by itself. This relationship has been a concern, however, of those who perceived the growth of central government financing as a threat to the independence of local government. 'He who pays the piper, calls the tune' was an adage frequently quoted. The Layfield Committee on Local Government Finance posed stark alternatives. Either finance local services from central funds and cease to pretend that local autonomy exists, or increase the ability of local authorities to raise their own income. They argued: 'whoever is responsible for spending money should also be responsible for raising it so that the amount of expenditure is subject to democratic control' (Layfield 1976:283). The rates were incapable of bearing the burden in their view and they expressed cautious support for a local income tax. The government in its response to Layfield (DOE 1977e) refused to accept the logic of the alternatives presented: they believed, as

TABLE 6.3 Relationship between grants and rates as a source of local authority current income

	1973 (%)	1974 (%)	1975 (%)	1976 (%)	1977 (%)	1978 (%)	1979 (%)	1980 (%)	1981 (%)	1982 (%)	1983 (%)	(1983)* (%)
Grants	60.1	60.3	65.7	67.2	64.4	63.8	62.9	61.5	59.3	57.3	59.8	(57.4)
Rates	39.9	39.7	34.3	32.8	35.6	36.2	37.1	38.5	40.7	42.7	40.2	(42.7)
	100.0	100.0	100.0	100.0	100.0	100.0	100.0	100.0	100.0	100.0	100.0	100.0

Source: National Income and Expenditure (HMSO 1984), Summary Tables.
*From November 1982, the figures are affected by the introduction of the housing benefit scheme. This has the effect of transferring some £1,750 million from central to local expenditure. This expenditure is met by a grant from central government. The figures for (1983) remove this element to give a comparison with earlier years.
Note: Percentages may not exactly total 100 owing to rounding.

politicians are wont to do, in the possibility of finding less radical compromises. In the event, as we have seen, the Layfield Report was published at the high point of the importance of government grants as a proportion of local income. Thereafter, both Labour and Conservative governments reduced the proportion, but there has been no indication that they are less inclined to 'call the tune'.

General grants

A full discussion of the methods of distributing the general grant is beyond the scope of this book. In their major work on local government finance, Foster and his colleagues describe it as the 'mystery of mysteries' (Foster *et al*.1980:4) while Bennett in more prosaic style simply refers to it as 'very complicated' (Bennett 1982:3). The difficulties arise in attempting to devise a formula that will distribute the grant so as to equalise its effects on the needs and resources of all local authorities. These difficulties are compounded when the government uses the grant system as a method of disciplining local authorities who overspend centrally determined targets.

The methods of distributing the general grant have varied over time. From 1967 the grant was known as the rate support grant (RSG) and contained three elements described by Bennett as follows:

(i) *Domestic rate relief*: a per capita subsidy to local residential taxpayers as opposed to commercial and non-domestic taxpayers.
(ii) *Resources equalisation*: a component aimed at equalising differences in the tax base of different local authorities.
(iii) *Needs equalisation*: a component aimed at equalising differences in the expenditure requirements of different local authorities (Bennett 1982:3).

Domestic rate relief was introduced in 1967 as a result of concern at the regressive nature of the rates and the burden they were thought to impose on ratepayers. From 1975 the amount has been the equivalent of a rate of 18.5p in the pound in England. This amount has also been applicable to Wales since 1982 although for several years before that date the subsidy in Wales had been approximately double that paid in England (Bennett 1982:80). The amount paid in Scotland has at times been higher than in England and it continued to increase after the English subsidy was stabilised in 1975 (Foster *et al*. 1980:315). In more recent years the domestic element in Scotland has been reduced and in 1983 it was the equivalent of a rate of 3p in the pound.

In 1981 the resources and needs elements of RSG were combined to form a block grant which is paid direct to all local authorities. An individual authority's entitlement is the difference between its total expenditure and the amount it is deemed able to raise from rates to finance that level of spending. This amount is its rateable value multiplied by a grant-related poundage (GRP) set by the Secretary of State for each category of local authorities. The grant does not, however, represent a blank cheque. The government makes an assessment of the grant-related expenditure (GRE) for each local authority, and expenditure in excess of this figure qualifies for a reduced proportion of grant and eventually for financial penalties. These adjustments are made by variations in GRP.

The GRE for a particular local authority is the government's assessment of how much it would cost that authority to provide a typical standard of service, having regard to its general circumstances and responsibilities. The basic approach is to analyse the national totals which are then examined to identify measurable factors which influence the cost to authorities of providing various services and to assess the relative importance of the different factors for each service. There are a large number of factors but they fall into five broad categories: the population of the area; the physical features of the area; social and environmental problems; differences in the costs of providing services between areas; and special requirements for particular services. Each factor has a unit value and the product of the numbers of the various factors by the appropriate unit values gives the GRE for each local authority (Bennett 1982:104–9).

Students who find the previous paragraph difficult to follow are in good company. The approach to needs assessment used in the former RSG has been described as 'a brilliant device provided one does not inquire too closely into what it means' (Foster *et al.* 1980:423) and the block grant system presents some of the same difficulties. The principal problem is the lack of precise measures of need. Simple per capita assessments, such as the number of schoolchildren, give a very crude measure of need. The assessment has to be refined, to continue the example, to take account of special needs posed by different circumstances or types of children. These adjustments to measurable criteria may be made by reference to research studies or to 'expert' judgement. In some cases statistical techniques (regression analysis) are employed that may use past expenditure on particular services as a proxy for need. This produces something very close to a circular argument: a local authority 'needs' to spend more because it spent more previously!

In Scotland a different method of assessment of need has been adopted in response to 'a desire to avoid the heavy dependence on statistical method implicit in the regression analysis approach in England' (Midwinter 1984:67). The Client Group method takes the number of clients for each service in each local authority and multiplies these by the average expenditure per client based on national figures. Various adjustments are made to allow for special circumstances affecting local costs of providing particular services. This approach has been criticised on similar technical grounds to the assessments of need in England and Wales. In addition there is the conceptual difficulty of defining clients for some services such as the police or highways.

The assessment of needs is not, therefore, a matter of objective measurement. The assessment is riddled with judgements made on the

basis of professional experience or political choice; special arrangements are introduced for London; and various changes are introduced
each year that may have important consequences for the assessments of
individual local authorities. Such a subjective process is controversial by
its very nature and becomes more so when it is used as a basis for
penalising local authorities perceived as 'overspending'.

LOCAL GOVERNMENT AUDIT

The accounts of all local authorities are subject to annual external audit.
Until 1983 the District Audit Service carried out most of this work in
England and Wales with the balance being audited by commercial
auditors approved by the Secretary of State for the Environment. From
1983 an Audit Commission absorbed the District Audit Service. Local
authorities no longer have the power to appoint their own auditors. The
commission is independent of both central and local government
although the Secretary of State has a power to issue directives and local
councillors are included among its membership. The new arrangements
for England and Wales were anticipated in Scotland following local
government reorganisation in 1975. A Commission for Local Authority
Accounts in Scotland 'is required to appoint a Controller of Audit and
to secure the audit of all local authority accounts, either by directly
recruited officers of the Commission or by private practitioners
appointed by the Commission' (Layfield 1976:100).

The requirements for local authority audit are wider than those
appropriate for commercial accounts. The code of practice for the
former District Audit Service referred to four additional responsibilities. First, the auditor must be satisfied of the legality of items of
account under the strict rules governing *ultra vires* expenditure (see Ch.
1). Second, there is a duty to ensure that different sections of the public
have been fairly treated. Third, there is a specific responsibility to
uncover fraud. Fourth, there is a general duty to report on matters
arising from the accounts that should be brought to the attention of the
council and the public. The auditor, therefore, 'must be concerned not
only with the form and regularity of the accounts but also with issues of
substance arising therefrom, such as the possibility of loss due to waste,
extravagance, inefficient financial administration, poor value for
money, mistake or other cause' (Layfield 1976, App 1:188).

The Layfield Committee received complaints about the difficulties of
providing safeguards against inefficiency when a local authority is
acting within its legal powers. Ultimately, this responsibility must rest
with the electorate, but they do not always receive the information
necessary to make judgements. The Audit Commission originated in
these concerns of the Layfield Committee, but its role has been widened

to encompass general questions relating to efficiency in local government. A member of the commission writes of four main differences from the previous arrangements:

1. The Audit Commission will have resources to do more work on value for money;
2. It has no powers to impose solutions on a local authority, but it can insist on adequate publicity for its reports;
3. It has the powers to investigate the impact of central government actions on economy, efficiency and effectiveness of a local authority. Local government has frequently complained in the past of the adverse effect of some legislation and ministerial directives. In the future they can ask the Audit Commission to investigate the effects;
4. Above all it has the authority to create the atmosphere for an improvement in the efficient use of resources from which all of local government can benefit (Shaw 1983:21).

The commission should not be concerned with local authority policy decisions, but in how these decisions are implemented. The distinction may on occasion be difficult to discern. Decisions on management structures may themselves be decided on political rather than efficency grounds (see Ch. 5). Accountants are not professionally qualified to distinguish between the lack of cost effectiveness arising from legitimate political decisions of councillors and that arising from management failures (*The Times* 5.4.83). In these respects and in matters concerning central – local government relations, the Audit Commission has found itself even more involved than its predecessors in matters of political controversy.

DISCUSSION – ALTERNATIVES TO THE RATES

Some form of property taxes are an almost universal source of income for local government, but in many parts of the world they are accompanied by other forms of taxation. The variety is immense. Local sales taxes, motor vehicle duties, poll taxes, taxes on industry, on commuters, or on tourists, are all used somewhere in the world – and local income taxes are common. In Britain the only local tax capable of local adjustment to be levied has been the rates, but there has been constant discussion of possible alternatives or supplements to this traditional tax.

Any local tax should meet several criteria if it is to be introduced. The Layfield Committee suggested two principal considerations. First, any new source of revenue should be capable of producing a yield large enough to provide for the possibility of a substantial reduction in both grant and domestic rates. Second, in order to enhance accountability local taxation should 'be clearly perceptible. Thus the level, and most importantly the change in the level, of any source of revenue should be set locally ... ' (Layfield 1976:184). In addition to these considerations of Layfield, the collection of the tax should not be excessively costly or present substantial new administrative problems. Finally, a local tax should interfere as little as possible with the ability of central government to pursue its economic policies (Foster *et al.* 1980:483–4).

When measured against these criteria most of the alternatives to the rates are less than convincing. A local tourist tax, for example, would produce little revenue in most parts of the country. On the other hand, a local sales tax which could produce high revenues would be complex to administer, and difficult for the local elector to disentangle from value added tax or prices in general. Moreover, variations in a local sales tax, or in a tax on vehicles or petrol could lead to unwanted distortions in trading patterns. Some people already move house to escape high rates: it would be even easier to change shopping habits to escape higher sales taxes. After a careful examination of all these factors, the Layfield Committee concluded: 'a local income tax (LIT) on personal incomes, levied according to where people live, is the only serious candidate for a new source of local revenue that could give a substantial yield and at the same time maintain or enhance accountability' (Layfield 1976:190–1).

The advantages of introducing LIT would be considerable. The tax base would be buoyant, that is, it would increase as incomes grew, and the amount paid could be related to income to produce a proportionate or progressive yield instead of the fundamentally regressive impact of rates. A LIT would also be immediately visible to a much wider section of the population – income-earners – than the rates which are levied on householders and other occupiers of property. The revenue raised could be substantial.

Despite the advantages British governments have not considered it either desirable or possible to introduce LIT. The reasons are political, economic and practical. The political difficulties lie in the relationship between LIT and national income tax. The level of income tax is a sensitive political issue. Movements in the basic rate of tax are part of the campaigning rhetoric of general elections. The public would not easily distinguish between local and national tax payments. In any case a government committed to a reduction in taxes on incomes would not welcome the substitution of LIT for domestic rates (DOE/Welsh Office 1983a:13).

In the evidence to the Layfield Committee, the Treasury outlined the economic implications of LIT. Such a tax would, they concluded, both 'constrain and complicate the government's ability to manage the economy' and 'carry some possible risk to incentives and to the encouragement of inflationary wage demands' (Layfield 1976, App 8: 211). Two academic members of the Layfield Committee have subsequently described this as 'just the centralist orthodoxy that should be challenged' (Jones and Stewart 1983b:100), but it is at present firmly entrenched.

The practical difficulties of introducing LIT have been stressed by the Inland Revenue. The existing income tax system in this country is more complex than in other countries. This would complicate the administration of LIT. The differences also mean that references to countries that already have LIT are not as persuasive as would at first appear. Another difficult problem to overcome is the lack of an appropriate address list from which to allocate LIT payers to appropriate local authorities. The Inland Revenue keeps no up-to-date list and to use the Electoral Register might encourage people to omit their names and hence lose their vote (Layfield 1976:199–201; App 8:138–42). The administrative difficulties led the Inland Revenue to argue that unless the national income tax system was made simpler the addition of LIT 'would be too much' (Layfield 1976, App 8:185; cf. Bonner 1977). The Confederation of British Industry after examining the extra work for employers described themselves as 'horrified' at the thought of LIT (Layfield 1976, App 8:249).

For the present these views are likely to prevail despite Layfield's conclusion that LIT was 'feasible' (Layfield 1976:207). The government decided against further work on LIT and accepted 'that rates should remain for the foreseeable future the main source of local revenue for local government' (DOE/Welsh Office 1983a:14). Moreover, the growing dependence of local government on central grants that so concerned the Layfield Committee has been reversed. The proportion of local authority expenditure supported by grants has been reduced to a figure Layfield thought could only be reached with the aid of LIT (Layfield 1976:184). This reduction has, however, been accompanied by stringent central controls rather than an increase in local independence. The arguments for LIT from those who wish to see local autonomy preserved will, therefore, continue (Jones and Stewart 1983b:99–102). The discussion about the merits of LIT that began with the introduction of the modern local government system at the end of the nineteenth century is more likely to stand adjourned than be ended.

The clamour of disgruntled ratepayers caused the government to produce yet another discussion document in 1986. They suggested a 'community charge' to replace domestic rates. This charge would be a form of poll tax expressed as a single amount per head of adult population. Considerable opposition to this proposal was immediately expressed by a wide range of people: not least because it could be intepreted as a tax on the right to vote if the Electoral Register was used as a basis for the tax. Even assuming its acceptance, the new scheme would not be fully implemented before the end of the century. Rates will be with us for a long while to come.

Part Two

THE POLITICAL CONTEXT

Chapter seven

LOCAL COUNCILLORS, PARTIES AND PEOPLE

Local authorities in Britain are part of a wider democratic system of government. As such there is controversy about the extent to which it is justifiable to describe them as political systems in their own right. Cox and Morgan define a political system as 'a set of structures and processes, the core of which is an authoritative centre of decision making' (Cox and Morgan 1973:21). Local authorities possess in the full council meeting a 'centre of decision-making', but they do not control all public policy decisions within the geographical area in which they operate. Many decisions are taken by local and regional offices of national government departments and other agencies. These provide a network of public services complementing those provided by local authorities. In some instances, such as the payment of various National Insurance benefits, the national services are unrelated to the activities of local government. In other cases there is a close interaction between national and local government responsibilities. We may instance transport, where there is a complex relationship between a central government department, local authorities and British Rail. The Manpower Services Commission's involvement in vocational training in local authority colleges of further education provides a further example. In addition to these complications of overlapping jurisdictions within the locality, local government itself is constrained by central government influence and control in a manner we shall discuss in Chapter 10.

Despite these possible obstacles to defining the boundaries and content of a local political system, local government has traditionally shown two characteristics of autonomous behaviour which have been reflected in different policy outcomes between local authorities of otherwise similar conditions. These two characteristics are control over an independent source of taxation and the legitimacy conveyed by popular election of the local council. Local government finance was dealt with in Chapter 6, and we now turn to the relationship between the elected councillors and their constituents. The interaction of local government with national institutions and central government will be considered in Chapters 9 and 10.

Local government is based on the system of representative democracy: councillors are elected to make policy on behalf of the general population. One justification often advanced for local government is the opportunity thus presented for wider sections of the population to become involved in political responsibilities than could be accommodated at a national level. Representative democracy, however, whether at national or local level, must be distinguished from the participatory approaches that provide for direct involvement in the policy-making process (Pateman 1970). The number of councillors is small relative to the size of the population they represent; and the ratio has grown still larger since local government reorganisation in the 1970s reduced the number of local authorities and hence of councillors. In considering a local representative system it is necessary first to discuss the nature of both the electoral practices and the people who become elected. Second, we are concerned with how the representatives perceive their role and how they organise themselves to fulfil their tasks. Finally, we need to know how the representatives relate to the people they serve. These relationships between politicians, parties and people form the basis of the chapter. We conclude with a brief discussion of the interaction of some recent participatory initiatives with the local representative system of democracy.

THE LOCAL ELECTORAL SYSTEM

Councillors are elected in a similar manner to Members of Parliament. The same Electoral Register is used for both types of election and much the same criteria for inclusion and exclusion are applied. There are some differences, however, and these are best understood if we consider first those who may vote in local elections and second those who may be elected as councillors.

Every British citizen (or citizen of the Republic of Ireland) who is over the age of eighteen is entitled to vote unless disqualified for a specific reason. A Register of Electors is compiled each year listing those people resident in the area on the 10 October. The new register comes into use the following February. Registration is compulsory – though voting is not – but there are still some people who are not registered either by accident or because they wish to avoid declaring their residence. People disqualified from voting include those convicted of corrupt and illegal practices in elections during the previous five years; those imprisoned for felony or treason; and those detained in psychiatric hospitals. Members of the House of Lords appear on the Electoral Register for local and European electoral purposes only: they are allowed neither to vote in parliamentary elections nor to serve as Members of Parliament.

Conditions for voting in local and national elections only became fully assimilated following the Representation of the People Act 1969. Before that Act non-residents could register for the vote in local elections if they occupied property in the area with a rateable value of at least £10 per annum. This provision now applies in the City of London only. The link between ratepaying and voting went back to the foundation of the present local government system. 'In 1853 the Municipal Corporations Act had established the rule that the right to choose the borough councillors should be restricted to those who, as ratepayers, made a direct contribution to the funds which the councillors would control' (Keith-Lucas 1952:224). The local government reforms following 1888 established new authorities with a franchise almost identical with the municipal boroughs. After 1945 the local franchise was extended to all residents in the area but the right to qualify by occupation of property remained until 1969.

Bryan Keith-Lucas has described how during the nineteenth century the local government franchise gradually became based upon general Acts of Parliament rather than on a 'medley of jurisdiction and authority' deriving from the common law and local Acts (Keith-Lucas 1952:221). During this process some women first lost and then gained the right to vote. At common law married women were excluded from the vote along with many other privileges that were open to men. 'The position of single women was less clear ... in some boroughs they voted on an equality with men' and although there was no general rule women could vote in many parish vestries (Keith-Lucas 1952:165). The Municipal Corporations Act 1835 specifically excluded all women from the local borough franchise, but single women continued to enjoy the vote and even the right to be elected in many parishes and important local bodies, such as the Poor Law Guardians, associated with them. The emphasis on property-holding, and hence liability for rates, as the basic qualification for the franchise in local elections was thus an advantage for some women in the struggle for the vote. Several Acts of Parliament in the latter part of the nineteenth century extended the right of women to vote in local elections if they were otherwise qualified. By 1911 the size of the local electorate in England and Wales excluding London was 3,265,000 of which about 419,000 were women (Sheppard 1982:20). These precedents contributed to the campaign for the parliamentary franchise although full equality with men was not achieved in either local or national elections until 1928 (Keith-Lucas 1952:165-9; Keith-Lucas and Richards 1978:18-19).

CANDIDATES

The qualifications necessary to enable a person to stand in a local election are more extensive in some instances and more restrictive in others than those which enable a person to vote. A registered elector over the age of twenty-one may be a candidate if not disqualified, but in addition people may stand for election if they have occupied property, been resident or had their main place of work in the area for at least twelve months. In addition to the disqualifications that apply to voting, a person may not be a candidate if he or she has been declared bankrupt within the previous five years, has incurred or authorised unlawful expenditure by a local authority above £2,000, or is a paid employee of the local authority.

The disqualification of employees from standing for election to their own local authority rests upon the need both to avoid a possible conflict of interest and to preserve the political neutrality of local government officers. The Committee on Rules of Conduct in Local Government after considering the case for a relaxation of this disqualification concluded 'that there should be no change in the existing law' (Redcliffe-Maud 1974:32). This view is not accepted by the trade unions and the Labour Party. They argue that the conflict of interest may be no greater for employees of a council than for people who have business connections with the local authority. The public interest in the latter case is protected by a general rule that they must declare their personal interest in any matter that comes before the council and must not then take part in the proceedings. The argument based on the desirability of senior officers preserving a stance of political neutrality is also contested. The considerations involved with senior officers are not so obvious when extended to employees who have no part in the preparation of policy advice. A bus driver, for example, or a school caretaker is unlikely to compromise the performance of his or her duties by a public declaration of political opinions. Their immediate superiors might be embarrassed by the reversal of roles, however, if junior staff became elected councillors. Some of these difficulties could be avoided by adopting rules governing the political activities of local government employees similar to those that apply to national civil servants. Different rules could apply to employees at higher and lower grades to protect the political neutrality of senior officers, and employees who became councillors could be prevented from serving on committees concerned with their own services.

The existing disqualification applies only to becoming a candidate for the local authority which employs a person. From 1974 every area in the country, with the exception of the Scottish Islands, was covered by two local authorities: a county or region and a district. An increasing minority of local councillors were elected who were employed by another local authority in their area. A bus conductor could serve on a district council, for example, and a school caretaker in a metropolitan district could serve on the county council. The system is evolving without the benefit of a fresh look at the implications and principles involved and will be further complicated by the abolition of the GLC and the metropolitan counties.

COUNCILLORS

Two national surveys have given details of the types of people who are elected as councillors. The field-work for the first was conducted in 1964 as part of the research for the Committee on the Management of Local Government. The terms of reference of this committee referred to the need for local government to 'continue to attract and retain people ... of the calibre necessary to ensure its maximum effectiveness' (Maud 1967, Vol I:iii). The second survey was conducted in 1976 for the Committee of Inquiry into the System of Remuneration of Members of Local Authorities (Robinson Committee). The question of payments to councillors will be considered below but first we shall look in more detail at the results of the two surveys.

Both surveys were conducted in the context of a perceived need to encourage able people to put themselves forward for election. This concern about the calibre of councillors has a long history. George Jones has quoted from *The Times* of 1880 to show that it existed before the creation of the present local authorities (Jones 1969:150). John Dearlove in his critique of the reorganisation of British local government reviews a literature that consistently points to a decline in the standards of councillors. He quotes Hennock who wrote, 'It seemed to many observers that there had been a change for the worse since 1835!' (Dearlove 1979:80).

The view that the concern about the declining calibre of councillors has much in common with the opinion that *Punch* is not as good as it used to be, and the well-known response that it never was, can be supported from the details given in Table 7.1. Councillors have better educational qualifications and are more likely to work in non-manual occupations that the population at large. In 1976 half the councillors had received higher education and this proportion had more than doubled since 1964. Of course, we cannot draw conclusions about the calibre of a person simply from his or her occupation or education, but these figures do not support the view that councillors lack either the education or administrative experience to perform their duties. Table 7.1 shows several other changes between 1964 and 1976. The proportion of owner-occupiers among councillors increased in line with the general growth in this form of tenure and they continued to exceed the general population in this regard. Council tenants are substantially under-represented on local authorities. The proportion of female councillors increased during the same period from 12 to 17 per cent, and the average age of councillors declined. These changes, together with the improved educational standards, are related to the reorganisations in the 1970s. Many older councillors took this opportunity to retire or failed to gain nomination to the new local authorities. In particular the abolition of the office of alderman removed many elderly people from places they had occupied by virtue of indirect election by the councillors. Aldermen

TABLE 7.1 Profile of councillors compared with the general population

| | Councillors | | Population* |
	1964 (%)	1976 (%)	(%)
Sex			
Male	88	83	48
Female	12	17	52
Age			
21–44	20	26	43
45–64	57	54	33
65+	22	20	25
Dwelling tenure			
Owner-occupier	66	76	53
Rented from local authority	16	16	31
Rented privately/rent free	18	8	16
Education			
Higher education	23	50	8
Other qualifications	28	13	25
No qualifications	49	37	67
Employment status			
Economically active			
Full-time employment	66	65	—
Part-time employment	5	7	—
Other	—	3	—
Economically inactive			
Retired	20	16	—
Housewife	7	7	—
Other	1	2	—
Type of employment (economically active males only†)			
Manual	—	33	60
Non-manual	—	65	38
Other	—	2	2

Sources: Robinson 1977, Vol II; Maud 1967, Vol II.
*The percentages for the general population refer to the nearest year to 1976 for which comparable figures are available. Full details are given in the source.
†The population figures have been recalculated as if the population had the same age distribution as councillors.

were elected for six-year terms of office in counties and boroughs in the proportion of one-third of the number of councillors (one-sixth in London). They were often remote from the day-to-day politics of ward parties and this handicapped them in the search for nominations in the elections to the new authorities.

A thumbnail sketch of the average councillor would present him as male, middle-aged, middle-class, and with a higher than usual level of education. This profile does not differ either from similar sketches of Members of Parliament or of those who participate in other forms of local public life (Boaden *et al.* 1980, 1982). Indeed despite the small proportion of women councillors they are rather better represented in local councils than in Parliament where the proportion has never reached 5 per cent (Stacey and Price 1981:41).

PAYMENTS TO COUNCILLORS

Both surveys of councillors show approximately two-thirds in full-time employment. Such councillors face two problems. First, they may have difficulty in obtaining the permission of their employers or colleagues to absent themselves from work while on council business. Second, they may suffer financially through loss of earnings during their absences. Robinson found that this applied to about one-third of all councillors (Robinson 1977,Vol I:26). These two problems may merge to produce even greater difficulties for prospective councillors. Employers may be expected to allow reasonable opportunities for their employees to engage in public service, but substantial demands for time off may either be refused or constitute a block to career advancement. When a person is seeking employment, council membership and the demands it imposes are unlikely to recommend him or her to prospective employers. There may be many councillors, therefore, who suffer substantial though undefinable loss of job opportunities through their council membership.

Two remedies for these difficulties have been advanced. First, the payment of various forms of allowances to council members, and second the transforming of the role into a full-time occupation similar to that of a Member of Parliament. The Robinson Committee reviewed the historical background to the remuneration of councillors:

> Prior to the Local Government Act 1948 no comprehensive or uniform scheme of members' allowances existed. Councils had a limited power to pay certain travelling expenses, and in some cases subsistence allowances, to their members, but only Scottish county councils could pay their members any allowances for the time taken off from their ordinary employment to attend to council business. Chairmen of county councils and mayors of boroughs in England and Wales could receive some remuneration, but this provision was not extended to Scotland (Robinson 1977, Vol I:3).

The 1948 Act established two new principles: council members should be eligible to receive payments for loss of earnings or necessary expenses; and these payments should relate to the performance of 'approved duties'. The allowances were varied over the years to take account of inflation, but were never particularly generous. The loss of earnings allowance approximated to the average male industrial wage. 'Approved duties' included council and committee meetings and other duties approved by the council in accordance with its functions.

With only slight amendments these arrangements continued until the reorganisations in the 1970s. Following the legislation in 1972 (England and Wales) and 1973 (Scotland) councillors are 'entitled to receive an attendance allowance as of right, without the need to demonstrate financial loss, for the performance of duties approved by his local authority' (Robinson 1977, Vol I:15). Both the maximum daily amount that may be paid and the limits of discretion in defining approved duties are subject to central government advice or regulation. Co-opted members of council committees continue to be entitled to a financial loss allowance if they can show loss of earnings resulting from council work. Later legislation, the Local Government Planning and Land Act 1980, gave councillors the choice between the two systems of allowances: loss of earnings allowance or attendance allowance. For the financial year 1983/84 the maximum attendance allowance was £15.07 per day and the financial loss allowance was £21 for a full day or £10.50 for periods up to four hours.

The Robinson Committee were very critical of the attendance allowance system which they considered was 'widely misunderstood' and 'distributes the money available on a wholly wrong basis'. A system based solely on attendance does not take account of the range of a councillor's duties; leaves some councillors better off than others (depending on their employment situation); and does not adequately reflect the added responsibility carried by senior councillors. For these reasons the committee recommended the abolition of the attendance allowance and its replacement by a combination of a basic payment, a financial loss allowance and a special responsibility payment for councillors occupying certain senior positions (Robinson 1977, Vol I:45–8). The government did not accept fully these recommendations but as we have seen they gave councillors the choice between claiming an attendance allowance or financial loss allowance. The same legislation provided discretionary powers for local authorities who wished to pay special responsibility allowances to councillors holding such positions as committee chairs. The total amount available varies with the size of the local authority. The maximum in 1983/84 was £11,300 for the largest authorities which they were free to distribute in accordance with their own policies (Skelcher 1983).

One alternative to the present system of allowances would be to pay councillors a full-time salary. The Wheatley Commission were in favour of this approach (Wheatley 1969:224–5) but councillors generally have not been in favour and the Robinson Committee rejected the possibility (Robinson 1977, Vol I:45). The objections are of both a constitutional and a financial nature. If all councillors became full-time politicians then this would restrict the range of people coming forward for election and could alter the balance of the relationship between them and the officers of the council. It would also be expensive if realistic salaries were paid and the existing number of councillors retained. In countries such as Japan and the USA where salaried councillors exist there are typically far fewer seats available. Despite these objections to creating full-time salaried councillors, the demands placed on those elected can be considerable. In 1976 councillors spent an average of seventy-nine hours a month on their duties (Robinson 1977, Vol II:20). This figure had increased substantially since 1964 and, of course, conceals considerable variations for individual councillors. A senior position on a major local authority is virtually a full-time job. There is a growing number of councillors, particularly in the larger cities, who have no other paid employment and who rely on attendance allowances for their livelihood. The recompense is meagre, but when combined with ideological enthusiasm it helps sustain a new type of local politician.

COUNCILLOR TYPOLOGIES

Councillors differ in their attitude to their role and this has led to the development by political scientists of typologies to describe the variations. The most elementary division is between those who concentrate on the representative function of a councillor by looking after the interests of individual constituents and those who prefer the managerial function of determining policy and ensuring its implementation. In 1976 councillors spent on average thirteen of their seventy-nine hours a month on electors' problems. For the rest of the time they were concerned with broader matters (Robinson 1977, Vol II:20). Unlike Members of Parliament, all councillors are formally responsible for policy decisions through attendance at full council or committee meetings. The 1964 survey showed about a third of councillors preferring to deal with the problems of individuals with 43 per cent preferring broad policy matters. The remainder would not or did not distinguish between these two aspects of their work (Maud 1967, Vol 2: 139). The preferences were shown to relate to various characteristics. Men and people in managerial or professional occupations preferred the policy-making aspects, while women and people in manual occupations preferred dealing with the problems of individuals. A later survey in Sheffield showed how membership of a majority party, and consequently the opportunity to implement policies one agreed with, could influence these preferences. Women with power, for example, were much less likely to conform to their role stereotypes than those without (Hampton 1970:193).

A more sophisticated analysis is presented by Kenneth Newton in his study of Birmingham. He examines six different dimensions of the councillor's role:

(1) attitudes towards the nature of representation, (2) behaviour within council groups, (3) preference for governing the city as a whole or looking after the interests of a ward, (4) preference for dealing with general policy issues or with individual problems, (5) preference for specializing in one aspect of council work or generalizing over them all, and (6) attitudes towards the involvement of community organisations in the government of the city (Newton 1976a:114).

From their attitudes to these six dimensions, Newton constructs five role types among Birmingham councillors. The *parochial* is concerned exclusively with individual problems arising in the ward he or she represents. *People's agents* extend this concern for individuals to a more generalised opposition to injustice and oppressive bureaucracy. *Policy advocates* are concerned with running the city as a whole in line with policy preferences expressed, for example, in a party manifesto. *Policy brokers* are less ideological than *policy advocates*. They are more likely to perform the classical political role 'of mediator and reconciler of different interests'. Finally, the *policy spokesman* speaks 'on behalf of his constituents on general policy matters'. He is a generalised *parochial* (Newton 1976a:137–42).

The new urban left
Such abstract typologies help us to understand the behaviour of councillors as a group but they do not necessarily apply to individual councillors who may exhibit characteristics drawn from several of the main types. Moreover, different configurations may arise at various times. One such development is the councillor who is associated with the 'New Urban Left' (Gyford 1983b). From the early 1970s a new attitude towards local government was introduced by sections of the left-wing of the Labour Party. Their disillusion with the reformist nature of the Labour governments of the 1960s, and the excitement generated by the world-wide social unrest of 1968, led them to look for the possibility of social change in local protest movements. By the early 1980s this strategy had been linked to the idea of local government acting as a mobilising force for working-class organisations and radical action groups of various kinds (Blunkett and Green 1983; Gyford 1983b; Boddy and Fudge 1984). Some of the policies pursued by councils where the New Urban Left gained control will be referred to in Chapters 12, for the present we are concerned with the nature of the new type of councillors.

Using Newton's typology, the New Urban Left councillor shows some of the characteristics of both the *policy advocate* and the *policy spokesman*. There is strong commitment both to a detailed election manifesto and to decentralising policy discussions throughout the local Labour movement (Fudge 1981, 1984). These attitudes lead them to adopt an interventionist style in the management of local authorities that differs in many ways from the more orthodox approaches discussed in Chapter 5. In some places policy units have been established that are staffed by known sympathisers with the views of the councillors. The councillors themselves often have professional expertise in the detail of local government services. A survey in 1982 found that a third of the left-wing Labour councillors either worked for another local authority (including teachers) or were full-time councillors living off their allowances. None of the Conservative councillors worked for a local authority in any capacity (Gyford 1983b:9).

POLICIES AND PARTIES

The incursion of party politics into local government is sometimes deplored but it is not a new development. The vestries that pre-dated the modern system of local government were sometimes centres of party political activity at the beginning of the nineteenth century, and this activity was carried forward into the town councils and other local bodies in Victorian England. As Derek Fraser points out 'whether the pavement was drained and swept, whether the poor should be incarcerated in workhouses, whether Dissenters should pay church rates depended upon the exercise of power. . . . Politics intruded into the whole urban experience . . . ' (Fraser 1976:9). The major party contests of the time were, of course, between the Tories and Whigs or, in the latter part of the nineteenth century, their successors the Conservatives and Liberals. The emerging Labour movement also threw itself into local politics with enthusiasm. Indeed for a short while in 1849 the Chartists obtained a majority of the elected members of the Sheffield council (Salt 1971:38). Later in welcoming the new county councils in 1888 the Fabians argued that a 'democratic State cannot become a *Social*-Democratic State unless it has in every centre of population a local governing body . . . ' (Shaw 1889:188).

The impact of the Labour Party on local elections in the years after 1918 caused the formation of many 'anti-socialist' coalitions under such names as 'progressives', 'citizens' or 'ratepayers'. The conclusion is sometimes drawn, therefore, that the rise of the Labour Party was responsible for introducing national party politics into local govern-ment. Such a view ignores the history of nineteenth-century local government and has been challenged for the twentieth century by Ken Young. He argues that some Conservative leaders were predisposed to fight local elections on party lines from the moment that the modern system of local government was introduced. He documents the influence of the national Conservative Party through the London Municipal Society and suggests 'the reader may draw his own conclusions as to the degree to which the Conservative and Unionist party shares with the Labour and Liberal parties a responsibility for the decline of local politics', and the 'nationalisation' of local political contests (Young 1975:33).

Whoever bears the responsibility, the domination of local government by party politics is now almost complete. The metropolitan areas in England were contested on party lines from the first elections in 1973. In the shire counties two remained non-party or dominated by independents, but 'by 1981 only Cornwall remained in this category' (Gyford and James 1983:2). In the rural areas of Wales and Scotland the tradition of non-partisan elections continues in some areas, but even so the role of the parties has been growing consistently since local government reorganisation (Gyford and James 1983:2; Keating and Midwinter 1983:107–13).

The Labour Party gains its most consistent successes in London and the other major cities. The former LCC was a Labour stronghold. Although its larger successor, the GLC, changed hands regularly – from Labour in 1973 to Conservative in 1977 and back to Labour in 1981 – London remains the strongest source of Labour support in the South-East of the country. The GLC, of course, was abolished in 1986 (see pages 198–201). The Greater London boroughs have been divided in the past between the Labour Party which predominates in the inner-city and the Conservative Party which controls most of the outer suburban area. In more recent elections the growing strength of the Liberal/Social Democratic Party Alliance has produced a number of councils without a clear party majority and a few with Alliance control. The actual number of Greater London boroughs controlled by each party naturally varies from election to election and is strongly affected by the national political climate. For example, the balance switched from Labour to Conservative in the majority of the thirty-two boroughs between 1974 and 1978. Labour lost further seats in 1982, but regained a lot of ground in 1986. After the elections in May, 1986, the Labour Party controlled fifteen boroughs (eleven after the previous elections in 1982), the Conservative Party eleven (16), the Alliance three (–), and there was no clear majority in the remaining three (5). The Labour strength in the inner-London boroughs allows them to control the Inner London Education Authority which is still based on the former LCC area.

The Labour Party controlled all six metropolitan counties when they were formed in 1974. Control was lost in four of them in 1977 but the Labour Party regained its monopoly of these strategic authorities in 1981 before they were abolished in 1986. In most years, the Labour Party also controls most of the metropolitan districts. Elections take place for a third of the councillors in each year that there is not a county council election. After the elections in May, 1986, the Labour Party controlled twenty-eight of the thirty-six metropolitan districts (twenty-four in 1985), the Conservative Party one (5), and there was no overall control in seven (7).

In contrast to the Labour dominance in the larger cities, the

Conservatives, sometimes in alliance with groups of independent councillors, have traditionally controlled most of the non-metropolitan or shire counties in England and Wales. The major exceptions have been counties in the mining areas where there has been a basis for Labour support. From the early 1980s, the position began to change as first the Labour Party and then the Alliance increased their vote at the expense of the Conservatives. By 1985, over half the forty-seven counties were without a clear overall majority. The Conservative Party controlled ten councils (nineteen after the previous election in 1981), the Labour Party nine (14), the Liberals one (1) and Independents two (3). The remaining twenty-five (10) were run by various coalitions or arrangements between minority parties.

In Scotland, independent councillors still retain their position on some local authorities. The three Islands Authorities have been controlled by Independents since their formation in 1975. Of the nine Regional Councils, Independents controlled three after the elections in 1986; the same number as after the previous elections in 1982. The Labour Party controlled four (3), the Conservatives none (2), and in two (1) there was no clear majority.

Unionists of one grouping or another control most of the twenty-six district councils in Northern Ireland. The elections are complicated, however, by the large number of small parties who contest a system of proportional representation. Moreover, the councils are sometimes used as 'weapons' in the wider political controversies in Northern Ireland. In 1986, for example, the Unionists suspended the normal working of seventeen local authorities they controlled as part of their opposition to an agreement reached between the governments of the United Kingdom and the Republic of Ireland. Under pressure from the High Court some of the councillors subsequently voted to resume normal working but the action was undoubtedly a severe embarrassment to the central government.

Electoral behaviour
The influence of national political considerations on local electoral behaviour is so marked that Newton considers that 'the term "local election" is something of a misnomer. ... Local elections are a sort of annual general election' (Newton 1976a:16). He estimates that no more than 10 per cent of the variance between the local election results in Birmingham and the national averages can be attributed to local factors (Newton 1976a:14–15). A rather different result was obtained by Geoffrey Green when he examined election results in Sheffield and Leeds for the years between 1951 and 1966. He identified three components of local voting and attributed 73 per cent of the swing between party support to national factors, 6 per cent to city-wide

factors, and the remainder to purely local factors at a ward level (Green 1972:51). His results have been criticised by Newton for underestimating the effects of city size on the proportion of Labour voters. These effects may express themselves differentially locally depending on the size of the city, but they are essentially national in character and reduce the influence attributable to local factors (Newton 1976a:17).

Even if Newton's criticisms of Green are accepted there remains a local component in local elections upon which both would agree. The dispute is about its importance (Bruce and Lee 1982). Moreover the smaller scale of the local political system allows minor parties and independents more opportunities than on the national stage. These are likely to be more important in rural than in urban areas (Stanyer 1975) but Green himself once obtained 773 votes as an independent candidate supported by a residents' association in a ward election in Sheffield (Hampton 1970:291). A major local issue, such as a redevelopment plan, or a sudden increase in the rates, as occurred in many areas in the mid-1970s, can cause the formation of a purely local party that enjoys some success at the polls (Grant 1977). Such successes may be short-lived, but the possibility of it happening at all is a dimension to be considered by the major political parties.

THE ROLE OF POLITICAL PARTIES

The role of political parties in local government is similar to their role in national affairs. They recruit and support candidates for election and by preparing local manifestos present a choice between several coherent approaches to policy. In view of the influence of national political factors on local electoral behaviour this choice is perhaps of more significance as a guide to the officers *after* an election than to the electorate *beforehand*. When a party emerges with a majority the focus of policy-making is clearly defined. This is now the position in most local authorities though there have been important examples of 'hung' councils in recent years including many shire counties after the elections of 1985 and Liverpool and some London boroughs. The experience in Cheshire suggests that when in these circumstances 'decisions depend on the construction of a political majority on each occasion', it is not possible to revert to procedures adopted in the former rural or smaller authorities. The parties are now present in a 'highly charged political atmosphere' when there is no clear party majority and this places special demands upon the officers. The lack of clear policy direction leads to a 'slower and more cumbersome' decision-making process and 'inhibits forward planning' (Elcock 1982:85–9; Keating and Midwinter 1983:110–11; Wendt 1983:4,5).

Political party groups on local authorities organise themselves with a greater or lesser degree of formality. Increasingly they are all adopting the full procedures accepted in major cities for many years (Green 1981). The group appoints a leader who becomes leader of the council when in a majority (Jones and Norton 1978). The group meets before council and major committee meetings to determine policies and tactics; disciplined voting is expected. A visit to the town hall in a large authority will reveal offices for the leader of the council who will be provided with secretarial and sometimes policy support in a local version of a ministerial private office in Whitehall. There may also be offices provided for the Whips and the minority party leader.

The relationship between the party group on the council and the wider party organisation is sometimes one of tension. The parties vary in their attitude to this relationship. The Conservatives maintain a formal constitutional position that accepts the independence of the councillors from outside party control on the grounds that they are answerable to the electorate alone (Gyford and James 1983:26). The Liberals accept a similar position strengthened by both an emphasis on the right of their representatives to adopt independent policy positions and their rejection of rigid group discipline. These attitudes do not, of course, prevent controversies arising in these parties but they are not usually as public or as bitter as those that can occur in the Labour Party (Hampton 1970 Ch. 10; Gyford and James 1983:183).

Labour groups on local authorities operate within a party framework that in recent years has placed an increased emphasis on the accountability of elected representatives to their party as well as to the electorate. In some cases major policy issues will be considered at the district party meetings and 'guidance' given to the party group. It is not unknown for the draft budget of the local authority to be presented to the district Labour Party and amended as a result. In formal terms the local Labour Party determines election policy and provides a panel of prospective candidates for the council elections. The Labour group is concerned with the practical application of policy and, when in power, with day-to-day management. To facilitate good communications between the group and the district party there is often a presence at each others' meetings. This possibility has caused anxiety for officers of the council who may attend group meetings to give professional advice (see Ch. 5). In his guidelines for chief executives in their relationship with party politics, Sir John Boynton suggests that they 'should not attend party political group meetings at which there are persons present who are neither elected members nor officials of the Authority' (RIPA/PSI 1980:50).

PUBLIC ATTITUDES TO LOCAL GOVERNMENT

Public attitudes to local government in Britain are ambivalent. On the one hand, a considerable amount of local sentiment can be aroused in opposition to any changes in local authority boundaries. The strength of this feeling was recognised by the minister when introducing legislation providing for local government reorganisation in 1888. He asked Members of Parliament to 'understand that a sentimental grievance is by no means the least difficult to overcome ... ' (quoted in Hampton 1966:463). More recently, Rutland fought a spirited battle to avoid assimilation into Leicestershire in the 1960s – a battle which was lost in the 1970s; and Cheshire conducted a campaign around the symbolic figure of Mr R E Mote in opposition to proposed boundary alterations during the discussions leading to the Local Government Act 1972. Such sentiments can smother party differences as local Conservatives and Labour Party members come together to defend 'their' local independence (Lee and Wood 1974: Ch. 3; Jones and Norton 1978:163).

Despite the passion aroused by local campaigns concerning proposals to change local boundaries, the general public displays little interest in the regular work of local authorities. The normal turnout in local elections is about one-third. Until the 1974 reorganisation introduced larger local authorities, and a consequent spread of party activity, even this figure of electoral involvement was misleading as many elections in the rural areas were not contested (Byrne 1981:287; Keating and Midwinter 1983:108–10). The lack of electoral participation is matched by a general ignorance of council procedures and responsibilities. A survey conducted for the Committee on the Management of Local Government found that 'one in five of the electorate were unable to name any of the services which were provided by their local authorities ... ' (Gyford 1984:99). Gyford goes on to quote a 1982 'survey commissioned by *New Society* [which] found a still fairly low level of awareness of which services were provided wholly or partly from the rates, with one person in four unable to give any answer' (Gyford 1984:99).

One aspect of local government upon which most local people have an opinion is the level of the rates: they generally consider them too high! Even so, the public have been unlikely in the past to exhibit a detailed knowledge of the local rate, let alone of other aspects of local government finance. In a survey conducted in Sheffield in 1967 only 5 per cent of the respondents could give the correct rate poundage and less than half could state accurately whether the rate had gone up or down in the previous year (Hampton 1970:129). These results were obtained, of course, before the sharp rate rises in the mid-1970s. These rate increases were accompanied in some areas by the formation of a new style of ratepayers' parties which contested elections against both Conservative and Labour opposition (Grant 1977). The higher salience of rates in local election campaigning after the Conservative victory in the General Election of 1979 also produced increased awareness of the issues in some areas. In one ward in Wolverhampton in 1980, 80 per cent of the electors could identify the correct rate increase from a list of four possibilities.

Bristow considers the rates issue affected voting behaviour in the election, but the direction of the effect was not uniform across the borough. The Labour Party who were in control had increased the rate by 50 per cent. They lost support in Conservative areas but gained it in traditional Labour wards where, presumably, the level of service was as important to the electors as the level of rates (Bristow 1982).

Corruption

Public confidence in local government was not enhanced in the early 1970s by a series of prosecutions for corruption. These prosecutions were mainly concerned with planning matters and achieved considerable publicity. Following the principal court cases, a committee was appointed by the Prime Minister to examine local government rules of conduct under the ubiquitous chairmanship of Lord Redcliffe-Maud. The judgement of the committee was 'that standards of conduct in local government are generally high'. Between 1964 and 1972 'a total of ten members and twenty-two employees were convicted of offences under the Prevention of Corruption Acts, and sixteen members were convicted of failure to disclose a pecuniary interest under the Local Government Acts' (Redcliffe-Maud 1974:3). These figures must be seen in the context of the 48,000 members and over 2 million employees of local authorities at that time. The committee prepared a Code of Conduct in which the key advice for councillors was probably the injunction to 'do nothing as a councillor which you could not justify if it became public' (Redcliffe-Maud 1974:47).

Maladministration

The public may suffer unjustly from inaction or actions of local authorities that are not contained within the definition of corruption. The content of this 'maladministration', as it is called, has been described as coming within the five categories of bias, delay, inaction and error, facts, and information and consultation (Lewis and Gateshill 1978:20). These concepts were first developed in the United Kingdom when a Parliamentary Commissioner (commonly known as an 'ombudsman' from the Scandinavian origins of the office) was established in 1967 to consider complaints of maladministration at a national level. The national ombudsman was specifically excluded from receiving complaints against local government but pressure soon developed to extend the concept into this area of public service. In 1969 a Commissioner for Complaints was established in Northern Ireland as part of the attempts to reduce the tension in the province. He 'was empowered to investigate acts by local authorities which appeared to involve either maladministration or discrimination' (Elcock 1982:41; see also Elcock 1972). Following local government reorganisation in Britain, Commissioners for Local Administration were appointed for England (3) and Wales (1) in 1974 and for Scotland (1) in 1976.

Local commissioners are not, of course, concerned with the content of a decision but with whether it has been made in the proper manner. They are not a court of appeal against the political decisions of a council nor against administrative discretion that has been properly exercised. There are other limits to their powers. They are excluded from complaints about commercial transactions, personnel matters, certain educational matters and actions taken in connection with the prevention of crime or concerning the commencement and conduct of legal proceedings. In the first four years, 'the English Commissioners received nearly 7,500 complaints' of which 331 were found to have involved injustice through maladministration. Similar amounts of maladministration were discovered in both Wales and Scotland (Lewis and Gateshill 1978; Byrne 1981:259).

DISCUSSION: PUBLIC PARTICIPATION IN LOCAL SERVICES

A reading of the academic literature on local government in Britain would lead to the conclusion that the attitude of the public is one of ignorance and indifference tinged with suspicion. Yet local loyalties remain high and activism on local issues appears to have increased considerably since the mid-1960s. A consideration of this conundrum has led the present author to perceive a difference between 'a community in a social – almost anthropological – sense, and a political community' (Hampton 1970:121). The formalities of representative democracy seem unable to capture the enthusiasm of the public at a local level. At the same time there has been a growth of both official encouragement for methods of enabling public participation in local services, and public demands for such opportunities. A discussion of public participation within local representative democracy provides, therefore, a fitting conclusion to this chapter.

From the late 1960s legislation has provided for direct citizen involvement in several local services. The legislation was initiated or supplemented by reports from many official committees and considerable public discussion has taken place. A key document in this respect was the Skeffington Report on Public Participation in Planning (1969) which defined participation as 'the act of sharing in the formulation of policies and proposals' and the public 'as an aggregate comprising all individuals and groups ... without limitation' (Skeffington 1969:1). The Skeffington Committee was established to provide guidance on the implementation of the Town and Country Planning Act 1968. This Act included provisions both for structure and local plans to be publicised and for local planning authorities to receive representations from the public (Sections 3 and 7). The word 'participation' was not included in the Act. The approach of the Skeffington Committee was not easily assimilated into a representative system of local democracy and the government drew back from implementing its more radical proposals (DOE/Welsh Office 1972:Annex; Boaden *et al.* 1980:24–5).

Other local services where official reports recommended increased public participation included personal social services and education. The Seebohm Committee on Local Authority and Allied Personal Services expressed 'a belief in the importance of the maximum participation of individuals and groups in the community in the planning, organisation and provision of the social services' (Seebohm 1968:151). The consequent Local Authority Social Services Act 1970 endorsed most of the administrative changes recommended by Seebohm; and although the Act did not embody the spirit of the participatory ethos of the report the growth of community work within the new departments provided an impetus in this direction (Sainsbury 1977:75). The Taylor Committee on the Management and Government of Schools similarly recommended extensive community participation in the governing body of each school: 'it should be an equal partnership for all those with a legitimate concern, local education authority, staff, parents, where appropriate pupils, and the community' (Taylor 1977:xii). These recommendations followed developments already occurring in the Inner London Education Authority (ILEA), Sheffield (Bacon 1978) and elsewhere. The Education (No 2) Act 1980 provided for the implementation throughout England and Wales of the main recommendations for parental and teacher participation in governing bodies. These provisions were introduced over the following years. A subsequent Green Paper proposed that parents should form a majority on boards of governors though this suggestion received little support from local education authorities, teachers or national organisations representing parents (*Parental Influence* ... 1984; 'Lukewarm response ... ' 1984).

Boaden *et al.* (1982) explored the relationship between the development of public participation in local services and several themes which have affected their provision in recent years. The themes include the growth of central government control over local affairs; the influence of departmentalism on service provision; the introduction of more corporate approaches to local government management; and the steady growth of professionalism among the officers administering the services. They identified several perspectives from the point of view both of the public and of those with power from which public participation might be judged (Ch. 10). First, there are the perspectives of the mass of the people. Participation in service provision can be seen as a means by which individuals may protect their rights as consumers of public goods and services; it can be described as the right to consultation; or it can involve the full Skeffington concept of people sharing in the processes of policy-making and service provision. From the perspective of those already in positions of power rather different objectives may be emphasised. These élite perspectives may be concerned either with legitimating particular decisions by involving the public in their consideration; or with gaining the local detailed knowledge from the public that will enable better policies to emerge. The élites expect to retain the final power of decision to themselves.

Several studies in individual services including education (Bacon 1978) and planning (Young 1984) and of neighbourhood councils (Cockburn 1977; Hain 1980) have stressed the importance of the legitimating function of public participation. Councillors and officers need to incorporate local people into their policies if large-scale plans are to succeed: the reorganisation of local government into larger units made it more difficult to use traditional representative devices for this purpose. Yet the general public, especially those from professional and managerial backgrounds (Boaden *et al.* 1980: Ch. 8; 1982:34), have also gained from the greater opportunities for participation. Some local government services are now conducted in a more open manner and decisions, even when not changed, have to be justified more thoroughly. At the very least, the general public benefits from a certain degree of 'consumer protection'.

From the wider viewpoint of balancing the outcome of public participation against the basic political question of 'who gets what, when, and how?' an assessment is more difficult. The 'major élites' (Boaden *et al.* 1980:19) were prominent in the participation in planning exercises (Young 1984); middle-class parents are active on school boards (Bacon 1978:132–3); and there is little opportunity for client participation among those who most need the help of social work departments (Boaden *et al.* 1982:146–7). The location of power has not changed despite the hopeful expectations of the radical advocates of the participation movement in the early 1970s: local representative institutions have absorbed the participatory experiments. For the time being enthusiasm for public participation has waned from both official and radical sources.

Chapter eight

GROUP ACTIVITY IN THE LOCAL POLITICAL PROCESS

Political scientists have long understood the importance of group activity in national politics. The part groups play in the local political process has only more recently been recognised. In 1967, for example, A H Birch commented on 'the relative scarcity of well-organised local pressure groups' and concluded: 'This aspect of local democracy does not appear to flourish in England' (Birch 1967:241). At the time this view was widely accepted. The local organisational life that was known to exist was interpreted mainly in sociological terms. The major concerns of most of these organisations were remote from the daily round of local politics thus making them invisible to political scientists. The activities of the chambers of commerce and trades councils in some areas were seen as the exceptions that proved the rule.

The number of educational, environmental and other pressure groups at the local level grew rapidly in the 1960s. With this growth came a change in the perceptions of political scientists. There is now a considerable interest in local group organisation. From the expanding literature we have selected two topics for discussion. The earlier part of the chapter is concerned with the extent of local group membership and the increase in the number of groups formed with specifically political objectives. We deal also with the relationship of these groups to the local political system and their involvement in public participation exercises. The second part of the chapter is devoted to local government trade unions and ends with a discussion of industrial democracy in local authorities.

LOCAL INTEREST GROUPS

The view is often expressed that if two Britons were marooned on a desert island the first thing they would do would be to form a club; and the second thing would be to elect a committee! The richness of local organisational life goes a long way to support this statement. Groups exist for an almost unlimited range of purposes from athletics to yoga – and no doubt there are some zither players who would complete the alphabet. Several surveys have provided evidence of the density of membership of these groups. The Community Attitudes Surveys conducted for the Royal Commissions on Local Government in England and Scotland found that nearly two-thirds of the population belonged to at least one organisation (Redcliffe-Maud 1969, Research Study 9:53; Wheatley 1969, Research Study 2:27). Similar proportions ranging from one-half to two-thirds have been found by many local surveys (Birch 1959:196; Hampton 1970:145; Stacey *et al.* 1975:50; Bealey and Sewel 1981:110). The active minority who run these organisations form a significant proportion of the population. Fourteen per cent of the respondents to the Maud Committee survey claimed office or committee membership in at least one organisation. The survey report suggests that 'this figure may seem a little high and it is possible that some people may have been exaggerating their present positions in their organisation' (Maud 1967, Vol III:119), but an identical figure was obtained in a local survey in Sheffield (Hampton 1970:150). In her study of Banbury in 1950, Margaret Stacey counted 1,026 committee members of voluntary or church organisations out of a total population – not electorate – of less than 19,000 and she confessed that 'inevitably some associations have been overlooked' (Stacey 1960: p 76 and Table 16).

The importance of these groups for the study of local politics is obvious. The theory of representative government is often presented as a relationship between an individual elector and his or her elected representative, but in practice the reality is very different. Kenneth Newton points out,

> For most people, participation of any weight or consequence in modern politics means organised and collective participation. With the exception of a few, rare people of unusual wealth, or power, or status, individuals who act on their own count for very little, whereas large numbers of individuals organised into a church or a trade union or a tenants' association may count for a great deal. For most of us, political power means joining an organisation (Newton 1976a:32).

Membership of any group enables an individual to develop the skills of organisation and communication that are necessary for effective political action, but some groups are naturally more regularly involved than others in local politics: the chambers of commerce and trades councils have long been perceived in many areas as an integral part of the local political process. From the mid-1960s new types of organisation began to relate to, and in many cases contest, particular aspects of local policy or service provision. At the same time central government began to show concern about consultative procedures in local government and to encourage the creation of local groups where none existed in particular policy areas (Cousins 1977:43–5). These newer groups have been particularly active in education, housing and environmental issues.

The traditional parent – teacher associations were 'arrangements for telling parents about the school's activities, or possibly for raising funds for some new facility like a swimming pool, but not to provide a channel of influence over what goes on in a school' (Regan 1979:57). From the 1960s they were supplemented by local branches of such organisations as the Confederation for the Advancement of State Education (CASE). These new organisations 'mainly pitted themselves behind progressive modes of education' (Kogan 1978:133) and were active in local controversies leading to the introduction of comprehensive education (Hampton 1970:239). They were also influential in creating a climate of opinion that led to the inclusion of a greater number of parents on school governing bodies during the 1970s. In a statement of objectives in 1974, CASE stated: 'There should be detailed information available about every school, choice of schools, parent – teachers' associations where the majority of parents want one, and parents and teachers represented on school governers' (Kogan 1974:127). These objectives have largely been achieved through the provisions of the Education (No. 2) Act 1980 (Boaden *et al.* 1982:157–61). One consequence of including parents on the governing bodies of schools is to change the function of the parents' associations. If governors report regularly to such groups then discussions of educational policy as it effects the school may supplement the traditional fund-raising activities. Such a development is not unwelcome to many politicians, but teachers regard it with some apprehension.

Housing provides another basis for local group organisation. The local authorities established by the Local Government Act 1888 received powers in 1890 and 1900 to build and subsidise housing for the working classes (Darke and Darke 1979:15). At first these powers were little used but from the 1920s successive governments gave legislative and financial encouragement to the building of 'council houses' that are no longer restricted to the 'working classes'. By 1976 council houses represented 30 per cent of the total housing stock in England and Wales and 54 per cent in Scotland (Darke and Darke 1979:43). Most council housing is provided on estates that sometimes reach the scale of new towns containing populations of many thousands. Such estates provide a 'unified and identifiable social base' for the thousands of tenants' associations and federations of tenants' organisations that exist and have existed in Britain (Lowe 1986: Ch. 3). The proviso 'have existed' is significant. Tenants' associations appear rapidly in response to some crisis such as a threatened change in the method of rent payment or deterioration in the standards of repair and then gradually decline as the immediate battles are either won or lost. The associations do not necessarily cease to exist. A study of fifty-eight groups in London in 1962 found that 'thirty-nine had been in existence for longer than ten years, and a further eighteen for more than five years' (Boaden *et al.* 1982:101). They do, however, change their character as they adopt a social role that is often associated with the management of a community hall or similar facility. The creation of tenants' associations received a fresh impetus from the end of the 1960s as rents were increased and means-tested rent rebate schemes were introduced (Hampton 1970: Ch. 10; Moorhouse *et al.* 1972). There was also considerable opposition among tenants to the Housing Finance Act 1972 (Sklair 1975). Further activities developed 'in the late-1970s in response to some new issues – the possibility of a Tenants' Charter, dampness, repairs and heating being the main concerns' (Lowe 1986: Ch. 3).

In addition to the growing number of groups formed among parents and council-house tenants, the 1960s witnessed a fresh interest in the environment. A survey of amenity or civic societies conducted in 1974 found 'eighty-five per cent of responding societies [had] begun since 1957', the year the Civic Trust was formed nationally (Barker 1976:21). Like the tenants' associations, many amenity societies come into existence in response to a particular issue: a major planning development such as a town centre, or a road or other traffic scheme (Barker 1976:23). Amenity societies as such seldom engage in social or welfare activities but the growing number of neighbourhood associations or 'action groups' often combine these functions with a concern for the local environment. Once again there has been a spectacular increase in the number of such organisations since the late 1960s (Lowe 1986: Ch. 4). Community workers often play an active part in the organisation of such groups whose principal focus may range from elderly people to vagrants, and whose environmental concerns may be the missing benches in a local park or the total redevelopment of Convent Garden (Butcher *et al.* 1980: Hain 1980).

IMPACT ON THE POLITICAL PROCESS

The growth in both the number and the range of local organisations since the 1960s has introduced a new dimension into local politics in many areas. The impact of this development must not be exaggerated: 'councillors can be remarkably well insulated from public sentiment' (Gyford 1984:130); but the new organisations contribute to a climate of greater openness in local government affairs. We need to ask how groups become involved in the political process and how the local authority reacts to them.

Kenneth Newton looked at the political activity of formally organised voluntary associations as part of his study of politics in Birmingham. He counted over 4,000 and admitted that the 'list is certainly not complete'

(Newton 1976a: 36). Organisations were included if they had a formal structure of office-holders; a voluntary membership; a private basis; had non-profit-making goals; and had a focus on the city or region. Political parties and branches of larger organisations were not included. The organisations were placed in thirteen categories: sports, social welfare, cultural, trade associations, professional, social, churches, forces, youth, technical and scientific, educational, trade unions and health (Newton 1976a:38). Approximately 30 per cent of these organisations had been politically active in the previous twelve months. Politically active in this context could mean anything from asking for information to conducting a campaign to change public policy, but it implied recognition that the local authority was concerned with matters affecting the interests of the organisation.

As one would expect, the different types of organisation varied in their propensity to take political action. Most active were the social welfare, health and trade union groups; but although a smaller proportion of the sports organisations were active the large number of such groups – over 50 per cent of the 4,000 – caused them to produce many which were politically active (Newton 1976a:38). In other words, political activity was distributed throughout the thirteen categories; unevenly distributed, but distributed none the less. The concept of a type of organisation that is inherently non-political depends simply on the definition of political being employed.

Organisations differ in the resources they have available and this will affect their ability to engage in political activity. A large membership provides the funds to engage paid staff who can meet local government bureaucracies on their own terms and at their own times. Such organisations are more likely to be politically active then less developed or smaller local organisations (Newton 1976a:43). The importance of congruence between the mode of operation of a pressure group and the institution it is seeking to influence is one reason for the appointment of community workers. When the DOE supported an experimental environmental liaison officer in Birmingham one councillor commented: 'he provided the posh words to put over the residents' points so that the officers could understand them' (Hampton 1978:32).

The councillor, of course, was making a tongue-in-cheek comment on the ability of professionals to describe their activities in a jargon that makes communication with lay people difficult. There is, however, a deeper issue involved in the concept of congruence and its significance in regulating the relationship between a local authority and the general public. John Dearlove, in his study of councillors and interest groups in the Royal Borough of Kensington and Chelsea, pointed out that governments cannot 'give detailed consideration to all the demands they receive, still less are they able to respond favourably to all demands. They need to develop, and cannot avoid developing, rules-of-thumb which they can use to categorise demands' (Dearlove 1973:173). He suggests that councillors use three criteria in categorising interest groups:

1. The source of the demand: *the group*.
2. The policy content of the group demand and its implications for council activity and resource commitment: the *demand* itself.
3. The method of articulation adopted by the demanding group: the *communication method* (Dearlove 1973:157).

These three criteria are worth considering in more detail. We have already seen that the number of interest groups that may approach a council is very large. Some will be familiar to councillors: others will be unfamiliar. The groups will, therefore, be received with an initial response deriving from the previous knowledge and expectations of the councillors. Dearlove chose a cross-section of twenty groups involved in the local political process and asked Conservative councillors – the majority party – how helpful they felt these groups were in making the borough the sort of place they would like it to be. The interest groups with a favourable image were those whose general aims were either non-controversial or in tune with the councillor's own background: the Housing Trust, a playspace group, charities, district nurses, the Women's Royal Voluntary Service and the Chamber of Commerce. Those with an 'unhelpful' image included the Inter-Racial Council and the Council Tenants' Association (Dearlove 1973:159).

We may easily imagine that the attitudes of Labour councillors in a northern city would differ from those of the Conservatives in Kensington and Chelsea: the Chamber of Commerce might be replaced in their estimation by the Trades Council or the Confederation of Shipbuilding and Engineering Unions. In both areas the councillors would be responding more favourably to those interest groups that reflected their own experience and expectations. The Conservative councillors in Kensington and Chelsea, for example, were generally in favour of groups that were 'actually doing a job of work' rather than making demands upon the ratepayers (Dearlove 1973:163). Groups that approached the council with demands for changes in council policy would be received less favourably than those whose activities were generally supportive of the council.

In addition to their predisposition towards a group and their attitude to the particular 'demand' being made, councillors are also influenced by the method by which the demand is communicated. Councillors in Kensington and Chelsea identified certain methods such as approaching a ward representative or committee chairman as 'proper', and others such as raising the issue in the local press or demonstrations as 'improper' (Dearlove 1973:161). The dislike of matters being raised in the local press rather than through the 'proper channels' is widespread among councillors and similar opinions are quoted elsewhere in the literature. The press are sometimes accused of distortion or of colluding with publicity seekers to embarrass the council (Cox and Morgan 1973:125–6; Dunleavy 1981:335–6). Demonstrations are also seen as an illegitimate means of protest. They represent a challenge to the authority of democratically elected councillors. Groups adopting illegitimate methods of presenting their views may be dismissed as pursuing selfish sectional interests that are contrary to the common good (Dunleavy 1981:336).

The criteria suggested by Dearlove can be combined to form profiles of different kinds of interest groups which may expect different responses from the council. Groups from a similar environment to the councillors presenting views supportive of council policy through formally recognised channels will be regarded as 'helpful' and will be favourably received. On the other hand, groups from backgrounds unfamiliar to the councillors making demands for changes in council policy through public agitation will be regarded as 'unhelpful' and disregarded. Put like this the conclusions seem commonplace, but they have important implications for local democracy and the opportunities for local people to participate in local affairs. Although a wide range of interest groups exist with formal equality of access to the political process, some are in practice excluded because their general background and approach are incongruent with those in positions of power. It is not simply a matter of conflict between different views of policy. The very structure of power may exclude certain groups. The organisation of society and its political structure is not a neutral, ideal state into which all sections of the population can enter on equal terms. It is a social construct which recognises the hegemony of precisely those groups of people who are most visible in the political process: male, middle-aged, middle-class and white. The formalities of ballot elections, minute-keeping and annual general meetings that occupy a central place in the thinking of councillors and officers may be unusual in some working-class, black or women's organisations. These organisations are not necessarily less democratic: they are simply part of a different ethos (Goldsmith 1980:74–5; Boaden *et al*. 1982:39–40).

Organised groups were understood to be particularly important in the more open planning system which followed the Town and Country Planning Act 1968. Many local authorities drew up lists of environmental and other groups to be approached for their views during public participation schemes. These lists usually consisted of two types of organisations. First, there were those organisations that had to be consulted if the proposed plan was to be acceptable to those who would be involved in its implementation: neighbouring local authorities, statutory undertakings, central government departments and major local industries. Second, there were the many citizens' groups that we have been discussing in this chapter. As we would expect, the consultation with the first type of organisation was much more successful than with the second. These groups understood the issues and the consultation procedures were congruent with their own internal arrangements. The citizens' organisations by contrast were less easily involved. Attempts to reach a wide range of such organisations were costly and achieved only a limited success. When these organisations did become involved they were frequently at odds with the attitudes of the local authority (Boaden *et al*. 1980:77–80). Patrick Dunleavy has noted a similar distinction between the influence of major established interests and the exclusion of many citizens' groups in his study of housing policy (Dunleavy 1981:335–8).

The growth in the number of local interest groups since the late 1960s has not, therefore, produced a pluralist political process in which competing groups arrive at compromise or consensus policies from positions of comparable strength. The representative system is dominant. The local authority can influence the type of interest groups which gain access to policy-making arenas. Other groups will be excluded. By adopting 'unacceptable' methods of expressing their views they will then justify their exclusion in the opinion of those in positions of power.

LOCAL GOVERNMENT TRADE UNIONS

Local authorities employ some 3 million people in many different occupations from part-time dinner assistants to highly paid executives. The organisations they belong to form a very important source of group influence on local authority policy. Poole estimates that 'there are well over 100 organisations which local government employees may be eligible to join' (Poole 1978:193). Some of these are professional organisations that recruit generally within their profession, such as the Royal Town Planning Institute, others are restricted to local authority employees, such as the Association of Directors of Social Services. There are trade unions catering both for local authority manual workers and white-collar staff. And there are organisations, such as the National and Local Government Officers' Association (NALGO), which combine both professional and trade union functions. The relationship between professional staff and policy-making has been referred to already in Chapter 5 and will be mentioned again in Chapter 9. In this section we consider the position of trade unions in local government and their growing militancy over policy matters since the 1960s.

Local authority employees have a long history of trade union organisation and of the formation of professional associations which adopt trade union functions. The Municipal Employees' Union (MEU), for example, was formed for manual workers in 1894, the National Union of Teachers (NUT) in 1870 following the Education Act which

Group Activity in the Local Political Process

introduced state primary education and NALGO was formed in 1905. From these early days trade unions in local government have achieved a high density of membership both in manual and white-collar occupations (Thomson and Beaumont 1978:24). In 1948 the proportion of eligible employees in local government and education who had joined trade unions was 69.4 per cent; by 1979 the proportion was 77.5 per cent (Price and Bain 1983:54). The contrast with private industry is particularly marked for white-collar employees. In manufacturing industry in 1974 only 32 per cent of white-collar employees were members of a trade union (Price and Bain 1976:342).

Trade union density, that is, the proportion of the eligible workforce in membership, is commonly greater in public sector employment than elsewhere. Several authors have identified the reasons for this from a combination of the following factors:

> public services are provided by a small number of individually large undertakings, the bureaucratic operation of such undertakings, which follows from their large size and the fact of being subject to parliamentary scrutiny, the ready willingness of governments to recognise unions, and the fact that union membership extends so far up the employment hierarchy in the public sector that senior officers are relatively well disposed towards unionism (Thomson and Beaumont 1978:26, quoting Clegg 1976).

Bain developed a similar thesis to explain differences in white-collar trade union density in various occupations (Bain 1970:124–5). Although the technical aspects of his arguments have been criticised (Jackson 1982:44–50), his views remain influential. Of particular importance has been the attitude of the state or local authority to trade union membership among public employees whether manual or white-collar. This attitude has usually been more favourable than the attitude of private employers and has affected the bargaining procedures adopted.

The development of systematic national bargaining in the aftermath of the First World War (see Ch. 9) encouraged trade union membership. It was consistent with a bureaucratic style of trade union leadership that relied heavily upon the role of full-time officials. Since the early 1960s, however, there have been two developments within local government trade unions that bear directly on the concerns of this chapter. The first of these is the movement towards full trade unionism among white-collar workers and the growth of militancy among both these workers and their manual colleagues. The second is the increasing readiness of local authority trade unionists to join general political campaigns including those affecting their own services.

Both NALGO and the NUT emphasised from their inception their role in enhancing the professional standing of their members and the contribution they could make to the development of local government. They were also concerned to provide a variety of services to their

137

members of a social and commercial character. This was particularly true of NALGO which by 1930 had developed a 'correspondence school, students' library, and summer schools for the ambitious junior; the Approved and Provident Societies for the lower and middle grades; specialised legal protection for the seniors; the Benevolent Fund, insurance company, cruises, cheap holidays, and discount trading for all ... in many towns, the "NALGO Dance" ... was ... the biggest event of the social calender' (Spoor 1967:107). There was no feeling among the membership of such associations of any affiliation to the wider labour movement. Indeed, the founder of NALGO, Sir Herbert Blain, later became Principal Agent for the Conservative and Unionist Party. Among the teachers there was a belief that their commitment to the education of the young precluded any open expression of opinion on controversial social or political topics. The manual workers were naturally not so inhibited in their political commitments. The MEU was part of the amalgamation that produced the National Union of General and Municipal Workers (NUGMW) in 1924 (Clegg 1954:16–23). The NUGMW, however, became a byword for orthodoxy among the trade union and labour establishment.

By 1960 the non-militant traditions of the major trade unions in local government were under pressure both from changing social and political conditions and by competition from rival unions. Central government introduced a succession of incomes policies that challenged the independence of the bargaining process. Public sector workers were expected to set an example in pay restraint to employees in private industry. The example was not always followed and there was a consequent deterioration in the relative status and standards of public employees (Levinson 1971: 74–7). At the same time the government was developing its corporate links with the trade union movement through the National Economic Development Council ('Neddy') which was formed in 1961. The trade union representatives on this body were nominated exclusively by the Trades Union Congress (TUC). The government refused to include any other trade unions despite attempts by NALGO, the NUT and sixteen other white-collar unions to form a non-TUC constituency from which representatives could be drawn. They told the Chancellor of the Exchequer 'the unions we represent generally repudiated striking and pinned their faith on collective bargaining and arbitration. The government's actions ... were destroying that faith ... '; but the Chancellor was unmoved (Routh 1967:202–3). Following this rebuff the white-collar unions steadily affiliated to the TUC over the following few years: NALGO joined in 1964, the Association of Teachers in Technical Institutions (ATTI) in 1967, the National Association of Schoolmasters (NAS) in 1968 and the NUT in 1970 (Spoor 1967:Ch. 33; Coates 1972a:Ch. 8). Local government trade unions are now among the largest unions affiliated to the TUC.

The developing militancy of local government trade unions in the 1960s was led by two unions that had been formed in the 1920s as a result of divisions in other unions. The National Union of Public Employees (NUPE) originated in a split within the MEU (Clegg 1954:18), and by adopting an 'industrial union' approach – that is, it aspired to organise all public employees whatever their specific occupation – found itself in constant conflict with both the general unions of manual workers and NALGO (Clegg 1954; Craik 1955, and 1968; Spoor 1967). The membership of NUPE trebled between 1960 and 1980 (Table 8.1) and during the 1960s they were involved in a number of disputes as other unions accused them of poaching members in the NHS and local government (Hepple and O'Higgins 1971:69). Also NUPE benefited by mergers with other smaller unions including in 1965 the National Ambulance Services Association (Craik 1968:90).

At the same time as NUPE was disturbing the established influence of the NUGMW and NALGO, the NUT was under increasing challenge from the NAS. This union had been formed in 1922 as a breakaway from the NUT and the larger union had successfully excluded it from the negotiating machinery. In 1961 following the first national strike by teachers in England and Wales the NAS secured representation on the Burnham Committee. The membership of NAS grew rapidly (in 1975 it joined with the Union of Women Teachers to form the NAS/UWT) and provided a constant spur to the NUT (Coates 1972a:Ch. 6).

The growing militancy among local government trade unions was accompanied by an increasing readiness to adopt actions and procedures common among other trade unionists. In 1961 NALGO

TABLE 8.1 Membership of selected trade
unions which organise in local government,
1960–80 (thousands)

	1960	1970	1980
NUGMW	796	853	916
NUPE	200	373	699
NALGO	274	440	782
NUT	245	311	232
NAS/UWT	(23)	(57)	124

Sources: TUC Annual Reports; Bain 1970,
Table 3A1; Roy 1968, Appendix III.
Notes: The growth in membership is affected
by amalgamations with other unions. The
figures indicate, however, the relative strength
of these major unions. The NAS/UWT was
formed in 1975: the membership given in the
table for 1960 and 1970 refers to the NAS
only.

altered its constitution to allow the union to call a strike. The first strike of NALGO members took place in Glasgow in 1964 (Spoor 1967:521–32). The teachers became more willing to use sanctions in pursuit of their salary claims and called a series of strikes in 1969–70 (Coates 1972a:62). Even ambulancemen and firemen became willing to withdraw their labour during disputes. First in 1969–70 and then again in the 'winter of discontent' in 1979, local authority employees were engaged in major industrial battles with their employers and with the government departments that stood behind them (Hepple and O'Higgins 1971:168–72; Thomson and Beaumont 1978:146–9; Pimlott and Cook 1982:206–7). By 1984 some branches of NALGO were encouraging their members to take part in a 'day of action' in support of a miners' dispute, and teachers were engaged in selective strikes in areas represented by Conservative Members of Parliament. Such actions were far removed from the 'non-political' attitudes of the 1950s.

Towards the end of the 1960s national bargaining began to be increasingly supplemented by local negotiations (Thomson 1982:125–7). Several unions including NUPE and NALGO appointed workplace representatives or shop stewards for the first time (Terry 1982). Local bargaining sometimes originated in imprecise national agreements which reflected divisions among the employing local authorities. It also came from pressures from lay shop stewards and activists who sought to improve the conditions set out in national agreements.

From this survey of the development of trade unionism in local government we may distinguish the influences it has on the policies of local authorities. These influences are of two types. First, there are those that arise during the process of collective bargaining. Coates points out that 'strikes by teachers are a political rather than an economic sanction ... to bring political pressure on their democratically elected employers' (Coates 1972a:79). The same point is true of most other local authority strikes. Electors expect their children to be taught and their dustbins to be emptied and vent their dissatisfaction on councillors if these expectations are not met. The trade unions, therefore, may secure by essentially political means conditions that constrict the policy-making function of the councillors. An obvious example is the prevalance of agreements which contain 'no redundancy' clauses (Thomson and Beaumont 1978:141). At a time of falling school rolls or financial stringency such an agreement can severely restrict a local authority's policy options. In some cases the agreement is applied by local trade union activists to a particular type of occupation or trade union. 'No redundancy' becomes 'no job loss' which in turn becomes 'every specific job protected'. The consequences for local authorities seeking to introduce new technology or a departmental reorganisation are obvious. Such policy issues become a matter of collective bargaining. Other examples are the disputes that occurred when some local authorities introduced private contractors to perform certain services.

Second, trade unions may seek to influence public policy through general campaigns or through the local political process. Dunleavy writes of 'the considerable, if largely unstudied, influence of public unions on urban politics via professional channels, party political links and local Trade Councils' (Dunleavy 1980a:69). Teachers, for example, have always been active in campaigns concerned with educational policy. Coates reports that 'as early as 1852, a deputation was sent from the Metropolitan Church Schoolmasters' Association to oppose the education policy of Lord Derby's Government . . . ' and the NUT lobbied the minister from the year of its formation (Coates 1972a:8–9). More recently, in the 1960s the teachers' unions formed an Alliance for Educational Advance to press for greater public expenditure on education (Coates 1972a:Ch. 7). They were also active with other local government trade unions in the campaigns against cuts in public expenditure in the 1970s. Many of these campaigns have an obvious connection with the employment interests of the trade unionists, but they are conducted in the political arena rather than through collective bargaining.

In the 1980s these campaigns became even more broadly based. Local government trade unions joined with local councillors in many parts of the country in opposition to central government policies for both the abolition of metropolitan counties and the imposition of restraints on the powers of local authorities to levy rates ('rate-capping'). Once again these campaigns were directly connected with the protection of local authority jobs, but the unions were ready to remind councillors of the support they had given to such campaigns during negotiations over other issues. In some areas the unions built upon this 'partnership' and expected to be consulted about the council budget before it was determined.

Councillors associated with the 'New Urban Left' (see Ch.7) provide a new dimension to a consideration of local authority trade unionism. The councillors are committed to a close working relationship with the trade unions, but at the same time they are committed to changes in the policies of local authorities. Trade unions, on the other hand, are essentially defensive organisations. Sheffield provides a good example of the difficulties that can arise. A Joint Works Group was established in response to central government pressures on Direct Labour Organis-ations. The group brought together 'a delegation of elected trade union shop stewards from the workforce, a delegation of tenants' represen-tatives . . . and Labour councillors'. The group worked on a wide range of issues,

> making the working arrangements in the Department more efficient and
> effective; making the workings and work of the Department more
> accountable to tenants and workers; exploring the causes and cures of
> dampness in housing; the inefficiency and inequality of the bonus system
> of wages payments; monitoring private contractors; trade union and

141

tenants' education; induction and training of workers; and publicity campaigns in support of the Works Department (Blunkett and Green 1983:19).

Included in this list are managerial, political and collective bargaining issues and there were 'problems reconciling the involvement of the workforce in the political direction of the Department with the needs of management ... ' (Blunkett and Green 1983:19). The NALGO representatives withdrew from the group for a time, thus emphasising the tension that may exist between manual workers and white-collar trade unionists who often occupy supervisory positions.

In a later dispute in Sheffield which started over the introduction of new working procedures in the housing department, the councillors claimed a right to manage in accordance with their policies. This dispute was one of several in 1984 between left-wing councils and local authority trade unions. The different approaches of these two sections of the labour movement were summed up, perhaps a little unfairly, by a shop steward who argued, 'Party policy isn't sacrosanct. It's got to be negotiated' (Wolmar 1984:15). The difference between authority derived from the ballot box and the role of trade unions to obtain the best possible agreement on behalf of their members lies at the heart of discussions of industrial democracy in local government. Public institutions have public responsibilities that distinguish them from private industry in the context of such discussions.

DISCUSSION – INDUSTRIAL DEMOCRACY IN LOCAL GOVERNMENT

Employees of a local authority are precluded from seeking election to their own authority. This disqualification does not prevent them serving on other authorities for which they may otherwise be elegible. The exclusion from their own authority is justified by the need to preserve the fundamental distinction between the roles of the elected members and employees of a local authority. The Local Government Acts 1972 and (Scotland) 1973 provide that 'A member of the authority may not become an employee of it while he remains a member or for twelve months thereafter (1972 Section 116 and 1973 Section 67); and an employee of the authority is disqualified for membership of it (1972 Section 80(1)(*a*) and 1973 Section 31(1)(*a*)' (Redcliffe-Maud 1974:27). These provisions have prevented local authority employees developing any form of 'worker participation' that involved membership of committees or full council. The one exception to this rule is the right of teachers to be co-opted as members of the education committee.

Despite the constitutional difficulties the TUC agreed in 1975 to support employee representation on council committees. The representatives would be drawn from and elected by trade union members and they would have voting rights. They would form not more than 20 per cent of any committee with a minimum of two representatives (NALGO 1977:7–8). These proposals would be in addition to normal consultative machinery and, of course, the regular involvement in developing policy which forms part of the job of some individual local government officers.

The TUC proposals were a response to more radical suggestions from NALGO for employee representation both on committees and on the full council. The representatives on the full council would 'have the right to speak and influence decision-making but should not have voting rights and by this means would not disturb the balance of power of the local authority'. Also, NALGO considered that a workers' council elected by trade union members within a local authority should be the basis of industrial democracy in local government. The workers' council would appoint the worker representatives on both committees and full council (NALGO 1977:Annex A).

The TUC and NALGO were both contributing to a debate surrounding the Committee of Inquiry on Industrial Democracy (Bullock 1977). The terms of reference on the committee were confined to private sector companies, but in welcoming the report the Secretary of State for Trade mentioned further consideration of the position of employees in central and local government (NALGO 1977:3). The Secretary of State was cautious and the Labour Party (to which he at that time belonged) shared his attitude. The party did not fully support the proposals coming from their trade union colleagues. A joint working party of the appropriate committees of the TUC and Labour Party issued a statement in February 1977. The TUC proposals mentioned above were amended to remove the voting rights of employee representatives on committees with the exception of teachers on the education committee who had enjoyed such rights since the end of the nineteenth century (Gosden 1977). The TUC and Labour Party reiterated however their policy 'that the law should be amended to end the disqualification of local government employees (with the exception of the chief officers and their deputies) from standing for election to the council of the local authority which employs them' (NALGO 1977:Annex B).

Since these discussions in the 1970s, there has been little movement towards an extension of employee participation in local government. A few authorities 'such as Slough, Hereford and Worcester, and Basildon have permitted employees to become members of committees in an advisory capacity' (Thomson 1982:130), but no legislative changes have been proposed.

The arguments in favour of employee representation on local authority committees or full council are rather different from those for allowing employees to stand for election as councillors. Employee representation is sought as an extension of the involvement implied in collective bargaining or consultation. The removal of disqualification, on the other hand, is seen as an extension of the civil rights of local authority employees. Despite these differences in the arguments in favour of the two sets of proposals, the arguments against are very similar. Redcliffe-Maud outlined 'three fundamental reasons' for maintaining the existing position:

> The first reason is the need to avoid a conflict of interest, or the appearance of a conflict of interest, between the individual's public duty as an elected member and his personal interest as an employee. The second is the need to preserve the political impartiality of officers. The third is the need to maintain sound working relationships at all levels in the authority's organisation and to avoid divided loyalties (Redcliffe-Maud 1974:32).

As we have seen in Chapter 7, these reasons are not entirely convincing. Proponents of change argue that there are well-established procedures for dealing with the conflicts of interest that may arise for councillors. These could be adapted for employees. The necessity for party political impartiality could be secured by restrictions on certain senior officers rather than on all employees.

The third reason outlined by Redcliffe-Maud applies very specifically to the discussion about 'industrial democracy'. Any developments in this direction would imply a movement away from hierarchical forms of management. The conventional role of senior and supervisory staff will 'become very difficult ... if all ranks of employees are involved in decision making' (Long 1976:55). The person who becomes an equal member of a committee is likely to show less deference to senior members of staff in other circumstances. For the New Urban Left this erosion of hierarchy is a positive advantage. They wish to see officers working with an understanding that their role is essentially one of 'community action', of politics with a small 'p'. They want to 'open up a freer, more creative dialogue between councillors and the whole range of local authority workers, getting away from the traditional system where policy is decided between chairmen and chief officers' (Blunkett and Green 1983:26). When considered in these terms 'industrial democracy' moves from the narrow trade union concerns of the 1970s into a wider political perspective that would change the whole nature of local democracy. The potential conflict between representative and participatory modes of democracy with which we ended Chapter 7 is once again exposed.

Chapter nine

THE NATIONAL LOCAL GOVERNMENT SYSTEM

The previous two chapters have considered aspects of the local political system within which local government operates. There is, however, a wider political system that local authorities have to consider. Many organisations and institutions at national level have a direct concern with local authorities or originate within local government itself. The interaction of these various bodies is often referred to as the national local government system. In this chapter we describe the links between national political parties and local government, the process of national collective bargaining, the role of professional associations, and the organisation of local authority associations. In Chapter 10 we turn to the vital matter of local authority relations with central government.

NATIONAL PARTIES AND LOCAL GOVERNMENT

The political parties maintain central facilities for the discussion and co-ordination of local government affairs at national level. The form and extent of these facilities vary with both the attitude of each party to local government and the resources each party has available. In the Conservative and Labour parties, the local government interest has a place within the formal framework of the constitution of the party. In the Liberal Party since 1977 the co-ordinating function has been provided by an Association of Liberal Councillors 'rather than as an organisational unit of the party; it has members, who each pay a £6 annual subscription' (Gyford and James 1983:75).

Political parties are not simply hierarchical organisations with one centre of power. The local government interest, therefore, fits within the bargaining framework that forms the decision-making process in the major political parties. This framework represents various interests that can draw on different sources of legitimacy. The party conference represents the party activists in the constituencies; elected representatives in Parliament and on local authorities represent their electorates; and ministers, when the party is in government, can claim constitutional authority as ministers of the Crown. The Conservative Party is always careful to observe the constitutional niceties by emphasising the predominance of the parliamentary leadership; but even the Labour Party, with its greater emphasis on the role of the party conference, has careful procedures for balancing the relationships between party organisations and elected representatives in Parliament or local authorities.

In their full account of the relationship between national parties and local politics, from which most of the details in this section are taken, Gyford and James provide a four-cornered model. At the corners are, respectively, the party at the centre, the party in Parliament, local party units and local authority party groups. There are linkages between these four groupings within a party to form a square in which the corners are also linked diagonally. This gives six lines of linkage (Gyford and James 1983:7). Even this model, though more complex than simple models of a chain of command from party leader to local party member, does not give the full picture. The role of the trade unions within the Labour Party, for example, adds another dimension to its intra-party politics.

THE CONSERVATIVE PARTY

The Conservative Party reflects its origins as an electioneering organisation supporting the party in Parliament by maintaining a dual structure. The National Union of Conservative and Unionist Associations represents the party membership: the Conservative Central Office serves the parliamentary leadership. A simplified view of the place of local government within this structure is given in Fig. 9.1. Like all such

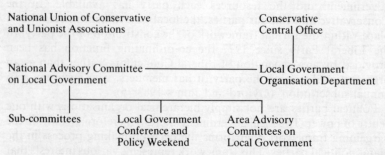

FIG. 9.1   Local government within the Conservative Party at national level

diagrams it is in some respects based upon aspirations rather than realities. The area advisory committees, for example, are not uniformly active throughout the country.

Since 1975 the National Advisory Committee on Local Government has had a membership of approximately 100, 60 per cent of whom are Conservative leaders on local authorities. Also included are a number of Members of Parliament and a member of the House of Lords. The committee is an advisory body within the party organisation and acts 'as a link between the Leader and all branches of the Party' (Gyford and James 1983:31). The large membership of the Advisory Committee results in the use of subcommittees including the Policy Liaison Group which is 'charged with securing liaison between, and co-ordination of, the party's activities in local government, Parliament and Central Office' (Gyford and James 1983:31). The local government conference is an annual one-day opportunity for councillors to listen to Conservative front-bench speakers and to express their opinions in return. The policy weekend is a smaller affair that considers current local government issues.

The Local Government Organisation Department services the National Advisory Committee and the Conservative groups on the local authority associations. In addition the department provides advice on electioneering and party proceedures to local councillors. Its role in policy formation is restricted not only by its constitutional position within the party but also by the size of its staff. There are 'rarely more than two professional staff, plus secretarial staff and an occasional voluntary assistant' (Gyford and James 1983:40).

THE LABOUR PARTY

The Labour Party has a unitary structure for the purpose we are considering. At the annual conference of the party a National Executive Committee (NEC) is elected which appoints a number of committees including the Home Policy Committee and the Organisation Committee. Until 1983, the Regional and Local Government Sub-Committee reported in appropriate circumstances to either of these main committees and thence to the NEC (Fig 9.2). The subcommittee has now been established as a main committee. The Local Government Committee consists of both NEC and local authority representatives. The committee meets roughly once a month and has an advisory function to assist the NEC in all matters concerned with local government. The Home Policy Committee continues to play a leading role in specific matters of new policy. As in the Conservative Party, attempts to establish advisory committees in the regions have been only partially successful. The committee arranges the annual local government conference. Since 1982 this conference lasts for three days

147

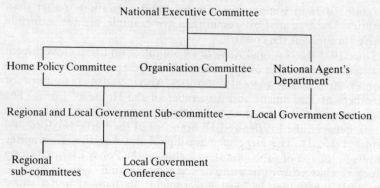

FIG. 9.2 Local government within the Labour Party at national level; 1983

and 'is in some ways a combination of the two events which the Conservatives separate – the rally, and the policy weekend' (Gyford and James 1983:60).

A local government section previously located within the National Agent's Department was transferred to the Research Department in 1984. The headquarters is responsible to the NEC and not, as in the Conservative Party, to the leader of the party. The local government section is of similar size to the corresponding department within the Conservative Party – that is, very small. It performs similar functions to its Conservative counterpart being concerned with both the servicing of the subcommittee and the preparation of background and information papers. In one respect the two party organisations are dissimilar. The staff in the Labour Party headquarters are far more likely than those in the Conservative Central Office to take an active interest in internal party controversies (Gyford and James 1983:65).

Despite the apparent neatness of the communication flows within the two organisational charts shown in the diagrams, we must remember the greater complexity of political reality. This complexity is inherent in the Gyford and James four-cornered model. For example, party members in local government may approach their colleagues in Parliament as either ministers or opposition front-benchers thus bypassing the party machinery. They may also persuade the constituency parties to pursue particular topics at the party conference. And, of course, they may use their own network of contacts within the party on a personal basis. The skill of a politician lies in using all such resources as are appropriate in the circumstances of each particular case and he or she will not be constrained by formal procedures if other opportunities are available.

NATIONAL COLLECTIVE BARGAINING

Each local authority is responsible for recruiting and maintaining its own staff. There is no unified local government service to provide a national corps of local government employees. In the past this has meant that local authorities could differ considerably in the terms and conditions of service they offered, but gradually over the years there has been a movement towards uniformity. Today the trade unions police a series of national agreements that provide a basis for employment policies from one end of the country to another. There is, however, still room for local variations within the national agreements. These variations may again be growing with the decentralisation of union activities and the development of a shop steward structure within local government trade unions (see Ch. 8). Local authorities will not wish, however, to move too far away from the national agreements, and the district auditor will restrain any major improvement on national payments.

The present system of national collective bargaining dates from the aftermath of the First World War. A committee established to consider relations between workers and employees 'recommended the establishment of a system of Joint (National) Industrial Councils, District Councils, and Works Councils' (Hepple and O'Higgins 1971:32). A further report extended these recommendations to central and local government. The councils became known as Whitley Committees after the chairman of the committee that had recommended their establishment. A similar committee concerned with teachers' salaries became known as the Burnham Committee after its first chairman.

At first 'many local authorities ... held aloof' from the Whitley Councils (Hepple and O'Higgins 1971:89). The growing trade union movement engaged in some negotiations at both national and local level, but 'bargaining between authorities and workers was random and piecemeal' during the 1930s (Poole 1978:69). In many areas trade unions were denied recognition for specific groups of workers. The unions themselves pursued an orthodox and cautious policy with the exception of NUPE which increasingly contested the established positions both of employers and other unions. During the 1930s NUPE extended union membership among previously unorganised groups of low-paid workers, such as county council roadmen, and by a series of local agreements gradually forced its way into the official bargaining machinery (Clegg 1954; Craik 1955, 1968; Spoor 1967). The resulting confusion of part national bargaining, part local agreements, and wide areas of non-recognition of trade unions and collective bargaining continued until the Second World War. The confusion was removed by the effect of 'wartime legislation. Primarily intended to prevent strikes and lockouts the legislation also required the observance of "recognised terms and conditions of employment" by all employers' (Hepple and O'Higgins 1971:88–9). This gave a great advantage to trade unions seeking recognition (Spoor 1967:193–5). Decisions by provincial Whitley Councils 'had to be observed by all local authorities, whether members of the Council or not' (Hepple and O'Higgins 1971:89). Finally an improved National Whitley Council was formed in 1943.

The present system of collective bargaining in local government consists of five groups of national negotiating bodies dealing respectively with administrative, professional, technical and clerical (APT & C) staffs; manual workers; teachers; police; and fire brigades. Each of these five groups is a complex organisation giving a total of some forty national pay bargaining bodies. Sixteen provincial councils exist for APT & C staff and manual workers. The employees' sides of these negotiating bodies are drawn from appropriate trade unions who may argue long and hard between themselves about the exact balance of their representation. The employers' sides 'are drawn, according to the character of the Negotiating Body, from the Associations of Local Authorities, the Greater London Council, the Associations of Local Authorities in Scotland, Provincial Employers' Sides, Government Departments and Voluntary Organisations' (Poole 1978:217). The employers' side is co-ordinated through the Local Authorities' Conditions of Service Advisory Board (LACSAB). The board was established in 1948 and provides a secretariat and advice to the employers. It also presents statements on general local authority manpower matters to government bodies and thus itself forms part of the national local government system (Poole 1978:77–9; Rhodes 1986:Ch.5).

The functions of the Whitley machinery vary with the particular council being considered. Some are concerned with the 'collection of statistics, encouragement of the study of administration methods, recruitment and training, and co-operation with other joint councils' (Poole 1978:74). Others are less expansive in their activities. The Burnham Committee deals exclusively with pay negotiations. The employers are represented in discussions about conditions of service for teachers by the Central Council of Local Education Authorities (CLEA).

Negotiations within the Whitley machinery are increasingly conducted in the presence of clearly defined central government pay policies (Rhodes 1986:Ch. 5). At times these have taken the form of 'guidelines' applicable to all pay negotiations, public and private alike. More recently in the public service the government has simply assumed a certain percentage increase when fixing the grant it will pay to local authorities or other institutions, thus imposing a 'cash limit' on any settlement. Negotiators, therefore, conduct their affairs with the ghost of the minister in the room. In some cases, the police and teachers for example, the minister has had a more solid presence and has either been represented on the committee or approved any agreement before it was implemented (Coates 1972b).

THE ROLE OF PROFESSIONAL ASSOCIATIONS

Local government is responsible for the delivery of services and not simply for deciding policies governing the provision of such services. Local authorities employ refuse collectors, bus drivers and a host of other manual workers: they also employ many people who may be described as professionals. The definition of a professional is a controversial topic (Johnson 1972:Ch. 2), but for our present purposes we may concentrate on two characteristics that are usually associated with the status. The first of these is the identification of professionalism with an ethic of public service rather than an exclusive concern with private profit. The other is the claim by professions to define and control the practice of the ethics thus adopted. Professions such as medicine and law provide the most complete examples. Doctors subscribe to the Hippocratic oath binding them to serve the welfare of the sick, and lawyers are the servants of the courts in the pursuit of justice. We are not concerned at this point to test the empirical validity of these claims by professionals: particular individuals or professions as a whole may persuade themselves that the best interests of their clients are served by enhancing the position of their profession. The significant point is the reference to a source of authority outside the professional/client relationship. The repository of this authority is the professional association. As Howard Elcock points out: 'Local authority officers are accountable in three directions: upwards, outwards, and downwards' (Elcock 1983:24). They are accountable upwards to senior officers and ultimately to members assembled in full council; they are accountable outwards through their professional associations for their professional standards; and they are accountable downwards to their clients. Individual citizens who suffer injury to their interests by a mistaken professional decision or incompetence may enjoy a range of remedies including political complaints, the intervention of the ombudsman, and court actions for damages if a legal liability is established.

The growth in the number of professionals employed by local government is a function of both the growth in the services provided and the aspirations of new groups of workers to full professional status. Thus traditional professions such as acrhitecture, law and engineering are supplemented by the local authority professions of municipal treasurers or public health inspectors. The number is constantly growing as groups such as housing managers, social workers, market managers and many others establish professional associations. 'There is also a distinctive set of Scottish professional associations' (Page 1980b:85). The associations conduct or validate examinations that define professional boundaries by entitling candidates to signify their success by an appropriate set of initials after their names. The associations also frequently publish journals that disseminate developments in professional practice.

The professional associations influence public policy in two ways. First, the general attitudes and ethos of a profession are absorbed by officers through their membership of an association. The influence of their peers then effects the behaviour of officers in the process of policy determination and implementation. An important network of communication exists through the professional associations. They link officers in different local authorities to each other. Sometimes this network extends to professional colleagues in central government departments and private practice. Officers meet in local branches of associations and at regional and national conferences. The associations foster a general feeling that officers owe a loyalty to the standards of their profession as well as to the policies of their local authorities.

Second, professional associations themselves form part of a national system of local government. The local authority associations (see below) 'have officer advisers appointed in consultation with professional associations' (Laffin 1980:23; Rhodes 1986:Ch. 3). These advisers have an influence on the development of national policy in relation to local government issues but their position depends more on their standing within their profession than on the support of their employers. The professional associations are also directly consulted by central government departments. They present evidence or provide members for official inquiries and Royal Commissions. In some cases they come to dominate the outcome of such inquiries. The Seebohm Report, for example, was heavily influenced by the emerging profession of social work (Laffin 1980:18–19). The views of the major professional associations are received with attention in the national news media. Thus officers who in their own local authority are expected to refrain from contributing to political controversies find their collective voice through pronouncements from their professional association or the editorial policy of their journal.

Examples of the importance of professional influence may be taken from housing and education. Patrick Dunleavy in his careful study of housing policy has analysed 'the role of local authority organisations, mainly the functional service associations in housing and planning, and of the local government press in combination with the influence of the design professions and the corporate section of the construction industry, in promoting high-rise, high-density housing solutions for the public sector' (Dunleavy 1980a:107). The professional associations in architecture 'tended to define an extensive scope for professional influence on housing construction policy. All sections in architecture were involved in public housing. The unity of the profession under the leadership of private architects was maintained' (Dunleavy 1981:14–15). Throughout his study, Dunleavy shows how local authorities in widely differing parts of the country adopted very similar solutions to their housing problems in the 1960s. The influence of the national local government system, and the self-interest of the construction industry, made a mockery of local autonomy. Many individual councillors had little understanding of what was going on, or were presented with reports from their professional officers that made particular decisions seem inevitable.

The 1960s were also a high point for a developing professional influence in the making of educational policy. In both Scotland and England new organisations were created in which teachers played a prominent part. The General Teaching Council established in 1965 'gave Scottish teachers a large measure of control over entry to their profession' (Bone 1974:51). In the first few years of its existence the council made a major contribution to discussions about teacher training and eliminated unqualified staff. In England the Schools Council for the Curriculum Examinations developed many new approaches to teaching and exerted steady pressure for the classroom teacher to have greater control over the nature and content of examinations. The Schools Council disseminated the results of sponsored research and curriculum development projects through publications and an information service. The governing body of the Schools Council contained forty-five teachers in a total membership of eighty. Perhaps it is understandable that by 1980 the General Secretary of the National Association of Head Teachers was speaking of a 'traditional partnership within the education service between Government, local authorities and teachers' (*The Times* 27.5.80).

THE LOCAL AUTHORITY ASSOCIATIONS

Individual local authorities have direct links with government departments and ministers. Representations and advice flow continuously in both directions. In addition to these individual links, local authorities have felt the need to organise collectively since the establishment of the modern system of local government in the nineteenth century (Keith-Lucas and Richards 1978:180). Although the need for collective action is recognised, it has not proved possible to reconcile the interests of different types of local authorities. There are, therefore, several local authority associations representing the various forms of local government in England and Wales and a separate organisation in Scotland.

The present system of local authority associations in England and Wales was constituted following local government reorganisation in 1974 (Rhodes 1986:Table 3.1). There are three major associations. The Association of Metropolitan Authorities (AMA) represents the metropolitan counties and their districts and the local authorities in London. The Association of County Councils (ACC) represents the non-metropolitan or shire counties. The Association of District Councils (ADC) represents non-metropolitan districts. These three associations continue the divisions apparent since the creation of the original local authority associations. The conflicts between them have been felt throughout the discussion about the appropriate structure for local government (Isaac-Henry 1975): the boroughs and the counties have seldom been in agreement. The conflicts have been continued since reorganisation both between the different associations and through the informal groupings of the larger towns and cities within the ADC (Ch. 2).

The Royal Commission on Local Government in England strongly recommended the formation of a single local authority association following reorganisation. They recognised differences that might arise between the various types of local authorities, but argued that there were many matters of common interest on which local government should speak with a united voice. They believed it would 'be a disaster if, when the new system is established, separate associations of main local authorities were formed' (Redcliffe-Maud 1969:Vol I 32). In taking this approach the Royal Commission avoided the very real conflicts of interest that can arise between the major urban centres and rural areas. In local government terms both the needs and resources of these areas are very different. Each has a vital interest in influencing government policy and the distribution of government grants to its own advantage. These real conflicts of interest find expression through the political parties. The Labour Party does relatively well in elections in the metropolitan authorities and in some non-metropolitan districts in urban areas. The Conservative Party is usually dominant in the non-metropolitan counties. These considerations led to the reconstitution of separate local authority associations following local government reorganisation. The arguments were never couched in party political terms, but the protagonists understood the issue involved. A single local authority association would be under continuous Conservative control owing to their strength in the rural areas. The Labour Party, on the other hand, could hope on occasion to control an association based on the metropolitan authorities. As might be expected, the Conservatives supported a single association while the Labour Party opposed the idea. The Labour Party also opposed any moves to separate the metropolitan districts from the metropolitan counties as this would weaken the association they hoped to control (Gyford and James 1983: 114–16).

The structure of the local authority associations is based on the model of local government. Each association 'has a Council (or meeting) which has the overall responsibility for managing the organisation. Each (including the ADC) has a well-developed committee system through which most of the work of the Association passes. Each has a secretariat with a chief officer ... ' (Isaac-Henry 1980:23). Committees are established for each of the major services provided by member authorities. They consist of both councillors and officers from these authorities. The officers are there to offer advice; they are not allowed to vote.

Since the late 1960s the political parties have organised within the local authority associations in the same way as they do within individual local authorities (Rhodes 1986:Ch. 3). The impetus for this development came from the Conservative Party members on the Association of Municipal Corporations (AMC) which was the forebear of the AMA. The Local Government Officer at Conservative Central Office at the time has subsequently explained the reason: 'It was obvious ... that ministers went to the local authority associations rather than to individual local authorities, and it seemed a bit ironical after 1967 that the AMC should continue to be Labour-dominated under a facade of independence' (quoted in Gyford and James 1983:112). Party groups on the AMA now meet to decide their attitude towards agenda items before association meetings; the controlling party takes the chair of both the full meeting and the various committees. The associations representing the counties and the districts have such a strong Conservative presence that changes in party control are unlikely, but they too have been affected by the growing influence of party politics. This growing influence has led to some dissatisfaction within the associations. In 1981, Derbyshire withdrew from the ACC. As a Labour-controlled authority they objected to the political bias of the Conservative majority in their support for the policies of the Thatcher government. Avon County Council also resigned and other authorities seriously considered their position. The DOE obviously regretted these developments; it had no wish to consult with a large number of individual local authorities and expressed a firm intention to continue to regard the associations as 'the accredited organisations to express views on behalf of local government generally' (Rhodes *et al.* 1983b:49).

The activities of the associations 'fall into three main categories. They are activities involved with government departments and Parliament, the provision of information, advice and other aids to member authorities and co-operation with other associations' (Isaac-Henry 1980:27). Consultation with government departments is both regular and detailed. It ranges from formal consideration of consultative documents to the ubiquitous telephone call. The associations also maintain regular contact with members of both the House of Commons and the House of Lords. Generally these friendly parliamentarians offer discreet support behind the scenes but occasionally the lobbying by the associations is more dramatic. In the early 1980s, for example, the associations sponsored major campaigns against aspects of the government's policy towards local government. Members of both the Commons and the Lords supported these campaigns, sometimes in opposition to their own party's Whip. Government policy was amended in some respects as a result of this parliamentary opposition (see Ch. 10).

Local authority associations co-operate in many joint organisations. The most important of these is the Consultative Council on Local Government Finance (CCLGF). This body was established in 1975 to formalise the discussions between ministers and local authorities about the grant allocation. Although primarily concerned with finance, the influence of the CCLGF extends into general policy matters with financial implications. These include manpower levels in local government (Rhodes 1986:Ch. 4). Other joint organisations include the Local Government Training Board and groups concerned with management issues. There is also a large number of advisory bodies for particular services. Isaac-Henry reports that 'in 1968 the AMC was represented on over 140 advisory bodies and committees on which it had over 200 representative places' (Isaac-Henry 1980:28). Most of these representatives are appointed by the appropriate committee of the association. In addition to the joint bodies comprising representatives of the associations, 'some local authorities with a common interest in a particular function have formed their own organisations independent of the associations (e.g. British Resorts Association, British Association of Conference Towns)' (Rhodes 1986:Ch. 2).

The establishment of joint organisations is not always a simple matter of administrative convenience. Education provides an example of a service where a joint organisation developed a major political presence that enabled it to compete with the local authority associations themselves. Before local government reorganisation the Association of Education Committees (AEC) was a powerful lobby for maintaining the relative independence of education within the local authority structure. The Secretary of the AEC was a powerful voice in national local government debates. It was he who 'spoke for the employing authorities on the Burnham Committee, and not the representatives of the local authority associations' (Keith-Lucas and Richards 1978:191). On occasion there was open disagreement between the AEC and the associations although both sides depended on the local authorities for financial support. When the present local authority associations were established after reorganisation the 'new national organisations ... were quite determined that education committees should have no national voice so the Association of Education Committees was forced out of existence' (Gosden 1982:119–20). The Central Council of Local

Education Authorities (CLEA) was established as a joint body of the AMA and ACC but it was 'not permitted to aspire to the position once occupied by the displaced AEC' (Gosden 1982:120; Rhodes 1986:Ch. 8).

SCOTLAND

The Royal Commission on Local Government in Scotland adopted the same attitude towards the local authority associations as its English counterpart. The report 'suggested that local government would be strengthened if it were represented by one local authority association and not, as existed under the pre-organisation system, four ... ' (Page 1983:54). In Scotland, unlike England, this recommendation was accepted. The Convention of Scottish Local Authorities (COSLA) was established in 1975 to represent all local authorities in Scotland. The subsequent history of COSLA has to some extent reflected the tensions that led to the continuation of separate associations in England.

The operation of COSLA is similar to that of the English associations. There is a general meeting of representatives from each of the sixty-five local authorities and a system of fifteen executive committees. These include a convention policy committee and committees concerned with particular local authority functions. In addition there 'are also Regional, District and Islands Policy Committees, which meet only rarely, and whose remit is more limited ... ' (Keating and Midwinter 1983:104). There is a small full-time secretariat to service the work of COSLA and its committees. In addition, there are part-time specialist advisers attached to each committee. These advisers 'are nominated by their professional associations, not by the elected members. The Society of Local Authority Chief Executives (SOLACE) and the Chartered Institute of Public Finance and Accountancy (CIPFA) are represented on every committee ... ' (Keating and Midwinter 1983:105).

The functions fulfilled by COSLA are similar to those of the English associations but there is room for some discussion about the relative effectiveness of the associations in the two countries. Keating and Midwinter consider that COSLA is not as well organised as the English associations in dealing with parliamentary legislation. The opposition to the government's legislation in the early 1980s 'was much fiercer and better orchestrated in England' (Keating and Midwinter 1983:107) which led Scotland to be the unwilling pioneer in central control over the rate levels (see Ch. 10). The wide variety of local authorities included in COSLA has also resulted in internal disagreements. On occasion these have prevented it making a reply to Scottish Office requests for advice (Page 1983:55). Such difficulties should not be exaggerated. Keating and Midwinter judge that 'there is still more unity than division' (Keating and Midwinter 1983:106). In any case it is arguable whether the occasional internal differences that lead COSLA to be mute are more damaging to the cause of local government than the capacity of the English associations to speak with several and various voices.

DISCUSSION – HOW SIGNIFICANT IS THE NATIONAL LOCAL GOVERNMENT SYSTEM?

The growing academic interest in the national local government system has enabled some aspects of it to be described in more detail than would have been possible a few years ago. There is still a need, however, to assess its significance in the study of local government and urban politics. The national local government system might influence local government in two ways. First, it might contribute to a decline in the ability of individual local authorities to influence policy outcomes in their own localities. Second, it might affect the influence of local government as a whole within the complex system of intergovernmental relations. These two aspects will be discussed in the context of the material presented earlier in this chapter. The latter part of the discussion forms a natural prelude to the full consideration of relations between central and local government that constitutes the central interest of Chapter 10.

First, we will consider the extent to which the national political parties, the national collective bargaining system and the professional associations limit the policy discretion of individual local authorities. The importance of national politics when considering voting behaviour in local elections is universally accepted even if the precise extent of the influence is disputed (see Ch. 7). Although people vote in local elections with national issues in mind this does not mean, however, that the national political parties necessarily have a strong influence on local politics. The national political parties have difficulty in exercising control over the activities of their own local party organisations. The large city parties in particular have often assumed considerable independence. In the past the London Labour Party elected its own delegates to the annual conference and the Conservative London Municipal Society maintained its own organisation and sources of finance. The reorganisation of London local government in the 1960s gave the national parties the occasion to incorporate these quasi-independent bodies into the mainstream of party organisation (Young 1972:44–9; 1975:210–12). Similar moves in the early 1970s attempted to restrict the role of the great provincial city parties. The emphasis was placed on the formal machinery of constituency and area or regional parties. Despite these attempts to assert central control many city organisations persist in form if not in name. Local Labour parties are not 'passive tools' of the party headquarters and in the Conservative Party 'the most salient point about the struggle between Central Office and the city parties ... is the weakness of the central organisation' (Wilson and Pinto-Duschinsky 1976:244).

The control that national parties can exert in their dealings with party groups on local authorities is limited still further by the legitimacy such groups can claim from the local ballot box. Gyford and James point out that, 'Constitutionally none of the parties possess any mechanisms whereby local politicians may be forced to comply with the wishes of the party at the centre ... ' (Gyford and James 1983:195). Nor can the local government departments maintained by the central parties compete with the resources available to councillors in a local authority. Even when a party forms the national government, local authorities of the same political persuasion may not necessarily comply with their wishes. Many examples could be given. These include the resistance in South Yorkshire to a Labour government's attempt in the 1970s to get them to increase fares on public transport (Gyford and James 1983:138–47). Another example would be the opposition of many Conservative councils to the government's proposals for rate-capping in the 1980s. Indeed, both these examples show the national party system being used with some success to support the policies of local authorities rather than to impose central priorities. There is no doubt some hesitance among local politicians about embarrassing their national leadership, but national politicians need to earn any respect that is available. In the bargaining that takes place between the national and local parties, local authorities do not seem unduly disadvantaged.

The development of national collective bargaining may be a more significant factor than the national political parties in limiting the discretion of local authorities. Poole quotes an American observer who points out that by accepting national collective bargaining 'local authorities have relinquished a degree of local autonomy far in excess of that taken from them by the remaining ministerial controls over officers or exercised by the courts in relation to the reasonableness of remuneration' (Poole 1978:70). The payment of their employees represents the major part of the expenditure incurred by local authorities. To a large extent an individual local authority is unable to decide for itself on the wages or salary to be paid to particular grades of employees. Negotiations are conducted through LACSAB within broad pay strategies determined by central government. This restriction must have a considerable impact on local policy outcomes; it removes one significant aspect of the debate from discussions over local policy options. Yet even here the removal of local discretion may not be as complete as it first appears. Earlier in the chapter the growth of local bargaining was mentioned. There is discretion in the number of people employed and in the point on the nationally agreed scales to which an individual is allocated. Teachers' salaries are determined by the

Burnham Committee, but pupil–teacher ratios, class sizes and contact hours for teachers – and hence the number of teachers employed – are decided locally. Indeed, when the Layfield Committee considered the possibility of central government paying teachers' salaries as a way of relieving the rate fund they concluded: 'the element of local discretion associated with the payment of teachers' salaries was sufficient to nullify the case for transfer' (Layfield 1976:110). If such discretion exists in education it is unlikely to be less marked in other areas of local authority employment.

Professional associations continue to be influential in local government affairs, but their position is not as secure as it appeared in the high days of corporatism in the 1970s. Corporate interests in policy-making have been challenged by both the interest in public participation and the more ideological approach of local and national politicians. These developments can be illustrated by returning to the examples of housing and education referred to earlier in the chapter. In an afterword to his study of housing policy, Dunleavy refers to the public rejection of the high-rise solutions adopted to housing problems in the 1960s (Dunleavy 1981:353–5). The great architectural showpieces of municipal housing are being either demolished or converted into student flats and other non-family accommodation. The policy of large-scale slum clearance which provided the occasion of the high-rise policy has been replaced by more sensitive and small-scale developments. In this new climate the public are more frequently consulted in an attempt to avoid the image of the professional planner so vividly contained in Jon Gower Davies's description of the 'evangelistic bureaucrat' (Davies 1972). The well-publicised corruption trials involving planners, architects and councillors in the 1970s must also have affected public attitudes.

Similar comments on the declining image of professionalism can be made with regard to education. The teachers' associations have pursued their salary and other claims with trade union energy and methods thus losing some of their professional mystique. At the same time, public opinion has become more wary of according their statements on educational policy full professional status. There is a belief, for example, that the pro-comprehensive views of the teachers' associations 'reflect the strong interest that teachers in the secondary modern schools – who are struggling to upgrade their jobs and status – have in redistributive education programmes' (Kantor 1976:319). Many parents now expect greater access to schools and have developed both national and local organisations to express their views on educational policy. The government has introduced legislation to enforce parental membership of school governing bodies and a Green Paper published in 1984 proposed that they should form a majority (see Ch. 7).

These developments both in public attitudes and governmental policy towards local authority housing and education have not, of course, resulted in a complete rejection of professional advice in favour of lay opinion. The examples counsel caution, however, in judging the extent to which professional associations can press their claims in the complex political process of policy determination. Professional opinion is more frequently challenged than in the past in many areas of activity.

The role of professional associations is also affected by the general climate of opinion within central government towards corporate institutions. The Conservative government first elected in 1979 pursued a strategy which included both reducing public expenditure as a proportion of the GNP and dismantling much of the state apparatus of advisory and other bodies – the so-called 'QUANGOS'. Whether the government was successful or not in its objectives is not here at issue; the climate changed within which professional associations operate. Proposals for the expansion of services were no longer part of the currency of policy discussions. Research and advisory bodies within which professional opinion was influential such as the Centre for Environmental Studies and the Schools Council were either closed down or substantially reorganised. These changes were not undertaken simply for reasons of economy. The Secretary of State for Education expressed his loss of confidence in the Schools Council when announcing its closure in 1982 and subsequent reorganisation. The decision was clearly political with a concern for the form and control of policy formation (Skilbeck 1982).

The interaction of the national local government system with the process of intergovernmental relations is complex. It is difficult to judge therefore, how far the national system influences the relationship between central and local government. We have just mentioned how Mrs Thatcher's government sought to reduce the corporate influence of professional associations. In the national political parties, however, local government became more salient as controversial policies affecting its relationship with central government were introduced. The Conservative Party brought several of its senior local government councillors into national prominence. Two former leaders of Leeds City Council entered the House of Lords: one to become a Vice-President of the party with responsibility for local government; the other to become a minister responsible for local government. Poachers sometimes turn gamekeepers, but these appointments indicate the stature of local government representatives in the eyes of the national party – a stature which has not always been recognised in the past. In the Labour Party the rise of the New Urban Left increased the influence of prominent local government personalities in the national party. The leader of Sheffield City Council, David Blunkett, was elected to the NEC as a constituency representative in 1983. He is the first non-parliamentarian to achieve this position since Professor Harold Laski at the end of the Second World War. Blunkett immediately took the chair of the Local Government Committee. In the Liberal Party, local government activity has become increasingly important in recent years. It has had an important part in sustaining 'the very existence of the party in the country and, specifically, to contribute to its revived electoral fortunes' (Gyford and James 1983:69).

The local authority associations are of key importance in considering whether the national local government system contributes to the influence of local government in intergovernmental relations. The intention to do so is, of course, the reason for their existence. There can be little doubt about the influence of the associations in the day-to-day business of government. They are in constant contact with civil servants and have ready access to ministers, although many of the matters on which they are consulted are not controversial. The significant question is whether their existence is important in the determination of *controversial* policy issues. In some cases the answer must clearly be no. If the local authorities are so divided among themselves that the associations either decline to give advice or express conflicting views to the minister then decisions will be taken on other grounds. The government may in any event have a clear policy it intends to implement. The associations, however, have clearly exercised a strong negative influence over some policy issues. For example, their inability to agree inhibited government moves to reform local government throughout the 1950s and 1960s. The reorganisation in the 1970s which was finally imposed met at least some of the views of existing local authorities (Rhodes 1986:Ch. 10). They also fought a sustained rearguard action against proposals to limit their rating powers in the 1980s. Examples of *positive* action on major policy issues are less easy to find. As with many interest groups, the associations come together under the threat of external attack, but find it more difficult to agree on other matters where the constraints under which they operate become more apparent (Rhodes 1986:Ch. 10).

CONCLUSION

The national local government system cannot be interpreted solely in terms of the constraints it places upon policy formation in particular localities (Dunleavy 1980a:105). Such constraints exist, but local authorities may also use the national system to influence the degree of independence they can exercise in relation to central government. In these circumstances the national system is a defender of local autonomy rather than a constraint. The national system may also be used during a conflict between an individual local authority and central government. The successful involvement of the Labour Party nationally in defence of the South Yorkshire transport policy is a good example. The minister was isolated within his own party. The political costs of continuing the battle led him to find a solution acceptable to the local authority (Gyford and James 1983:147). The national local government system may, therefore, be interpreted as an intermeshing of local and national structures of policy-making. The context within which this intermeshing takes place has obviously been affected by the radical restructuring of British society attempted by the Conservative governments led by Mrs Thatcher. These broader questions will be considered in the course of Chapter 10.

Chapter ten

CENTRAL–LOCAL
GOVERNMENT RELATIONS

The relationship between central and local government has assumed a particular importance in recent years. There are two reasons for this growing importance though these are obviously inter-connected. First, academic specialists have devoted much effort to research in various features of the relationship between the two levels of government. Second, the relationship itself 'has become strained and the dialogue that sustains it acrimonious' (Young 1983:1). The resulting torrent of academic literature and polemics, sometimes written by the same people, has had an influence on many aspects of the study of urban politics. The previous chapter was heavily dependent on recent research conducted in this context and other references are scattered throughout our text. Students should not assume, therefore, that the present chapter represents the complete content of the current approach to central–local relations. In some respects indeed this phrase no longer denotes a section of the subject-matter of urban politics but rather a different way of synthesising all the material available. Students should treat the polemics written in this area as a supplement to the academic literature. The authors of these tracts act as advocates whose emphasis in making a case allows clearer judgements to be made about the essential elements of the subject-matter.

The present chapter provides a guide through the recent debates by placing them within the context of earlier discussions of central–local relations. We start with an outline of the traditional approach before considering more recent models. We end with a discussion of the controversy surrounding the legislation introduced by the Conservative government in 1984 to contain the powers of local authorities to levy rates at a level of their own choosing.

THE CLASSIC APPROACH

The classic approach to the study of central–local government relations is found in Professor J A G Griffith's *Central Departments and Local Authorities*. He argues:

> ... it is important to emphasize three conditions which shape the relationship between the centre and the locality. The first is that the providers of services are the local authorities. ... Secondly, to speak of the relationship between the centre and the localities as one of control is a partial misdescription ... local authorities make their impact also on the departments. ... The third condition that shapes the relationship is the acceptance, for most services, of a general minimum standard which it is believed should apply to the whole country (Griffith 1966:17–18).

From such premises two rival models of the central-local relationship can be derived. Those who look at the law and the insistence on minimum standards describe local authorities as the *agents* of central government. Their task is to carry out duties delegated by the government of the day. Those who accept that there is a wide variation in the level of service provided, and note the complex interaction between local authorities and central government departments, prefer to write of a *partnership*. Within this partnership local authorities have an influence on the determination of central policy and exercise some discretion in their local activities. Whichever of these models is accepted the relationship between the centre and the locality may be analysed within the broad headings of legal, administrative and financial.

LEGAL

In Chapter 1 we described how local authorities are creatures of statute. Both their existence and the purposes they serve are prescribed by law. Actions for which they cannot point to statutory authority may be found *ultra vires* and any consequent expenditure disallowed. Griffith points out, however, that once an Act of Parliament has vested powers in a local authority then it becomes autonomous 'within the terms on which those powers are bestowed' (Griffith 1966:49). It is the government department that must then be able to justify any intervention by reference to statutory provisions. Central government – or any ratepayer – may wish to intervene either to prevent a local authority pursuing a policy for which it has no legal authority or to insist that it carries out a statutory duty. The intervention, in other words, may be either restrictive or promotional in its effect on local policy.

Several leading cases of the first type relate to transport. In 1953, for example, Birmingham Corporation resolved to provide free travel on their 'buses for certain classes of old persons. There was no statutory provision either authorising or prohibiting the scheme' (Jackson 1965:245). A ratepayer obtained a declaration from the High Court that the proposal was *ultra vires* as the local authority lacked the power to operate such a policy. The policy, therefore, had to be abandoned. Subsequently, an Act of Parliament gave local transport authorities a general power to operate such policies. In a later case the House of Lords ruled that neither this general legislation nor the London Transport Act 1969 gave the GLC the power to implement a supplementary rate to introduce a *general system* of heavily subsidised fares on tubes and buses. During the Appeal Court hearing of the case as it progressed to the House of Lords 'Lord Denning referred to the duty that the GLC had to promote "integrated, efficient and economic transport facilities" . . . which did not include "the question of social or philanthropic or political objectives". The GLC had not held a fair balance as it should between conflicting interests' (Wistrich 1983:28). In upholding the decision of the Court of Appeal, the House of Lords emphasised that 'although the GLC had powers to make grants to London Transport, they should not be for the purpose of social or transport policy but to cover any unavoidable deficit' (Wistrich 1983:28).

During the GLC case there was considerable discussion of the meaning of 'economic transport facilities'. The judges tended to interpret this as meaning facilities that did not make a loss, while the GLC interpreted it more widely in the context of a general economic policy. Indeed, the Transport Act 1968, which provided for provincial transport services spelt this out more clearly. It placed a duty on the metropolitan county councils 'to secure or promote the provision of a properly integrated and efficient system of public passenger transport to meet the needs of that area with due regard to the town planning and traffic and planning policies of the councils of constituent areas and to economy and safety of operation' (Section 9(3)). The different wording allowed Merseyside to succeed in the courts where the GLC had failed in defending a policy of subsidised fares. These cases illustrate the central role of the courts in central–local relations. The uncertainty that surrounded transport policies during the court proceedings was welcomed by neither the government nor the local authorities. Indeed, with the help of some minor legislation and compromises, a modified cheap fares policy was subsequently adopted in London without serious challenge.

The statutory relationship between central and local government is always subject to the power of the courts to interpret legislation in the light of previous cases and general legal principles. For example, even where statutory authority exists for a course of action, a local authority is expected to act 'reasonably' or face the possibility of an auditor disqualifying any expenditure involved. One of the most famous confrontations between local authorities and the courts illustrates this principle. In the early 1970s Poplar and several other East London boroughs adopted policies that provided for much better than normal conditions for their employees, higher benefits than usual for the relief of the unemployed, and a refusal to levy a rate adequate to meet their obligations. The councillors and Boards of Guardians in respect of the relief of the unemployed, were found to be acting unlawfully. The failure to levy an adequate rate led to the mayor and twenty-nine of the councillors being committed to prison for contempt of court (Keith-Lucas and Richards 1978:Ch. IV). This imprisonment, and the slogan adopted by the councillors of 'Guilty and Proud of It', has become one of the legends of local government.

The courts are more effective at preventing unlawful action than at enforcing the performance of statutory duties. A court order may be disobeyed. This may have unpleasant consequences for the councillors concerned but it will not ensure that the service is provided or the statutory duty fulfilled. These potential difficulties have caused the government to include further remedies in the legislation concerning some services. In these cases the government may take direct responsibility for a service if a local authority does not carry out its duties. A commissioner is appointed for the service and the full costs incurred are charged to the local authority. These costs are invariably higher than those that would have been necessary if the council had carried out its obligations. The presence of powers to take direct responsibility enables the government to place greater pressure on local authorities that are considering a refusal to carry out certain duties. The threat may be sufficient to ensure compliance. Griffith quotes the appointment of commissions to provide civil defence services where local authorities refused to comply for political reasons as occasional examples of the use of default powers. He concludes: 'Such powers are, in practice, rarely or never used' (Griffith 1966:58).

More recently the relationship between central and local government has on occasion become so strained that the installation of a commissioner has been a more significant possibility. The opposition to the Housing Finance Act 1972 provides well-documented examples. Several councils refused to implement the increases in council-house rents provided for in the Act. Housing commissioners were appointed. In most cases the arrival of the commissioner led the councils concerned either to change their minds and implement the Act or at least to allow the commissioner to implement it without further difficulty. In Clay Cross, however, a determined left-wing council maintained its opposition and refused to allow the housing commissioner to use council premises or facilities to carry out his task. The result was a long drawn out struggle illustrating the administrative and political difficulties that face central government when it attempts to administer local government services through direct intervention; and perhaps indicates why default powers are so seldom used. Professor Harry Street later argued that the housing commissioner's performance 'was so ineffectual and insignificant that one must assume that he was acting thus under the

167

Department's [of Environment] instructions. ... The Department obviously reached a decision of policy ... based no doubt on political considerations that it would not utilise its legal powers to have the defaulting councillors imprisoned' (quoted in Sklair 1975:289). Although not imprisoned, the councillors were made bankrupt and lost their seats on the council. Their example of intransigent opposition was undoubtedly present in the minds of both central government and left-wing councillors as they prepared for the battles over rate-capping in the 1980s.

ADMINISTRATIVE

Central government departments constantly communicate with local authorities with respect to specific services. The nature of the relationship varies, however, both between departments and within departments when they are responsible for several services. The variations in the character of the service obviously have a major effect on these differences in attitude. Griffith concludes: 'Three separate attitudes are broadly distinguishable: one is basically *laissez-faire*; one is basically regulatory; and one is basically promotional' (Griffith 1966:515). By *laissez-faire* he implies 'a positive philosophy of as little interference as is possible within the necessary fulfilment of department duties' (Griffith 1966:515). The former Ministry of Health is given as an example. The developing services for which this Ministry was responsible were considered to be better left to local initiative and discretion. By contrast the regulatory attitude was adopted by the Home Office when it was responsible for child care services. An inspectorate were appointed who were concerned both to advise local authorities and to see that the statutory regulations were kept (Griffith 1966:519). The promotional attitude is most clearly seen in the relationship of the Department of Education and Science with the local education authorities. Education is often referred to as a national service which is locally administered. The Education Act 1944 placed a duty on the minister 'to have a national policy which local education authorities execute under his control and direction' (Griffith 1966:523). Prominent in this process are Her Majesty's Inspectors of Education (HMIs) who advise, supervise and inspect the service with a view to maintaining and improving standards. The difference between the regulatory and promotional attitudes is one of degree, but the latter is more positive in its approach.

In the years since Griffith wrote his study, there have been major changes both in the organisation of central departments and in the structure of local government. These changes have been accompanied by an increasingly interventionist attitude towards local government on the part of governments of both political persuasions. Every local authority receives a flood of circulars from the central departments with which it has to deal. These circulars vary in formality from simple requests for information, through guidance on policy or technical questions, to explanations of new Acts or statutory instruments. Technically, these circulars constitute 'advice' but various administrative or financial sanctions can often cause a local authority to treat them with respect. The sheer size of this effort on behalf of the departments should not lead one to presume, however, that it always has the desired effects. It is common, as Griffith points out, 'for departments not to seek to know what action, if any, local authorities have taken as a result of such circulars' (Griffith 1966:559). Nor will the action when taken be uniform. A local study conducted in the 1970s found considerable variation in the response by different local authorities to circulars concerned with residential renewal (Goffin 1979).

There remain considerable and important areas of discretion available to local authorities. In education, for example, there are 'no national statutory pupil–teacher ratios, class sizes or contact hours for teachers; ... no national or core curriculum' (Crispin 1983:76). Alan Crispin was responding to suggestions by Professor Kogan that in the case of education 'there have been changes in the balance of power between institutional freedom and government authority' (Kogan 1983:58). Kogan accepts the difficulty of influencing such important matters as the curriculum – the minister cannot be in every classroom! – but suggests that 'collective norm-setting is certainly in the wind' (Kogan 1983-65). These changes are being attempted in several services through administrative as well as legislative means. Central government requires local authorities to provide it with more information and is more prone to initiate nationally preferred policies for particular services: whether through legislation, as with the sale of council houses; or through exhortation, as with the privatisation of refuse collection. There has also been a renewed tendency for central departments to require local authorities to prepare a scheme or plan showing how they propose to exercise their statutory powers or duties.

The requirement to prepare schemes of this kind represents a 'pattern of control which was common to many Acts passed during the Labour Government 1945–51' (Griffith1974:5) but became less significant in subsequent years. Its revival from the late 1960s 'has involved a proliferation of planning systems' which Professor Hinings listed in 1980 as follows:

> The ones that involve some form of relationship between local
> authorities and central government are PESC; Regional Reports
> (Scotland); Regional Strategic Plans; Financial Planning (Scotland);
> Transport Policies and Programmes; Structure Plans; Housing Plans
> (Scotland); Housing Investment Programmes; Community Land
> Programmes; Regional Recreation Strategies; Social Service Plans; Joint
> Care Planning; Police Service Planning. There are also Comprehensive
> Community Programmes and the Inner Area Partnerships and
> Programmes (Jones 1980:60).

The precise list will obviously vary over time but it represents a considerable and growing administrative interaction between central and local government.

FINANCIAL

A broad outline of the financial relationship between central and local government is contained in Chapter 6. Students should refer back to that chapter if some of the terms used below are unfamiliar. Three aspects of this relationship need to be reiterated in the present context. First, local authorities must obtain permission ('loan sanction') before they can borrow to finance any significant capital project and are subject to an overall limit on capital expenditure. A loan sanction does not of itself provide the capital: it is simply a permission to borrow. The control afforded by the system of loan sanctions obviously enables the government to control the capital expenditure of local authorities and to direct it into policies consistent with its existing priorities. The control may be exercised more subtly to influence decisions about policy values. For example, when the government was striving to introduce comprehensive education, local education authorities knew that loan sanction would be more readily forthcoming for a comprehensive school than for a school that fitted the existing tripartite pattern.

Second, central government may influence the current expenditure of local authorities by providing specific grants in support of particular services. A local authority is then encouraged to provide that service to the requisite standard as the grant provided cannot be transferred elsewhere. As we have seen (Ch. 6), specific grants have increased in importance since 1974.

Third, central government may use its general grant to local authorities both as a legitimation for a general influence on local policies ('he who pays the piper calls the tune') and as a method of influencing overall local authority expenditure. It is this later aspect of the financial relationship between central and local government that produced the controversies of the 1970s and 1980s.

Soon after the reorganisation of local government in 1974, local authorities received a circular from the DOE (171/74) announcing the need for expenditure restraint in the interests of national economic objectives. At first the government hoped for 'a co-operative approach from local authorities' but when this was not easily obtained they 'decided to use the grant as an instrument of control' (Greenwood 1982:46–7). From 1976–77 the government began to cut grant aid as a proportion of local authority expenditure in real terms. Greenwood outlines three main difficulties for this policy of 'using the existing Rate Support Grant (RSG) mechanism to reduce local authority spending' (Greenwood 1982:51). First, the cuts were made on a global basis affecting *all* local authorities irrespective of their performance in conforming to the government's requests for restraint. Second, the resources element of RSG, when adjusted to bring the claims for grant into line with the amount available, accentuated the tendency to penalise all local authorities for the actions of a few. Third, the complexities of the way the grant formula was devised favoured those authorities who spent the most: 'High spending authorities attracted grant because assessment of need to spend was assumed to be linked with the levels of spending throughout local government' (Greenwood 1982:52). There were no objective measures of need.

The Conservative government after 1979 introduced new proposals to meet these difficulties. First, they changed the basis of RSG, replacing the needs and resources elements by a new block grant which was related more closely to expenditure assessments for each local authority. Second, they introduced 'targets' which specified the expenditure each local authority should aim for in the forthcoming financial year. Third, they introduced a sliding scale of grant penalties for local authorities exceeding the government's expenditure requirements. The 'excess expenditure' would receive less support from government grants and would therefore fall more heavily on the rate fund. This would have the effect of improving the financial discipline attached to local spending decisions.

These revised procedures left several unresolved difficulties. With regard to capital expenditure, they did nothing to prevent the wild fluctuations resulting from the use of local authority capital programmes as an economic regulator for the economy. Such 'stop-go' measures hindered attempts at long-term rational planning. They were, and are, particularly damaging to the construction industry which relies upon local authority housing contracts as a basis for development. More worrying, from the central government's point of view, the new grant procedures could not prevent local authority current expenditure continuing to increase if councillors decided to make up any shortfall in grant by further increases in the rates. A number of high-spending local authorities, including several in London, were penalised to the point where they received no grant at all: the government then had no further sanction against continuing high expenditure. This was the difficulty that caused 'rate-capping' to be introduced. We shall return to the wider questions posed by 'rate-capping' in the final section of this chapter.

THE SECRETARIES OF STATE FOR IRELAND, WALES AND SCOTLAND

Our discussion of central–local government relations has not differentiated so far between England and the other three countries constituting the United Kingdom. In general this is understandable: the United

Kingdom is a unitary state and broad general principles can be outlined for the whole country. The three smaller countries have an institution, however, that distinguishes their intergovernmental relations from those of England. Each has a Secretary of State who normally serves in the Cabinet. There is no equivalent minister for England. Presumably the relative size of England reduces the need for a separate office in governmental institutions already dominated by the English – some would say the *southern* English – experience.

The Secretary of State in each of the three countries has a specific role which relates to the particular history and needs of the country concerned. We shall look briefly at these in a moment. All three accept a general responsibility within their country for most of the functions performed by local government. They interpose, therefore, a further layer in relations between central and local government.

The present Northern Ireland Office was established in 1972 when the United Kingdom government assumed direct responsibility for the administration of the province. It has, of course, much older antecedents in the troubled relationship between England and Ireland. The political and security difficulties that led to the 1972 assumption of responsibility continue to place graver responsibilities on the Secretary of State for Northern Ireland than on his colleagues in Wales or Scotland. It is not just a matter of security. The failure to reach political agreement on some form of power sharing in the province has meant that many services, including housing and education, are administered by special agencies rather than being the responsibility of local government (Norton 1984:230–7).

The Welsh Office was the creation of the 1964 Labour government. It owes something to the then current interest in regional economic planning, and rather more to the political need of the Labour Party to protect their stronghold from incursions by the Welsh Nationalists. The Welsh Office accepts fewer responsibilities than its Scottish counterpart. Its most distinctive contributions are concerned with the two issues of economic development and support for the Welsh language. In general, Wales shares most of its legislation with England and the Welsh Office may be seen as a relatively low-key contributor to the structure of central–local relations.

By contrast, the Scottish Office has assumed an importance over the years that has led one commentator to challenge 'the view of the "United Kingdom", which implies that all decisions emanate from Westminster and Whitehall' (Page 1983:56). Scotland also has a separate system of law and distinctive local government arrangements. The Scottish Office was created in 1885. It now comprises five departments: Agriculture and Fisheries; Development; Economic Planning; Education; and Home and Health. The last named is responsible for police, prisons, criminal justice and fire as well as for the NHS in Scotland. The Secretary of State is assisted by a number of junior ministers who accept responsibility under his general supervision for one or more of the functions of the

Scottish Office. The appearance of a separate government with the Secretary of State in the role of Premier of Scotland is seductive, but not completely persuasive. The degree of autonomy exercised by the Scottish Office varies with the policy being considered. Keating and Midwinter 'divide policy proposals into three types: Scottish Office proposals for Scotland alone; proposals from "UK departments" for England and Wales; and proposals for the whole of the UK (or Britain), in which the initiative and lead will almost invariably be taken by a UK department' (Keating and Midwinter 1983:19). Within this spectrum the role of the Scottish Office ranges 'from at one extreme, almost complete autonomy in policy making to, at the other extreme, complete dependence' (Keating and Midwinter 1983:20).

The Secretaries of State, like Janus the God of Gates, face both ways. They are members of the Cabinet and responsible, therefore, for both the formulation and implementation of central government policy. They cannot stray too far from the accepted views of the Prime Minister and their other colleagues. The existence of separate government departments located in the three peripheral countries, however, allows central policies to be refracted in their impact on local conditions. Page quotes several examples of ways in which the Scottish Office, in particular, can influence the implementation even of legislation that is not specifically Scottish (Page 1983:54).

The Secretaries of State represent the government in the periphery but they also represent the periphery in the Cabinet (Kellas and Madgwick 1982:27). Decisions concerning economic development or support for an ailing industry have often been made after intervention by one of these 'territorial' Secretaries of State. The significance of their advocacy will depend on the governmental and political importance at the time of the country concerned. The presence of such an advocate in the Cabinet, however, can only be to the advantage of the localities concerned: it is certainly envied by some of the deprived regions of England.

RECENT MODELS OF CENTRAL–LOCAL GOVERNMENT RELATIONS

The classic approach to central–local government relations, which presents models of agency or partnership as an explanation of the legal, administrative and financial interactions between levels of government, has been replaced in recent years by more sophisticated analyses. The new approach has been stimulated by the Social Science Research Council (now the Economic and Social Research Council) which in 1978 established a Panel on Central–Local Government Relationships. The panel developed a programme of research which recognised 'that there was more to the study of central–local relations than investigating whether and how central government was controlling local government. They were seen to interpenetrate in complex and subtle linkages ... ' (Jones 1980:3). The research commissioned by the panel comprised six studies:

1. A study of policy implementation as an aspect of central–local relationships ...
2. A study of policy planning systems as a means of relating central and local government ...
3. A study of the local authority associations and other central institutions of local government ...
4. A study of the nature, extent and consequences of party political linkages between central and local government ...
5. A study of local government professions as linkages between central and local government ...
6. A study of the influence of central grants on central–local interactions ... (Jones 1980:4–5).

The framework for this programme of research was provided by R A W Rhodes who used interorganisational analysis to produce a power-dependence model. Within this model he argued 'that the discretion and the relative power of the various tiers of government is a product of their resources, the rules of the game and the values and interests supporting both the rules and the existing distribution of resources' (Rhodes 1981:10; 1986:Ch. 2). Each of these factors deserves to be considered in a little more detail.

First, Rhodes (1981) identifies five sets of resources which while not exhaustive illustrate the range available to central departments and local authorities. The five sets comprise constitutional–legal resources, hierarchical resources, financial resources, political resources and informational resources. Some of these we have already discussed either in the previous section or in earlier chapters. The analysis emphasises the interdependence created by the distribution of these resources: central government does not have a monopoly of power nor is local government completely dependent within the framework of the power-dependence model. For example, Parliament is constitutionally supreme but 'only local authorities possess the statutory grant of powers to alter private rights so that central government policy may be promoted' (Elliott 1983:36). Central government could, of course, persuade Parliament to adopt such powers for itself but this might lead it into political difficulties. The controversies of the 1980s showed that political resources are available to local as well as to central government.

When it comes to the availability of information and professional expertise, local authorities are in a dominant position. As Griffith pointed out, 'the providers of services are the local authorities ... ' (Griffith 1966:17). The information and skill necessary to fulfil these tasks rest with their professional staff. The threat of non-co-operation with commissioners or successor agencies is a real one even if professional officers seldom adopt such an extreme sanction.

The rules of the game are those implicit understandings that Truman suggested 'set approximate limits within which discretionary behaviour may take place' (quoted in Rhodes 1981:105). Rhodes gives as examples of such rules the assertion of the value of local democracy or local self-government, and the expectation of consultation before central government imposes new policies. The importance of the rules of the game lies not in any legal significance – they seldom have any – but in the effect they have on behaviour. Thus Griffith quotes the County Councils Association in 1963 as accepting a rule that obliged local government 'to conform to the political, social and economic policies which are being pursued over the country as a whole' (Griffith 1966:507). The councils led by the New Urban Left in the 1980s rejected this attitude. The government then presented this failure to accept the rules of the game as a break with the constitutional conventions underlying central–local relations. This break, in their view, justified legislative intervention.

The values and interests that underlie both the rules of the game and the existing distribution of resources between central and local government reflect a broader consensus in society. Thus in Britain there is a presumption in favour of free elections and a suspicion of bureaucratic organisations. These beliefs sustain locally elected councils. For example, it proved politically impossible for central goernment to replace the GLC and metropolitan county councils by appointed bodies of a different political complexion as they prepared for the eventual abolition of these local authorities. The House of Lords carried an amendment to the Bill and the government found it expedient to accept the defeat (*The Times* 29.6.84 and 17.7.84). The abolition itself, and the complex arrangements for fulfilling the former functions of these second-tier authorities, proved to be among the most controversial policies adopted in Mrs Thatcher's second term of office.

The original framework prepared by Rhodes attracted a number of criticisms which he and his colleagues summarised in a later paper (Rhodes *et al.* 1983c). First, the framework lacks the historical dimension which is necessary if the changing nature of central–local relations is to be examined. Second, the emphasis on bargaining fails to give sufficient attention to the qualitative difference in the power available to central and local government. Central government is sovereign and in the last resort – or earlier if it chooses! – it can change the rules of the game. Third, there is a distinct lack of politics within the framework. There is too heavy a concentration on organisational rather than policy dimensions. In a review of the framework the present author asked: 'What does it tell us about the distribution of public resources: what do we learn about the central political question of who gets what, when and how? Where is the sniff of battle?' (Hampton 1981:64).

In their response to these criticisms Rhodes *et al.* remind us of the limited theoretical literature available on central–local relations when the framework was devised. There was a 'need to shake off the detritus of the past literature on central–local relations and build bridges to theories and issues of more general interest within the social sciences' (Rhodes *et al*. 1983c:42–3; cf. Rhodes 1986:Ch. 2). Implicit in the framework, they maintain, is a version of corporatist theory. This theory seeks to explain intergovernmental relations within the context of bargaining between major institutions – government, local government, industry, for example – over the realities of state power. Rhodes *et al*. accept that such a theory is itself open to criticism, and that most of the studies based on the framework dealt with less abstract matters. Nevertheless, they deny the charge of ignoring theoretical questions and hope that future work will 'focus on distributional consequences of the varied forms of state intervention in and through policy communities' (Rhodes *et al*. 1983c:44).

DISCUSSION – THE CONTROVERSY OVER RATE-CAPPING IN THE 1980s

Discussions about the relationships between central and local government have been conducted in the past in the context of a concern to encourage small local authorities to fulfil their functions effectively. To this end central government retained various powers and developed administrative procedures to monitor local government progress. As Professor Griffith expressed the difficulty: 'The argument for greater freedom for local authorities has often foundered on the fallibility of the weak authority' (Griffith 1966:540). The Royal Commissions at the end of the 1960s held similar views. Redcliffe-Maud, for example, believed a reorganised local government system would be able to exercise greater freedom to experiment and decide their own priorities (Redcliffe-Maud 1969:Vol I 30). To this end the report recommended: 'All main authorities should have a *general power* to spend money for the benefit of their areas and inhabitants ... the only limit on the use of the new power should be the wishes of the electors and such restrictions as have to be placed on local government expenditure in the interests of national economic and financial policy' (Redcliffe-Maud 1969:Vol I 84, emphasis added). Such a provision had it been fully accepted would have removed much of the impact of the rule of *ultra vires* on local authorities.

The controversies over rate-capping were concerned not with the defects of a weak local government system, however, but with the ability of strong local authorities to challenge central government priorities. To some extent the Redcliffe-Maud expectations were justified: the reorganisation of local government strengthened the position of many major authorities – especially in the metropolitan areas. Central governments did not welcome this development, particularly when the

New Urban Left grasped the possibilities of conducting their own experiments in new forms of local socialism (Boddy and Fudge 1984).

The Conservative Party won the 1979 election on a programme of reducing public expendiure as a corollary of reducing the burden of taxation in general and of income tax in particular. These policies were part of a general economic programme that stressed private incentives as a means to improving Britain's economic performance. In pursuit of these policies the government continued the reduction in grant support to local authorities that had begun under the previous administration. As the proportion of their expenditure covered by grant fell (Table 6.3, p 100) many local authorities could not, and some would not, reduce expenditure to the extent necessary to prevent rapid rate increases. These increases were seen to be against the government's general policy of reducing taxation. At first, the government sought to resolve its difficulties by changing the basis of grant allocation. A grant-related expenditure assessment (GREA) was formulated for each local authority. Expenditure above GREA attracted a reduced proportion of grant. When this change was not effective in reducing local expenditure quickly enough the government produced 'targets' for each local authority. These targets implied a reduction on the local authority's previous expenditure. The target could be above or below GREA depending on the local authority's previous performance – thus creating further anomalies. Failure to comply with the target led to further reductions in the proportion of grant until the reduction was in excess of the expenditure incurred. This procedure constituted a form of 'fine' on non-compliant local authorities.

By this time some local authorities were not receiving any grant at all and could not be penalised by further reductions. Other local authorities refused or were unable to meet their targets. The government, therefore, turned to the control of the other main source of local government income. Legislation was introduced in 1984 allowing the Secretary of State to impose a maximum rate for a particular local authority or for local authorities in general. This is the procedure referred to as 'rate-capping'. Subsequently, the system of 'targets' was ended in 1985.

The introduction of rate-capping provoked a debate that spread far beyond the normal party disputes in Parliament. Academics and local government officers joined in a political controversy in which the government was attacked by leading members of its own party. The government's argument was clear and relatively simple. New powers were necessary to control a minority of local authorities who refused to follow government policy and reduce local public expenditure. Lower public expenditure was expected to assist in reducing the rate of inflation and the general level of interest rates, thus making British industry more competitive. In the past, the government maintained, local authorities had accepted their duty to abide by government guidelines, but a few councils now rejected this convention. The problem applied only to a small minority: '75 per cent of this overspend can be laid at the door of just 16 conspicuously extravagant councils' (HC Debates 17.1.84: col 166). The remedy, therefore, needed to be selective so that the Secretary of State could apply it to the recalcitrant local authorities without penalising the others. The argument was often presented in crude political terms: the offending local authorities were socialist, 'mostly Marxist led': there were frequent attacks on councillors from the New Urban Left such as Ken Livingstone and David Blunkett (Conservative *Newsline*, Jan 1984:4–5; HC Debates 17.1.84: cols 249–50).

The opposition to the rate-capping legislation was concerned with both its economic assumptions and the constitutional implications of its remedies. The government's critics did not accept that local expenditure was 'out of control': it had 'been falling in real terms, but not as rapidly as the government would like' (Dawson 1983:23). The allegations of runaway extravagance could not be justified. The amount local authorities were spending in excess of government targets was less than £1 billion, which was about 0.5 per cent of total planned public expenditure. Moreover, local spending would have a negligible inflationary effect if financed entirely from taxation; even though any public expenditure might raise interest rates and adversely affect the exchange rate of sterling (Jackman 1983:33). An increase in local authority taxation would not of itself, therefore, interfere with the government's prime economic objective of reducing inflation (Dawson 1983:23; Jones and Stewart 1983a; 1983b:51–61). In these circumstances the remedy seemed likely to prove worse than the disease. The bureaucracy created to administer rate-capping would be less efficient and more expensive than the system it was intended to replace. The Director of CIPFA did not believe the proposals could in practice achieve the government's objective of reducing local expenditure by a significant amount (*The Times* 16.1.84). The experience of similar legislation in Scotland did not provide an encouraging precedent.

Scottish legislation gives the Secretary of State for Scotland the power to order a general abatement of RSG. Such a reduction of grant is intended to persuade local authorities to cut their expenditure. In addition, the Local Government (Miscellaneous Provisions) (Scotland) Act 1981 allows selective intervention by the Secretary of State in the expenditure decisions of individual Scottish councils. The 1981 Act was supplemented in 1982 by the Local Government and Planning (Scotland) Act which gives the Secretary of State greater freedom to decide on the sanctions to be applied to selected local authorities. Among these santions is a power to cause part of the rates collected to be returned to the ratepayers (Midwinter 1984:41). Whilst the use of these powers has had an impact on some individual councils, general spending by local authorities seems to have been relatively unaffected in the first few years. In 1983–84, Scottish local authorities budgeted to spend £144 million in excess of the RSG settlement. The Secretary of State ordered a general abatement of RSG of £54 million and imposed selective reductions of £18.7 million – 1.3 per cent of total rate-borne expenditure. These figures may be seen in the context of a total local authority spending in Scotland of approximately £2.5 *billion* (Midwinter 1984:55). In 1984/85, the Secretary of State took no selective action at all: he relied entirely on a general abatement of RSG to influence local expenditure. It is, of course, dificult to assess how far local authority decisions have been affected by the anticipation of action by the Secretary of State, but two years after the 1981 Act, a research team from the University of Strathclyde concluded: 'The Act has failed to achieve the objectives which central government appeared to have in mind. It has, instead, further eroded local autonomy and destabilized central–local relations in Scotland' (Midwinter *et al.* 1983:394).

These complex arguments drawn from economics and administrative effectiveness take a long while to consider, but they were not the major concern of many of the opponents of rate-capping. The constitutional issues were seen as more important. During the debate on the Second Reading of the Bill, Edward Heath explained the position very clearly:

> ... one of our main purposes in politics is to balance the power existing in our society. In particular, we have been opposed to the centralisation of power because we have throughout realised the intense dangers to freedom that that holds for everyone. The Bill deals with the balance of power between central and local government, and weighs it now heavily on the side of central Government (HC Debates 17.1.84: col 184).

Professors Jones and Stewart pointed out that for the Secretary of State to describe some local authorities as 'over-spenders', and to penalise them on that basis, meant that he was 'substituting himself for the local electorate' (Jones and Stewart 1983b:72–3).

The legislation was opposed during its passage through Parliament by the Labour, Liberal and Social Democratic parties; by the three local authority associations – the AMA (Labour controlled) and the ACC and ADC (both Conservative controlled); by individual members of the Conservative Party; by almost all academic specialists in local government; and by *The Times* newspaper among others: but the government majority enabled it to obtain its Act. At the time of writing it is too early to judge whether either the expectations of the government or the fears of its opponents will be realised.

THE STRUCTURAL CONTEXT

Chapter eleven

SPECIAL PURPOSE AUTHORITIES

In this final part we shall be concerned with the structural context within which local government operates, but over which it has only a tenuous or indirect influence (Dunleavy 1980a:56–7). The potential content of such a discussion of urban politics is very wide: international economics, changes in policy that result in the closure of defence bases, even the geological conditions that bring oil to one area and not another can all have a profound effect upon local government. We must perforce adopt a narrower perspective and have chosen three themes to illustrate the widening concerns of students of urban politics. The present chapter considers special purpose authorities; we then move to the problems of the inner cities and the economic initiatives of some local authorities; finally we outline some of the theoretical perspectives that are informing the academic development of the subject.

Chapter 10 considered central–local government relations in the context of the existing distribution of local authority services. There is, however, no settled pattern for the allocation of governmental responsibilities (see Ch. 4). Central government decides on the allocation and can thereby affect the powers exercised by local government in a fundamental manner. Dunleavy has estimated that 'a total of eighty-five organisational "births" in the period 1946–75 were based on powers transferred from local authorities or local authority organisations and committees; in contrast, there were very few "deaths" . . . due to reverse transfers back to local government' (Dunleavy 1980a:103). In this chapter we consider three services: water and sewage, health, and transport. At various times in the past each of these services has in part been the direct responsibility of local government. The main responsibility at present, however, rests with special purpose authorities or *ad hoc* joint boards. At the end of the chapter we discuss the controversy over the abolition of the GLC and the metropolitan county councils (MCCs) and the transfer of some of their services to special bodies.

Special purpose authorities take many forms and it is difficult to give a precise definition. Indeed, Stanyer and Smith consider it tempting 'simply to speak of "the rest" after government departments and local authorities have been described' (Stanyer and Smith 1976:55). Special purpose authorities range from the giants of the nationalised industries and the NHS to small industrial training boards and planning authorities for individual national parks. Such authorities in Britain may be distinguished from central and local government in a number of ways. First, they are concerned with a single or limited range of purposes rather than being compendious bodies. Second, their membership is appointed or indirectly elected. Third, special purpose authorities exercise a degree of independence from other public policy authorities. They include the Quasi-autonomous National Government Organisations (QUANGOS), whose members are appointed by ministers (Drucker *et al.* 1984:109–13), and joint boards of local authorities.

Special purpose authorities are created to avoid placing a service within the direct compass of central or local government. The reasons may be political or administrative (Self 1972:80–1; Stanyer and Smith 1976:151–2). Trading services such as transport, for example, are often thought to be better administered if removed from the daily rhetoric of party politics. For other services, technical or administrative reasons are given for the creation of a special purpose authority. The provision of water and the disposal of sewage, for example, need to be related to river catchment systems that bear little resemblance to any feasible local government structure. Once again these apparently rational explanations for the creation of a special purpose authority are sometimes the subject of controversy. They may be used to avoid discussing more cogent reasons for the establishment of the authorities. These additional reasons may include a desire on the part of central government to reduce the influence of local government for a particular service, as in the case of London Transport, or the power of professionals in the service to retain some measure of independence, as in the case of doctors in the NHS.

WATER AND SEWAGE

The origins of modern local government are closely connected with the health and sanitation needs of the growing industrial towns in the nineteenth century. The recognition by the middle of the century that cholera was associated with water contaminated by sewage led to the creation of *ad hoc* boards concerned with public health and sanitation. These boards formed part of the basis of the local government system introduced in 1888 and 1894 (Ch. 2). Even as late as 1969, the Royal Commission on Local Government in England considered that water and sewage 'are basic to a great deal of the work of local authorities: to planning, housing and general development. Plainly, within our definition of the purpose of local government these ought to be local government services ... ' (Redcliffe-Maud 1969:Vol 1 21). Yet by 1983 local authorities had lost their representation on Regional Water Authorities (RWAs) and the press and public had lost their right to attend meetings. These developments form the focus of this section.

In their study of the administration of the water industry, A G Jordan, J J Richardson and R H Kimber identify four main aspects of the service:

i) water conservation: the storing of surface and underground water plus transfers between river basins.

ii) water supply: taking water from sources, treating it and distributing it to consumers.

iii) sewerage: the transmission of sewerage and trade wastes including any treatment before discharge to the sewers.

iv) water reclamation: treatment of sewage and trade wastes to yield usable supplies. (Jordan *et al.* 1977:317).

As the services developed from the nineteenth century these different aspects were dealt with by a large number of separate agencies including local authorities and private water companies.

The difficulties arising from fragmented control soon became apparent. As the demand for water grew so the need for reclamation increased: but a sewerage authority had little incentive to improve its treatment facilities if the main beneficiary would be a quite separate water authority downstream. The water shortage was highlighted by a drought in 1934 when a Cabinet minister suggested that the 'defects were becoming more obvious as improved methods of transport brought about "the wider distribution both of industrial users of water and of a population with urban standards as to its domestic use" ' (Sheail) 1983:389). Despite the early recognition of the problem no proposals for reform were forthcoming until after the Second World War. The Water Act 1945 gave the Minister of Housing and Local Government powers to amalgamate water authorities and these powers were extensively used. Between 1956 and the late 1960s the number of water authorities was reduced 'from 884 to 192, 157 of the latter being either local authorities or joint boards of authorities' (Redcliffe-Maud 1969:Vol 1 20–1). These amalgamations, while providing stronger water authorities, did not unify various aspects of the service. In addition to the water authorities, 'sewerage and sewage disposal was dealt with by more than 1,300 authorities (county borough and county districts with a few joint sewerage boards). Water conservation and river management was the responsibility of 29 river authorities' (Jordan and Richardson 1977:43). By the end of the 1960s, therefore, more radical solutions were being suggested.

The Redcliffe-Maud recommendation that water and sewage should become the responsibility of the larger local authorities they were proposing was supported by the evidence they received from the Ministry of Housing and Local Government (Jordan *et al.* 1977:319). By the time Redcliffe-Maud reported, however, the Ministry was in the process of changing its mind. The technical needs of the industry were causing it to emphasise the managerial aspects of a reorganisation at the expense of local democratic control. But while the new approach from the Ministry implied 'that the service would be improved by removing it from local government, it did not wish to assume the responsibilities itself' (Jordan *et al.* 1977:323). The solution was the creation of a managerial board of the type used in other public utilities such as gas and electricity.

The Water Act 1973 restructured the entire management of water resources in England and Wales. The preamble to the Act stated that it was 'to make provision for a national policy for water, for the conferring and discharge of functions as to water (including sewerage and sewage disposal, fisheries and land drainage) and as to recreation and amenity in connection with water, for the making of charges by water authorities and other statutory water undertakers, and for connected purposes'. These duties are carried out by nine English RWAs and the Welsh National Water Development Authority. The boundaries of the RWAs are based upon the technical needs of river catchment areas. They are neither related to local authority boundaries nor uniform in size. The city of Sheffield, for example, is divided between the Yorkshire Water Authority and the Severn–Trent Water Authority. Even the Welsh border is not sacrosanct on this occasion. The Severn–Trent Water Authority extends into Wales and the Welsh authority extends into England. The areas of the RWAs vary greatly both in extent and population (Gray 1982:144–5). The Severn–Trent Water Authority, for example, touches both the Humber and the Severn; the Anglian Water Authority includes the whole of eastern England from the Humber to the Thames. Other RWAs are much smaller in size but not necessarily more respectful of local authority boundaries. The population covered by RWAs varies from over 11 millions (Thames Water Authority) to under 2 million (South-West Water Authority).

The emphasis on technical considerations in drawing the new regional boundaries of the water industry was paralleled by similar concerns in devising the management structure. The Act places a duty on the appropriate government minister to promote 'a national policy for water in England and Wales' (McLoughlin 1973:37/1). This duty is to be exercised through RWAs. The original intention was that these should be small bodies with 'only a limited representation from local authorities' (Gray 1982:158). The chief executive of the RWA was also to sit on the board (Jordan *et al.* 1977:330). Under pressure from local authorities the original proposals were modified. The chief executive was not to serve on the board and local authority nominees became the majority. The chairperson was appointed by the Secretary of State and the remaining members by either the latter or the Minister of Agriculture, Fisheries and Food.

The formula for appointing local authority representatives was complex. Both counties and districts were represented and various exceptions to the normal position were allowed for in London and other major cities (Gray 1982:159). The consequence was that the boards were rather large bodies consisting of between sixteen and sixty-two members. Within the new RWAs, the managerial orientation remained strong. Indirect elections from many different local authorities made it difficult to develop policy control by members of the board. Jordan *et al.* concluded: 'The links between local government and the new water machinery are tenuous – despite this nominal control through a majority of appointments' (Jordan *et al.* 1977:330).

The Water Act, 1973 also provided for the establishment of a National Water Council (NWC) consisting of a person appointed to the chair by the Secretary of State, the chairpersons of the water authorities, and not more than ten other members appointed by appropriate ministers. The responsibilities of the NWC included giving advice to the government on national water policy and assisting the RWAs in the performance of their duties. The NWC was in some respects a development of the Central Advisory Water Committee (CAWC) first appointed in 1937. The CAWC brought together the various interests associated with water. It was expected both to advise government departments and to make representations to them on such matters as it thought fit (Jordan and Richardson 1977:43).

Scotland
The problems facing the water industry in Scotland were not as acute as those in England. A lower density of population and other natural advantages enabled a review of water resources in Scotland to be entitled *A Measure of Plenty* (SDD 1973). In these circumstances the managerial approach adopted in England and Wales was not followed in Scotland. The Scottish reorganisation formed part of the general restructuring of local government in 1975 (Ch. 3 and Table 4.1, p 66–7). The regional and island authorities took over responsibility for water supply, sewerage and flood prevention. River purification became the responsibility of boards designated by the Secretary of State (OU 1975:114).

Northern Ireland
Water and sewage services were removed from local authority control in Northern Ireland in 1973. Since then these services have been administered centrally together with water conservation and pollution control (OU 1975:120).

WATER ACT 1983

The Water Act 1983 changed the existing position in three ways that are germane to our concerns. First, the size of the boards of the RWAs was reduced and the local authorities lost their majority representation. The Secretary of State appoints a chairperson, designates a deputy chairperson and, together with ministerial colleagues, appoints all other members of the board. The boards now have between nine and fifteen members. Second, the NWC was abolished. Third, the Public Bodies (Admission to Meetings) Act 1960 was repealed in so far as it related to water authorities. This means that neither the press nor the public have a right to attend RWA meetings. Although few people deny the technical nature of providing an integrated water service, the provisions of the 1983 Act caused some misgivings. The RWAs have responsibilities that affect property, especially land, and recreational facilities as well as the more obvious duty of providing adequate supplies of clean water. They spend hundreds of millions of pounds. Moreover, they raise this money not through a commercial pricing policy, but through taxation. The RWAs levy a rate which is now demanded separately from the rates levied by local authorities. The 1983 Act continued the movement away from local accountability that was begun in 1973. Early in 1986, the government announced plans to complete the process by selling the water industry to the private sector (*The Times* 6.2.86).

HEALTH

There is a vast literature on the health services in Britain. Although intrinsically interesting, much of it is irrelevant for our present purposes. We shall concentrate on the relationship of the health services to local government. Such an approach necessitates an emphasis both on the extent of the content of the services and on the problems of ensuring the accountability of the services to the general public.

The various health services originated either in voluntary effort – often linked to the churches – or in the Poor Law and the public health and sanitation legislation of the nineteenth century (Ham 1982:7–13). As the services developed, state involvement increased and local authorities accepted greater responsibilities. The range of services that could be considered in this context is very wide. The Royal Commission on the NHS started its report with the understanding that 'Health itself is not a precise or simple concept. ... It should be concerned with more than the treatment of disease ... with disease prevention and with helping people to achieve the wider benefits of good health' (Merrison 1979:8). Such a remit is almost infinite in its scope. For example, clean water supplies are essential to the prevention of disease; unemployment or poor housing may adversely affect health; welfare services may provide necessary support for the infirm; and public parks provide opportunities for healthy recreation. Health care, so broadly defined, touches many aspects of local authority service provision but the NHS was not intended to perceive its responsibilities in such a comprehensive manner. Its core objective has been 'to meet all the individual health needs of the population, whether in hospital, a doctor's surgery or their own homes' (Brown 1979:3). There is no pretence that even this wide coverage exhausts the content of the concept of health. There has continued, therefore, to be an interaction between the NHS and local authority services.

The foundation of the NHS in 1948 is seen as the centrepiece of the Welfare State developed by the Attlee Labour government. The scale of the service was not achieved, however, without a struggle in Cabinet. Herbert Morrison argued against the absorption of local government health responsibilities into the NHS. He pointed to the difficulties of public accountability that arise in any measure of centralisation and supported the democratic merits of local government. In words that could be applied to the other services we are considering in this chapter, he suggested:

> It is possible to argue that almost every local government function, taken by itself, could be administered more efficiently in the technical sense under a national system, but if we wish local government to thrive – as a school of political and democratic education as well as a method of administration – we must consider the general effect on local government of each particular proposal. It would be disastrous if we allowed local government to languish by whittling away its most constructive and interesting functions (quoted in Klein 1983:18–19).

In his response, Aneurin Bevan wrote of the need to establish a 'uniform standard of service for all' irrespective of local conditions (Klein 1983:19). He must also have been aware of the distaste with which the medical profession viewed local authority control.

The Royal Commission on Local Government in England referred to the transfer of local government hospitals to the NHS as 'a great misfortune' (Redcliffe-Maud 1969:Vol 1 20). They canvassed the possibility of reorganised local authorities taking full responsibility for the health services (Redcliffe-Maud 1969: Vol 1 92–3). Ten years later, the Royal Commission on the NHS again reviewed the relationship of local government to health care. They conceded that transferring the NHS to local government 'has many attractions' (Merrison 1979:265) but were not finally convinced. Neither of the Royal Commissions could consider the issue fully. The Royal Commission on Local Government had no remit to consider the NHS; and the Royal Commission on the NHS could not consider the structure of local government. The Merrison Commission, however, wrote of two difficulties in proposing a transfer of the NHS to local government. First, there is a great resistance within the NHS to the possibility of local government control: the professional interests stress the importance of clinical freedom. Second, the acceptance of responsibility for the 1 million employees of the NHS and for the further tenth of public expenditure involved would place great pressures on local authority administration and sources of finance. David Regan and John Stewart have contested both these arguments.

They point to the many professionals already employed by local government who have a need for independent judgement in the exercise of their duties. The medical profession could be accommodated with special arrangements to protect necessary clinical freedom. Similarly, the financial and administrative demands could be met if the principle of the transfer was conceded (Regan and Stewart 1982:37–40). They emphasise that the existing 'health authorities do not serve the interests of accountability in the NHS; if anything they tend to obfuscate it' (Regan and Stewart 1982:23). Moreover, 'uniform standards' throughout the country have not been achieved even forty years after Bevan created a *national* service (Ham 1982:131–44).

The complexity of the health services, the pressures for clinical freedom and the existing responsibilities of local authorities, enable us to understand why the 'NHS was born of bargaining and is a monument to compromise' (Klein 1974:8). Nor have the various compromises adopted been accepted as satisfactory on a permanent basis. The NHS in England has had three administrative structures since 1948. The other countries within the United Kingdom have adapted the general structure to their own local circumstances.

The 1948 structure established separate administrative arrangements for local authority health services, hospitals and general practice (Fig. 11.1). Local government retained responsibility for environmental health and the schools health service; Regional Hospital Boards (RHBs) and Hospital Management Committees (HMCs) ran the hospitals; and Executive Councils organised general practitioner services. Separate Boards of Governors were established for the teaching hospitals. The regions 'often cut across local government boundaries' (Brown 1979:4), but local links were established by appointing a number of councillors to the RHBs and HMCs.

By the 1960s the tripartite system of administration for the health services was coming under increasing criticism. Difficulties of co-ordination were apparent, particularly between local authorities and the NHS. The opportunity was taken, therefore, to reorganise the NHS at the same time as local government was reorganised in England and Wales in 1974. There were three objectives underlying the reorganisation (Brown 1979:40). First, to integrate the services provided by the NHS. The teaching hospitals and the Executive Councils were absorbed into the general management structure. In the case of general practice the absorption was more apparent than real. A Family Practitioner Committee (FPC) continued to represent the interests of general practice (Klein 1983:79). Second, the reorganisation sought a closer relationship between the NHS and the remaining health services provided by local authorities. The NHS took over responsibility for these services. Local authorities lost, therefore, their last direct involvement in medical care. At the same time, local authorities absorbed medical social workers from the NHS into their social work departments. Third, the reorganisation was intended to strengthen the

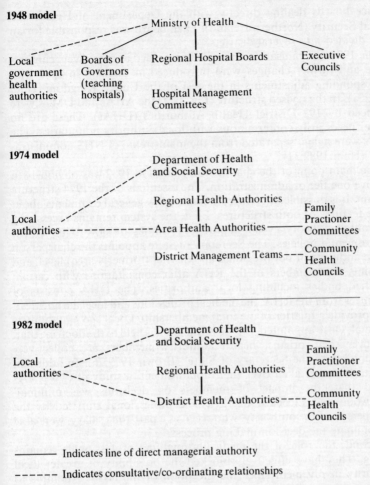

FIG. 11.1 The changing administrative structure of the National Health Service (England) (*Source*: Reproduced from Klein 1983:94)

local area control within the NHS. The RHBs and HMCs were transformed into fourteen Regional Health Authorities (RHAs) and ninety Area Health Authorities (AHAs). The new structure (Fig. 11.1) was completed by the creation of some 200 District Management Teams (DMTs) and Community Health Councils (CHCs) – and 'festooned with professional advisory committees' (Klein 1983:95). Regional authorities were only created in England. In Wales, the Welsh Office acted as a regional authority. In Scotland, the Scottish Office dealt directly with fifteen health boards which in some cases were divided into districts (Keating and Midwinter 1983:48–9; Mair 1983:54–5). In Northern Ireland a reorganisation in 1973 created four health and social

191

service boards dealing directly with the Department of Health and Social Security (Northern Ireland). Each board was responsible for an area divided into several districts.

The 1974 reorganisation was widely regarded as excessively cumbersome and further changes were introduced in England in 1982 with corresponding adjustments in the rest of the United Kingdom (Ham 1982:31). In the revised structure (Fig. 11.1) the AHAs and DMTs were replaced by 192 District Health Authorities (DHAs). These are no longer necessarily conterminous with local authority boundaries. The FPCs were again 'separated from the mainstream of NHS administration' (Ham 1982:31).

The main point of the changes introduced in 1982 was obviously to remove one tier of administration. The essentials of the 1974 structure remain. It is possible, therefore, to make a few general comments about some features of both structures. First, the system remains excessively centralised in theory, even if in practice localities are slow to implement governmental policies. The Secretary of State appoints the chairperson of the authority at both regional and district (formerly area) level, and appoints the members of the RHA after consultations with certain specified bodies including local authorities. The DHA consists of nominees from the RHA, the medical professions and local authorities – who provide a quarter of the total membership. Local accountability is minimal. Once appointed, the 'government has held to the doctrine that, whatever their origins, health authority members are collectively accountable to the Secretary of State' (Brown 1979:26). In addition, despite the care taken over their appointment, a study of two RHAs found that 'the impact of members on decisions was minimal' (Haywood and Elcock 1982:129). The professional staff led by the chairperson of the authority, who receives a part-time salary, were able to dominate the decision-making process.

Second, the role of the medically qualified professionals remains strong. They have effectively blocked the possibility of greater local authority involvement since the inception of the NHS. Attempts to integrate the general practitioners into the general administrative structure have failed. Each DHA contains a consultant, a general practitioner and a nurse. The mystique of 'clinical freedom' prevents any lay participation in medical accountability either in the assessment of professional competence or in considering complaints. As Klein points out (1983:165), medical practitioners are not alone in claiming the privileges of self-regulation, but their claims are more completely acceped than those of other professions.

Third, there is the general question of public accountability in the NHS. In formal terms this is achieved in Parliament through the appropriate Secretary of State, but there are other possibilities for local authorities and for the general public. Local authorities have representation at various levels in the NHS, but as we have seen their collective influence is weak. The general public has two further avenues of influence. First, a Health Service Commissioner (ombudsman) was appointed in 1974 to parallel similar appointments for central and local government. The commissioner is barred from considering complaints involving clinical judgement (Boaden *et al.* 1982:119–20). Another innovation in 1974 was the creation of CHCs. (In Scotland similar bodies are known as Local Health Councils.) Some 200 CHCs were appointed for the areas covered by the DMTs. This number has survived the further reorganisation in 1982. Members of each CHC 'are nominated, one-half from the local authority, one-third from voluntary organisations, and one-sixth by the Regional Health Authority' (Boaden *et al.* 1982:121). The membership of a CHC is not to overlap with that of a health authority. The CHCs are entitled to receive information from their DHA and to be consulted over important matters like hospital closures. The impact of CHCs on policy-making in the NHS is difficult to assess. Boaden *et al.* are doubtful about their 'real effect on health service decisions' (Boaden *et al.* 1982:126); but both Brown (1979:196–7) and Ham (1982:125) consider that CHCs have increased the accountability of health service managers.

TRANSPORT

Transport is a fundamental service in any society. It includes everything from cycling to international air travel. Such a wide topic cannot be considered in any depth in the present book, but there are some aspects of the subject that provide further insights into the relationship of local government to special purpose authorities. In the present section we shall first outline the nature of some of the issues that arise in connection with transport. Second, we shall discuss the institutional interaction between central and local government in this connection.

The introduction of a new mode of transport can have profound effects upon the nature of a society. The development of the canals and the subsequent growth of the railway network, for example, are among the topics most frequently considered by students of industrialisation. The advent of the internal combustion engine had equally important consequences for society. Motor cars, vans and lorries revolutionised transport facilities and had a considerable effect on urban life. Together with its undoubted benefits, motorised transport brought 'jams, frustrations, parking difficulties, confusion, noise and accidents' to urban areas (Buchanan 1963:9). The problems associated with 'traffic in towns' developed with the rapid growth in the number of vehicles after 1950. In that year the number of motor vehicles licensed in Great Britain was 2,272,000; by 1980 the number had reached 19,210,000 (Wistrich 1983:6). Over half the households in the country now have the use of a car and the proportion of goods carried by road compared with other modes of transport has increased dramatically. But it is not simply a matter of the proportion. The *total* volume of transport has increased. The roads have taken most of the increase while the share of the railways has declined (Wistrich 1983:11). In an early recognition of the problems, the government appointed a study group in 1961 under Mr (later Professor Sir) Colin Buchanon to examine 'the long term development of roads and traffic in urban areas and their influence on the urban environment' (Buchanon 1963:7). Their conclusions had an important effect on both public opinion and government policy. The group argued for the building of new roads and for the separation of traffic from pedestrian areas. The major road-building programmes of the 1960s and early 1970s, together with the widespread introduction of 'pedestrian precincts' were encouraged by their analysis.

From a longer-term perspective, the conclusions of the Buchanon group provided difficult problems for policy-makers to resolve. After a study of Leeds they 'concluded that there is no possibility whatsoever, in a town of this size and nature, of planning for the level of traffic induced by the unrestricted use of the motor car for the journey to work in conditions of full car ownership' (Buchanon 1963:94). They believed in 'the long run the most potent factor in maintaining a "ceiling" on private car traffic in busy areas is likely to be the provision of good, cheap public transport, coupled with the public's understanding of the position' (Buchanon 1963:195). The Buchanon estimate of the increase in the number of vehicles (27 million by 1980) was influenced by the current expectations of a continuous growth in both population and economic prosperity. Neither of these assumptions has been fulfilled and consequently the number of vehicles has reached little more than two-thirds of their estimate. Given the nature of the problem, however, the slower rate of growth in motor vehicles has only eased rather than avoided the dilemma facing public authorities. Once a road network is full, the number of vehicles that are surplus to its capacity becomes somewhat irrelevant. It is as difficult to get a pint and a half into a pint pot as it is to accommodate the traditional quart!

The economics of transport provide further complications for policy-makers wishing to influence the relative proportions of traffic using different modes of travel – the 'modal split' as it is described in planners' jargon. First, most forms of transport incur heavy fixed costs. Railways require expenditure on track and rolling stock; road transport must be provided with roads and vehicles. Once this capital expenditure has been incurred, the *marginal* cost of additional use is relatively small. The cost of one extra passenger on a train or one extra trip in a motor car bears little relationship to the *average* costs of such journeys. Second, road transport offers a convenience of flexibility that is not available to railways. Privately owned road transport has even greater advantages of flexibility. The convenience obviously has a value to the user that will be offset against the costs of owning private vehicles. Third, transport is a prime example of the economic problem of 'peaking'. The congestion of the morning and evening 'rush hour' is complemented by more moderate traffic flows during the rest of the day and unused facilities at night.

The combination of the three factors outlined in the previous paragraph means that the owner of a private vehicle will incur relatively low *marginal costs* for additional journeys and these costs will be further offset by the flexibility of private use. The public transport operator must, on the other hand, cover total costs which are inflated by the additional expenditure incurred by meeting peak demand (Tyson 1970, 1972a; Fletcher 1972). Public transport cannot compete with existing vehicle owners in the pricing of particular journeys without either incurring heavy losses or restricting the service to a few profitable routes. When the economic arguments we have sketched are related to the planning considerations advanced by Buchanon then the reason for public involvement in most forms of transport becomes obvious. In this brief survey we shall continue to concentrate on 'traffic in towns'.

The relief of congestion and other traffic problems can be met by either improved roads (within the constraints identified by Buchanon) or manipulating the 'modal split' between public and private transport – or by some combination of these approaches. The co-ordination of highways and transport responsibilities has, therefore, certain administrative attractions. The first attempts at co-ordination concentrated only on transport. In the 1920s there were 195 bus undertakings in addition to tramways and railways in London. Herbert Morrison, Minister of Transport 1929–31, provided the basis for the more unified, comprehensive approach that became incorporated in the London Passenger Transport Act 1933 (Wistrich 1983:19). The London Passenger Transport Board (LPTB) was a special purpose authority responsible to Parliament with a monopoly in the provision of public transport in London. Responsibility for highways remained with local government. Outside London many local authorities provided public transport services, but privately owned companies continued to operate. After 1945, a Labour government brought most forms of transport into public ownership; some of which were subsequently denationalised by Conservative governments.

Following Buchanon, transport policy developed within a climate of both growing interest in local government reorganisation into larger units, and a concern for strategic and corporate planning. The time seemed opportune for a co-ordinated approach. The 1968 Transport Act provided for Passenger Transport Authorities (PTAs) in the major conurbations. At first these were joint bodies incorporating representatives of appropriate local authorities. After 1974 the MCCs became the PTAs for their areas. Shire counties are not PTAs but have a responsibility of promoting adequate public transport services. The metropolitan counties were also, of course, the major highways authorities in their areas and were responsible for producing structure (i.e. strategic) plans. The Transport (London) Act 1969 gave similar powers to the GLC. The two Acts were slightly differently worded which became important in later controversies over subsidised fares (see Ch. 10).

The day-to-day operation of local transport rests with the Passenger Transport Executive (PTE). The PTE consists of professional officers whose statutory relationship with the councillors on the policy-making PTA is rather different from that obtaining in other local government services (Hovell and Jones 1975). The officers exercise certain powers in their own right and thus transport has become almost a hybrid of local government and special purpose authority control. Under the 1969 Act, the London Transport Executive (LTE) accepted a similar relationship to the GLC. The transfer of responsibility for London transport from the LPTB to the GLC was a rare example of the demise of a special purpose authority to the advantage of local government during the reorganisation years. The local government gain was short-lived. The London Regional Transport Act 1984 transformed the LTE into London Regional Transport (LRT). This new special purpose authority is responsible to the Secretary of State for Transport. There is no involvement of local councillors.

The creation of PTAs in the major conurbations was accompanied by other planning measures. County councils became responsible for drawing up structure plans. The term structure was used 'to mean the social, economic and physical systems of an area' and included measures for 'the management of traffic' (*Development Plans* 1970:18,89). County councils are also 'required to submit annual Transport Policies and Programmes (TPPs) to the Department of Transport for approval as a basis for the receipt of TSG [Transport Supplementary Grant]' (Wistrich 1983:58). The TPPs are intended to cover expenditure over the whole transport field including public transport, roads, parking, traffic management and pedestrians. Since 1978, shire counties have also been required to produce a five-year rolling public transport plan (PTP) that relates both to structure plans and TPPs.

The various measures we have just described provided a basis for a more co-ordinated transport policy but they did not avoid political controversy – quite the contrary. Two interlocking developments brought central government into conflict with local communities and their representatives. First, there was a public reaction against road systems which adversely affected the local environment. Major controversies arose around proposed trunk road developments in London and other urban areas (Boaden *et al.* 1982:82–5; Wistrich 1983:104–12). One commentator, indeed, has referred to the events in London between 1969 and 1973 as a 'kind of insurrection' (Thomson 1977:59). This public reaction, together with the less favourable economic climate in the 1970s, caused some local authorities to place less emphasis on road construction and more on other aspects of transport policy. This second development steadily stole the headlines as the earlier disputes over road construction receded. South Yorkshire provides a key example. South Yorkshire County Council (SYCC) included a cheap fares policy for public transport at the heart of its structure plan and similar policies began to be adopted elsewhere. The SYCC argued that their policy for public transport would reduce the expenditure and disruption caused by major urban road developments. Such developments were in any case difficult to achieve in Sheffield because of the topography. In these circumstances a greater reliance on public transport could be expected to benefit even those who travelled in private cars by reducing congestion and in other ways (Tyson 1972b). The SYCC were also interested in the redistributive effects of subsidised fares which they believed would enable poorer people, women and the elderly to have easier access to transport facilities: motor cars were more readily available to men 'of working age of a higher income level' (Wistrich 1983:9). In their three-year plan prepared for 1984–85 to 1986–87, the South Yorkshire PTE stated that between 1974–75 and 1982–83 both the annual bus mileage and the number of passengers carried had increased by 7.1 per cent. In the context of a national decline in the use made of public transport this represented a considerable success for the policy adopted by the SYCC.

Although the public in the areas affected have generally supported subsidised fares for public transport, successive governments have been alarmed at the effects on local public expenditure. The question of the balance a local authority is expected to keep between the interests of the users of a particular service and the generality of ratepayers has also been tested in the courts (Wistrich 1983:26–30). How high can subsidies go? The Transport Act 1983 resolved some of these matters by placing greater powers in the hands of the Secretary of State. Each year the PTE prepares a three-year plan of services and fare structures having taken account of any advice the Secretary of State may have given. The PTA approves or modifies the plan, again in the light of advice given by the Secretary of State, and determines any revenue grants that may be necessary to balance the transport accounts. In approving any such grants, a PTA 'shall have regard ... to the need to achieve a proper balance between the interests of the ratepayers in their area and the interests of transport users' (Transport Act 1983:Section 6(7)). After receiving the plan and such other information as is required, the Secretary of State gives guidance on the maximum amount of revenue grant that would be appropriate. If necessary the Secretary of State indicates the alterations to the plan that are needed to take account of his or her guidance (Section 4(5)). Between the role of the PTE in preparing the plan and the role of the Secretary of State in giving 'guidance' before approval, there appears to be relatively little space for PTA initiatives of the kind pursued by the SYCC. The role of local government in transport policies becomes even less significant with the abolition of the GLC and MCCs. We conclude the chapter with a discussion of the issues raised by such abolition.

DISCUSSION – THE ABOLITION OF THE GLC AND METROPOLITAN COUNTY COUNCILS

A Conservative government was re-elected in 1983 on a manifesto that included a commitment to abolish the GLC and the MCCs. Legislation was introduced in the session 1984–85 in the expectation that it would become effective in 1986. The discussion surrounding this policy was among the most acrimonious of the government's term of office with many of its usual supporters expressing strong opposition. At times the government seemed in total disarray as its proposals were attacked as unconstitutional by a former Conservative Prime Minister and defeated in the House of Lords. With friends like these one is tempted to the conclusion that a Conservative government had no need of enemies; but they were faced also by a very effective opposition organised by the GLC and the MCCs. These authorities financed a massive public relations campaign to sway public opinion in their favour and achieved considerable success.

Amid the dust of such a controversy it is difficult for a student of urban politics to distinguish the themes that will have a lasting significance. The position is complicated by the interaction of several of the discussion points raised in previous chapters. These may be summarised as follows. First, there is the argument between proponents of unitary and multi-tiered local government. Is there a need for strategic authorities covering a wide area and if so what services should they provide or what functions should they perform? Second, there is the consideration of the relative merits of compendious and special purpose authorities. Third, there is the whole question of central–local government relations and the growing ideological content of disputes between these layers of government. Each of these issues needs to be developed in a little more detail.

The Conservative government argued that local government re-organisations in the 1960s and 1970s were typical of 'a time when resources seemed to be freely available ... the heyday of a certain fashion for strategic planning, the confidence in which now appears exaggerated' (DOE 1983b:2). According to this thesis, the distribution of responsibilities left the GLC and MCCs with too little to do, but with access to large rating resources: 'This generates a natural search for a "strategic" role which may have little basis in real needs' (DOE 1983b:3).

The 'search' for a 'strategic' role was, of course, the main reason for the creation of the metropolitan authorities. The proponents of unitary authorities in the Royal Commission on Local Government in England accepted a need for a wider authority for some services in the metropolitan areas and for an authority that could prepare a strategic plan for conurbations. In this they were following the example of the reorganisation of London local government a decade earlier. The Royal

Commission's proposals for the conurbations survived the Conservative government's different attitude towards unitary local authorities and became part of an overall two-tier system. The MCCs thus created differed in at least two respects from the Royal Commission's recommendations: first the boundaries of the conurbations were much more tightly drawn; second, the number of metropolitan counties was increased from three to six. The metropolitan areas (both GLC and MCCs) consisted of strong boroughs or districts and relatively weak strategic authorities when looked at in terms of the services provided. The boroughs and districts were made responsible for high spending services such as education (except in inner London) and social services. The GLC and MCCs were responsible for strategic planning, refuse disposal, transport, fire and police (outside London). They shared some other responsibilities with the lower-tier authorities. Both the police and transport as we have seen were subject to special arrangements that differentiated their administration and policy control from the general procedures of local government.

Within their limited powers, the metropolitan authorities sponsored some important developments in their areas. For example, Tyne and Wear provided a modern rapid transit system using former suburban railway track. South Yorkshire sought to regenerate the declining industrial area of the Dearne Valley; and, of course, adopted an innovative, albeit controversial, policy for public transport. The authorities gave considerable support to regional cultural activities such as theatres, art galleries and orchestras. Above all the authorities sought to create a conurbation identity that could maintain morale and enable the stronger districts to support the weaker through times of rapid economic and social change. None of these developments would have been so easily attempted without the presence of a metropolitan strategic authority.

Despite their achievements, the GLC and the metropolitan county authorities occupied an uneasy position between powerful boroughs and districts and an emerging regional tier of special purpose authorities. The Royal Commission had recommended a regional tier as a necessary complement to a unitary system of local authorities. The London boroughs and metropolitan districts closely remembled the unitary authorities but they operated in a quite different regional context from that intended by the Royal Commission. The structure created in 1974 was supplemented by an increasing number of special purpose authorities. These authorities accepted powers that strengthened local or regional elected authorities might have been expected to obtain. The GLC and MCCs were thus weakened from the start and regarded as too small for some purposes and too large for others. Examples may be drawn from the earlier sections of this chapter. Health care was consolidated in the NHS and water and sewage went to new special purpose authorities in 1974. Transport was increasingly subject to central government responsibility after the London Regional Transport

Act, 1984. In addition, the GLC housing responsibilities were steadily transferred to the boroughs and such bodies as the Merseyside Development Corporation and the Docklands Corporation in London were given powers that effectively limited local government responsibilities in these areas (see Ch. 12). The perceptive comments of Morrison quoted earlier in the chapter were being justified. Local responsibilities were first whittled away and then the role of local government itself was questioned. Supporters of both unitary and two-tier local government were, therefore, united in opposition to the abolition of the GLC and the MCCs as it involved the allocation of their major functions to a special purpose or indirectly elected bodies. The abolition had the further consequence of leaving London without an elected representative body for the first time in a 100 years.

The White Paper preceding the abolition of the GLC and MCCs stated that on reorganisation the London boroughs and metropolitan district councils would 'acquire responsibility, individually or collectively, for the functions currently exercised by the GLC and the MCCs, with the exception of London Transport, flood protection in the London area [which went to the RWA] and a few minor aspects of other functions' (DOE 1983b:6). Subsequently, the government responded to public pressure and provided for an elected single-purpose authority to take responsibility for the ILEA. In the context of the present chapter our interest is with the collective arrangements for providing services thought beyond the scope of individual districts. Although the metropolitan district councils received additional powers under the legislation, the main services formerly provided by the MCCs, including police, fire and public transport, became the responsibility of joint boards comprising nominees from the district councils. These services had accounted for approximately two-thirds of MCC expenditure (Coopers and Lybrand Associates 1984:14). The joint boards have precepting powers on the district councils. As well as these precepting bodies there are numerous joint committees for other services where co-operation is needed over a wider area than the individual district. It is difficult to believe that such a mass of complicated inter-authority arrangements can achieve the objectives outlined in the government's White Paper. These were to 'streamline local government in the metropolitan areas ... remove a source of conflict and tension ... save money ... [and] provide a system which is simpler for the public to understand' (DOE 1983b:5). An independent study of the government's proposals for the MCC areas concluded both that the original case for abolition was overstated and that the 'structural changes cannot be expected to lead to savings in themselves ... there are further costs associated with losing the county wide nature for some of the services and the multi-function nature for others' (Coopers and Lybrand Associates 1983, 1984:6).

The abolition of the GLC and the MCCs has to be considered in the wider context of central–local government relations. Several of these authorities had pursued vigorous policies conflicting with central government priorities. This point was recognised in the White Paper (DOE 1983b:4) and perhaps had more salience in the government's thinking than the unquantified expectations of financial savings. The ideological commitment both of the New Urban Left in some of the major cities and of a government of the 'radical right' provided no basis for the carefully balanced conventions of previous central–local relations. The conflict over abolition led the government to propose a Bill 'paving the way' for a new system by cancelling the elections to the GLC and the MCCs due in 1985 and substituting nominees of the boroughs and districts. The government feared a complete lack of co-operation during the change-over. The attempt to substitute nominees (sometimes of a different political party) for elected councillors led to a government defeat in the House of Lords. A compromise was reached. The Local Government (Interim Provisions) Act 1984 extended the term of office of existing councillors until 1 April 1986. The Act also gave the Secretary of State powers both to obtain the information necessary to facilitate the transfer of duties from the GLC and MCCs to other bodies and to control certain actions of the existing councils in the interim period.

It is too early to assess the performance of the new joint bodies. We may safely assume, however, that they will not enhance local accountability. Indirectly elected bodies tend to develop a corporate identity of their own which obscures the responsibility of their parent authorities, particularly when they receive precepting powers. Nor will a network of single-purpose bodies find it easy to co-ordinate services either with each other or with the services of the districts or boroughs. There will no longer be a policy forum, for example, for considering the common interests of police, transport and highways authorities. The longer-term tendency may be for the joint boards to develop into fully fledged special purpose authorities in the manner of the water authorities. In any event the abolition of the GLC and MCCs and the distribution of their major services to special purpose authorities and joint boards can only be interpreted as a weakening of the role of local government.

Chapter twelve

LOCAL GOVERNMENT AND THE LOCAL ECONOMY

The character of a locality is heavily dependent on the nature of the local economy. A fishing port differs from a holiday resort; a commuter village from a mining town; and a city based on metal manufacture from a commercial capital. These differences affect the political life of the areas as people bring the attitudes and cultural expectations of their occupations into the political process. In Peterhead, for example, 'the attitudes inculcated in fishing and farming remained strong enough, ... in 1970, to impede the growth ... of a militant trade-union movement' (Bealey and Sewel 1981:28). By contrast, the dominance of manual occupations in heavy industry 'has caused Sheffield to be a radical city' (Hampton 1970:44). The style and partisan allegiances of local politics are not the only features of local government, however, to be affected by the local economy. The equalisation provisions contained in central government grants (see Ch. 6) do not prevent a local authority prospering if the local economy is booming and suffering if it declines. In other words, the structure of the local economy conditions the resources available to provide local services – as well as affecting the private well-being of the local population.

Despite these considerations, 'it would until recently have been unusual to consider local authorities as bodies with economic functions, still less as bodies with an economic policy' (Johnson and Cochrane 1981:1). Such a view of local authorities is no longer so unusual. The change of attitude was stimulated by two developments. First, the rediscovery in the 1960s of the poverty in which many people existed even in the midst of a relatively affluent society. Second, the underlying conditions facing the British economy began in the 1970s to express themselves in the long-term decline of many urban areas. Both central government and local authorities initiated new approaches to these problems of local poverty and inner-city decay. The approaches were small scale and largely experimental in character, but by the 1980s fundamental differences began to appear between some left-wing local authorities and a Conservative government. Local economic policies began to provide one of the most significant features of central–local relations and conflicts.

A full discussion of the causes of poverty and the decay of inner-city areas is not possible in the short space available – even if these causes were fully understood and agreed. The literature facing the student of these topics is extensive, often ephemeral and sometimes polemical. The objective of this chapter is the more modest one of outlining some major components of what has become known as the Urban Programme and showing how this programme has contributed to the growing interest in local economic policies. The expression 'the urban programme' is being used here as a generic term to include all the various initiatives for dealing with the problems of the inner cities including the specific response known as *the* Urban Programme – with capital initials. We end the chapter with a discussion of the economic policies pursued in several areas by the New Urban Left.

THE URBAN PROGRAMME

In their excellent survey, Joan Higgins and her colleagues identify 'four major influences on the genesis of the Urban Programme: the "rediscovery of poverty" and the re-emergence of selectivity in the early and mid-1960s; the American War on Poverty programmes; the growing emphasis on area-specific policies … ; and the … growing public concern over the issue of immigration and the (mainly) governmental anxiety about race relations from the mid-1950s on' (Higgins *et al.* 1983:49). A few words on each of these four points will assist in the analysis that follows.

The 'rediscovery of poverty' owes much to Professor Peter Townsend and his colleagues at the London School of Economics and the University of Essex. In a major distillation of their work Townsend considered the conceptual problems of defining poverty. He argued: 'Individuals, families and groups in the population can be said to be in poverty when they lack the resources to obtain the types of diet, participate in the activities and have the living conditions which are customary, or are at least widely encouraged or approved, in the societies to which they belong' (Townsend 1979:31). On the basis of this approach he studied the problems of unemployment, low pay, disability and handicap, single-parent families and old age. He concluded, 'poverty is more extensive than is generally or officially believed' (Townsend 1979:983). His views were supported by a growing number of pressure groups such as the Child Poverty Action Group, Shelter, the Disablement Income Group and Gingerbread. The universal provision that lay at the heart of the Welfare State established in the 1940s was thus mingled with a new concern for the special needs of selected groups.

The second influence on the developing urban programme was the aura surrounding the War on Poverty programmes launched by the Johnson administration in the USA in the early 1960s. The word 'aura' is used deliberately. Many aspects of the American programme were not conspicuously successful (Marris and Rein 1967), but the lessons were not learnt by those considering similar initiatives in Britain (Higgins 1978:40–1).

Third, in the 1960s a number of government reports 'showed that the major services had not been successful in making themselves equally as available to all social groups in need of the services' (Edwards and Batley 1978:15). A greater measure of positive discrimination was needed to compensate for the special disadvantages suffered by the deprived. Some of these disadvantages related to the personal characteristics identified by Townsend: other disadvantages related to decaying nineteenth-century environments. An area of multi-deprivation occurred when these various sources of disadvantage coalesced in a specific district.

The fourth and most dramatic influence on the development of the urban programme was the growing political salience of immigration and race relations. The American War on Poverty programmes are reputed to have been a response to the urban pressures created by 'the migration of large numbers of blacks from the rural South to the Northern cities' (Higgins 1978:28). Similarly in Britain the occasion for the announcement of the Urban Programme (in its more specific meaning) was the response by the then Prime Minister (Harold Wilson) to a speech by Enoch Powell. Powell 'forecast future problems from the concentration of coloured people in cities: "Like the Romans, I seem to see the River Tiber foaming with much blood … "' (Edwards and Batley 1978:25). An official review in 1980 concluded: 'Assisting ethnic minorities has been an implicit objective of the Urban Programme since its inception' (quoted in Stewart and Whitting 1983:14).

When considering the origins of the urban programme in the 1960s the omission of economic factors is noticeable. British cities were already beginning to be affected by a major restructuring of the economy. Traditional heavy industries in the North were declining while industries based on new technologies were developing elsewhere. Furthermore, changes in the pattern of overseas trade were shifting the focus of port activity from the West to the East, and the use of containers brought further problems for traditional dock areas. McKay and Cox consider that the effects of these changes on the inner cities were 'not appreciated within government circles in the mid- and late-1960s' (McKay and Cox 1979:237). The following ten years witnessed a complete change in attitudes.

The analysis of urban poverty upon which the government relied in the 1960s led to policy proposals directed at supporting individuals or regenerating the worst-hit areas. The argument was as follows: active and able young people were moving to new towns or peripheral housing estates leaving behind in the decaying Victorian terraces those who for one reason or another were unable to join in the growing affluence of the consumer society. The solution was to provide support for these areas and encourage the local residents to develop the self-confidence needed to participate in improving their own condition. The Local Government Grants (Social Need) Act 1969 made grants available to local authorities for 75 per cent of the cost of approved social and community projects. Local authorities met the remaining 25 per cent of the costs. This policy is usually referred to as the Urban Programme – with capital initials. In the first fifteen years grants of rather less than £100 million were made available to support about 5,000 projects. About a third of the projects were concerned with children: nurseries were particularly well supported (Higgins *et al.* 1983:69–73). The programme is, therefore, a relatively minor source of funds supporting worthwhile and usually un-contentious projects. Its effect on overall conditions in the inner city has been negligible.

More significant for our present purposes – though no more successful in halting the decline of the inner-city areas – were the research projects established to assess the possibility of improving conditions in specific areas of concentrated need. The strategy implied a redirection of local government services to such areas and included the assumption that local people would themselves be stimulated to make greater use of both their own resources and those available from public agencies. Of the various projects established, the two that had most effect on subsequent developments were the Community Development Project and the Inner Area Studies. These will, therefore, be considered in a little more detail.

THE COMMUNITY DEVELOPMENT PROJECT

The Community Development Project (CDP) became the most controversial of all the projects established in the inner cities. Indeed, the controversies started before the CDP teams were appointed. Some local authorities 'refused the invitation to set up projects in their areas' (Higgins 1978:45). These areas did not want the stigma of being thought in special need. They had some strong arguments on their side. Although the concept of concentrated pockets of multi-deprivation had proved persuasive in government circles, it was difficult to identify them on the ground: 'One third of the United Kingdom's population was implicated in the first definition of deprived areas!' (Edwards and Batley 1978:50). A sharper definition was obviously needed – 'needlepoint' was one analogy of the time. Twelve areas were eventually chosen to give a spread over the country as a whole but the problem of identifying them had suggested a deeper difficulty. Professor Townsend later commented: 'However economically or socially deprived areas are defined, unless nearly half the areas in the country are included there will be more poor persons or poor children living outside them than in them. There is a second conclusion. Within all or nearly all defined priority areas there will be more persons who are not deprived than are deprived' (quoted in Higgins *et al*. 1983:119).

The CDP teams began their work in the early 1970s, therefore, with a brief implying deficiencies in the people and areas concerned that did not match reality (McKay and Cox 1979:244). For example, the districts selected were not obviously more deprived than surrounding areas and contained many people who did not come within any of the categories defined as needing special help. Moreover, when it came to improving access to local services the difficulties were often found more within service bureaucracies than within the local populations. As a result of their experiences, therefore, the teams gradually began to locate the causes of urban deprivation within the structural constraints of a capitalist economy rather than within the faults and special problems of individuals or particular small areas. The majority of the CDP areas had experienced a decline in key local industries; in other cases redevelopment proposals had led to the disruption of settled communities. But whatever the specific local circumstances, the Inter-Project Report 1973 concluded: 'The 12 CDP areas have all, in different ways, experienced the negative repercussions of industrialisation and urbanisation ... changes in the pattern of industrial investment have imposed on these small areas negative costs which are felt in terms of jobs, housing and the environment, social provision and the overall quality of life' (CDP 1974:8). Reports from individual projects reflected this structuralist perspective. They included detailed research on landownership and investment policies in the areas. Such a broadening of approach was not welcome either to central government or to the local authorities hosting the projects (Higgins *et al*. 1983:34).

The CDP proposals for combating the causes of the problems they were analysing were even less acceptable to established politicians than the basis of their analysis. The Inter-Project Report presented three main models of social change:

(i) *Consensus* models of social change are based on the assumption that social problems are 'malfunctions' which can be cured by adjustments and rearrangements within the existing operating systems. The problems are defined mainly in terms of failures of co-ordination and communication, and the focus of change is thus on management and administration and the non-participant. The central tactic is debate.

(ii) *Pluralist* models of social change are based on the assumption that social problems arise from 'imbalances' in the democratic and bureaucratic systems. The problems are defined mainly in terms of failures of participation and representation of certain interests in the political process, and the focus of change is thus on politicians, policy-makers and the disenfranchised. The central tactic is bargaining and negotiation.

(iii) *Structural conflict* models of social change are based on the assumption that social problems arise from a fundamental conflict of interests between groups or classes in society. The problems are defined mainly in terms of inequalities in the distribution of power and the focus of change is thus on the centres of organised power (both private and public). The main tactic is organisation and raising of levels of consciousness (CDP 1974:23; cf. Benington 1975:182).

As the CDP teams came to adopt the third approach the sources of conflict with local politicians and the government increased. The projects were first curtailed and then allowed to serve their time with diminishing resources. In 1977 the CDP was terminated.

Amid the clamour of political controversy the CDPs were at first considered a failure. The areas remained much as before with all their problems and strengths: the potential role of community development had become associated with radicalism expressed in strident Marxist language. From a slightly longer perspective the positive achievements of the CDP have been assessed by Higgins and her colleagues (Higgins *et al*. 1983:45–6). First, the projects produced a mass of data, some 200 reports, on the economic, political and social influences on towns and cities suffering urban stress. Second, the projects provided the conditions of experimentation that enabled the emerging occupation of community work to test the possibilities and limitations of its approach. Many of the community workers employed by CDP later moved into work for which their previous experience was valuable. They included some of the pioneers of the more radical economic policies pursued by local government. Finally, and most important, once the dust had settled the climate was found to have changed. The 'social pathology' analysis that identifies the causes of urban deprivation in the characteristics of individuals or areas can no longer be advanced unchallenged. As we shall see, the CDP structuralist perspective was apparent in a revised approach to the urban programme from the end of the 1970s. The government, however, preferred to give most credit for this to the Inner Area Studies.

THE INNER AREA STUDIES

The Inner Area Studies (IASs) were a product of the newly created DOE in the early 1970s. Professional consultants were appointed to carry out research in inner-city areas in Birmingham, Liverpool and Lambeth. The study brief published in 1972 contained four objectives:

1. To discover by study a better definition of inner areas and their problems.
2. To investigate by experiments on the ground the actions affecting the physical environment of these areas which could usefully be undertaken for social and environmental purposes.

3. To examine whether the concept of 'area management' can usefully be developed and what the practical implications would be for the local authority.
4. To provide the basis for general conclusions on statutory powers, finance and resource questions and techniques (DOE 1977a:1).

These objectives were in many ways similar to those originally envisaged for the CDPs, but less emphasis was placed on action projects. Each IAS interpreted the brief rather differently. The three reports, therefore, have distinct emphases. They all, however, give particular attention to housing and employment issues. The IAS teams also allowed their interests to range rather more widely than the circumscribed boundaries of their study areas. Regional employment policies and industrial investment decisions were recognised as important determinants of the life opportunities of inner-city residents.

The reports of the IASs, though written in more circumspect prose, had much in common with the conclusions of the CDPs. There is the same avoidance of placing the blame for their own poverty on the personal characteristics of inner-city residents; and the same emphasis on broader economic issues. There is also a suggestion that inner-city poverty is related to a more general unequal distribution of economic and political power in society. This unequal distribution results in the inner cities receiving less than their fair share even of those public services which might be expected to provide a counterbalance to their general lack of prosperity. For example, the Liverpool study area contained 9.6 per cent of the total population of the city, but received only 6.1 per cent of the expenditure of the city council. Peter Walker, who as Secretary of State for the Environment had established the IAS, later referred to this as a 'horrifying fact' (Walker 1979:12). There are, of course, many and complex reasons for public expenditure varying from one area to another (Sharpe and Newton 1984). In the present context the crucial point is that any attempt to improve conditions in the deprived urban areas implies a major shift in the present distribution of public resources. The Birmingham study concluded:

> Changes in attitudes will not just happen. The more privileged people in society (most of whom live in collectively more privileged environments) cannot reasonably be expected to make concessions of privilege, either by the sacrifice of present advantage or by forgoing future opportunity, unless, first, they are made more aware of the 'unfairness' of the great disparities that still exist in the distribution of social goods and opportunities and, second, the disadvantaged themselves become more organised and articulate in pressing for a better deal (DOE 1977a:297).

The more radical CDPs had preferred to write of a fundamental conflict between social groups and of raising class consciousness; but behind the differences in language the message was remarkably similar.

The recommendations from the IASs included the need for a substantial switch of resources to inner-city areas, a new approach to economic development and a more co-ordinated programme of central and local government policies. The Liverpool study was quite specific in recommending 'a new agency; a semi-independent body, an economic development board, possibly set up by, and responsible to, the local authorities but relying for financial support on central government' (DOE 1977b:234). A weak version of such an agency formed part of the next stage of the urban programme.

PARTNERSHIP

The White Paper introducing a change in policy towards the inner cities referred to local authorities as 'the natural agencies to tackle inner area problems. . . . Local authorities now need . . . to stimulate investment by the private sector, by firms and by individuals, in industry, in commerce and in housing' (DOE 1977d:8–9). The subsequent Inner Urban Areas Act 1977 enhanced the powers to assist industry of local authorities with serious inner-area problems.

The new emphasis on the economic powers of local authorities was accompanied by a more co-ordinated approach to central and local responsibilities. In seven areas central government entered into 'partnership' arrangements with local authorities. These areas receive a share of urban programme resources which are allocated by a partnership committee comprising representatives of central and local government with a minister in the chair. The committee is supported by joint teams of officers. A further fifteen 'Programme' authorities also receive advance allocations of urban programme resources without the formal structure of partnership. The remaining local authorities continue to have access to the 'traditional' urban programme. Thus partnership arrangements led to a direct intervention by central government, and particularly by DOE officials, in the allocation of urban programme funds in the areas selected for special assistance (Higgins *et al.* 1983: 144).

During this brief survey of the urban programme since its inception in the late 1960s, we have drawn attention to two features that have importance for the student of urban politics. First, there is the gradual movement away from 'pathological' explanations of poverty in favour of structural explanations based on economic considerations. Second, there is the growing intervention of central government in the local policy process in inner-city areas. The urban programme started on the basis of 75 per cent specific grants which gave central government an influence in the type of special projects supported. By the end of the 1970s, the partnership arrangements provided for even greater ministerial interest in selected urban areas.

LOCAL ECONOMIC POLICIES

The major urban areas of Britain are clearly faced by a complex set of economic problems. Rising oil prices in the early 1970s triggered an economic recession throughout Western economies: unemployment rose to levels unapproached since the 1930s. The recession in Britain was, in the opinion of many people, accentuated by the adoption of monetarist policies by successive central governments. The monetarists place the reduction of inflation rather than the avoidance of unemployment at the heart of economic policies to strengthen the competitive position of the British economy. They argue that an increase in the money supply will, other things being equal, lead to increased prices: 'It is the old explanation of inflation – "too much money chasing too few goods"' (Barratt Brown 1984:72). The converse of this argument is the expectation that a reduction in the supply of money will lead to a reduced rate of inflation.

A discussion of the validity of monetarist theory would lead into academic avenues far removed from the boundaries of the present text. The implications of monetarist policies for local government have, however, hovered in the background of several of the topics we have considered in Chapters 6 and 10. A reduction in money supply has been sought by central government through a general reduction in public expenditure – including local authority expenditure. The special urban programme expenditures referred to in the first part of this chapter must, therefore, be seen against a general background of pressures on local authorities to reduce their demands on resources. Urban programme monies are only a small amount when compared with the general reductions in central government grants to local authorities since the mid-1970s: 'In 1981/82, for example, £40m extra money was made available to Merseyside through the Merseyside Development Corporation and the Urban Programme, while local authority expenditure was reduced by £65m in real terms compared to the previous year' (Parkinson and Duffy 1984:87; cf. Parkinson 1985).

A reduction in local government expenditure can have a detrimental effect on the local economy. Local authorities are often the largest employers in their areas. They spend large sums of money on goods and services. Any reduction in their activities puts people out of work both directly among their own employees and also indirectly among the employees of their suppliers. Such effects could, of course, be countered if a reduction of local government activity allowed a reduction in rates which in turn created increased economic activity in the private sector. The lower proportion of local authority expenditure covered by government grants, however, has made rate reductions difficult to achieve. Moreover, in the early 1980s, 'the general tilt in rate support grant in favour of inner-city authorities [was reversed]. This had a drastic effect on the main programme budgets of the London

Partnership authorities, in particular' (Higgins *et al.* 1983:154). In any event, the simple substitution of one type of economic activity by another is not inevitable either in total or in any particular locality.

Broader considerations of structural and locational change within the British economy compound the effects of general economic recession in the major urban areas. The traditional industries in Scotland, Wales, the north of England and the Midlands – the areas that London-based officials refer to as 'the regions' – are declining. The manufacturing base of many towns and cities has disappeared. The legacy of empty buildings and dereliction remains. These vacant sites are not attractive, however, to firms and industries that are expanding. Professor Doreen Massey (1979) has analysed these changes to show how developments in the economy at any given time produce particular distributions of economic activity throughout the country. The growth of large companies and technological changes in methods of manufacture produce different locational requirements from those of small firms based on individual craftsmanship. The multi-storied factories of the inner cities give way, therefore, to low density industrial complexes outside the urban areas. Britain's accession to the European Economic Community gives a further boost to the relative economic attractions of the south-east of England. This 'restructuring of capital thus entails the development of some local economies and the desertion of others ... industrial decline and urban deprivation [are] not exceptional but *normal* and even vital elements in the operation of advanced capitalist economies' (Pahl *et al.* 1983:90; cf. Young and Mills 1982).

Against this background of economic depression and industrial relocation, local authorities became increasingly interested in economic policies for their areas. The government, too, has pursued regional policies that have included specific arrangements with urban authorities. Each of these developments will be considered in turn before we discuss the economic strategy of the New Urban Left.

LOCAL GOVERNMENT AND INDUSTRIAL DEVELOPMENT

Local authorities responded to the effects in their areas of the problems facing the British economy by adopting policies for industrial development. In this they were encouraged by the new approach embodied in structure planning and the growing awareness of the structural nature of the problems with which they were faced. After the reorganisation of local government in the early 1970s, each county authority in England and Wales became responsible for producing a structure plan for the area. Although the Town and Country Planning Act 1971 is cautious in its wording (and DOE officials were often even more cautious in their advice), many local authority planners interpreted the legislation as providing a basis for plans that went beyond traditional land-use concerns. The plans included policies affecting social and economic developments through the provision of a beneficial infrastructure of roads, public transport and other local authority services.

Major investment in public service infrastructure is dependent upon central government permissions and policies. Local authorities have adopted other policies conducive to industrial development which are more within their immediate control. The adoption of such policies has been facilitated by Section 137 of the Local Government Act 1972 which allows a local authority to 'incur expenditure which in their opinion is in the interests of their area or ... inhabitants'. This partial relaxation of the *ultra vires* restriction on local authority expenditure is limited to the product of a rate of 2p in the pound. Such a rate can produce several millions of pounds in the larger local authorities and has financed many of the policies outlined below. The scale of these activities remains small, however, when compared with the finance available from central government regional development grants or, of course, private industrial investment. Even the expansion of local authority involvement from the late 1970s could not affect to any significant extent the relationship between local assistance to industry and the scale of capital formation shown in Table 12.1. The largest local authority in the early 1980s, the GLC, was spending at the rate of approximately £30 million per annum on economic policies.

TABLE 12.1   Financial assistance to industry; 1977

	(£m.)
Local authority activities	
Capital	30
Revenue	37
Government regional preferential assistance to industry	365
Gross domestic fixed capital formation by industry (manufacturing)	4,323

Source: Burns 1980:6

Most local authorities concerned with industrial development have emphasised 'the provision of sites and premises for industry. ... In particular there has been an upsurge of local authority involvement in the provision of small factory units' (Boddy 1983:34). By 1982 'over 80 per cent of district councils were providing sites and over half providing premises' (Boddy 1984:189). Other types of local authorities had a similar commitment. The sites available are often in local authority ownership following substantial clearance schemes in the late 1950s and 1960s; land can be assembled and prepared for industrial development in advance of market need. The provision of small factory units is another example of local authorities anticipating the market. Local authorities built many such units in the 1970s when the private sector found small developments unprofitable. These units were 'easily marketed locally' (Johnson and Cochrane 1981:47): by the 1980s private developers were again entering the market.

With so many local authorities providing sites and premises for the limited amount of new investment available, a degree of competition is inevitable. Local economic policies include, therefore, general promotional and publicity activities and the appointment of industrial development officers who give advice and information to prospective developers (Johnson and Cochrane 1981:48–53). Some local authorities are also willing to offer financial incentives to industrialists. They may provide loans on favourable terms or grants in support of the acquisition of sites and premises and for other purposes. For legal and financial reasons most of this activity is on a very small scale (Johnson and Cochrane 1981:54; Boddy 1984:161).

CENTRAL GOVERNMENT INVOLVEMENT

When a Conservative government took office in 1979, they confirmed the general development of urban policies as outlined in the 1977 White Paper *Policy for the Inner Cities*. The emphasis within these policies, however, began to change. In particular, the government wished to enhance the role of private enterprise in generating new economic activities in the inner city. No longer were local authorities to be regarded as 'the natural agencies to tackle inner area problems' (DOE 1977d:8). In some respects they were seen as part of the problem. Partnership arrangements provided for a direct intervention by central government in some of the worst affected areas, but the Secretary of State considered that the programme was 'unwieldy and over-bureaucratic' (Higgins *et al.* 1983:152; cf. HC 1983:xxx–xxxiii). The local Government Planning and Land Act of 1980 created, therefore, Urban Development Corporations (UDCs) for the Liverpool and London docklands. The UDCs operate as single-purpose agencies with special powers that place them outside the normal framework of local government. Their membership includes businessmen and other prominent local people who do not hold any elective office (Boaden 1982).

A further indication of the government's reliance on private enterprise to restore the prosperity of the inner cities was the announcement by the Chancellor of the Exchequer in 1980 that a number of Enterprise Zones (EZs) were to be created in urban areas. By 1982 eleven were in existence. The EZs are an attempt to encourage industry and commerce by the removal of certain taxes and the easing of planning controls. The main concessions, which run for ten years, are exemption from development land tax, exemption from commercial and industrial rates, exemption from industrial training levies, corporation

213

and income tax allowances of 100 per cent for capital expenditure on commercial buildings, priority processing of applications for certain customs facilities, relaxation of planning restrictions, and a reduction in government demands for information.

As with the UDCs, the EZs reduce the influence of local government within some parts of the urban areas and have provoked much controversy. Professor Peter Hall, who is credited with parentage of the idea, defends EZs as experiments that may generate economic growth in areas such as Liverpool where conventional approaches appear to have little chance of success. In a symposium in the *International Journal of Urban and Regional Research*, however, several critics denied the economic validity of the EZ approach and emphasised its political significance. Professor Doreen Massey in particular argued that the EZ idea was an ideological attempt to solve the crisis of the British economy by a 'change in the locus of political and economic power ... – in favour of capital' (Massey 1982:433).

The last central government initiative in an urban area (at the time of writing!) came in response to the urban riots in the summer of 1981. The worst violence occurred in the Toxteth area of Liverpool and the government sent the Secretary of State for the Environment for a two-week visit to Merseyside to assess the position. The Merseyside Task Force was created after this visit. The Task Force is yet another attempt to bring central government departments and private enterprise to the assistance of an area where local government is perceived as inadequate to deal with problems of economic decline. The Merseyside Task Force consists of thirty civil servants and a few people seconded from the private sector. Unlike some of the other initiatives, Task Force has no separate budget and must work through existing agencies – including local government. Its main purpose is to co-ordinate central government's urban policy for the area and to improve communications with the private sector (Parkinson and Duffy 1984:82–3). In 1985, the government announced the appointment of Task Forces in five other areas: Birmingham, Manchester–Salford, Newcastle–Gateshead, Hackney–Islington, and Lambeth. The new appointments involved no commitment of extra funds, but a fresh emphasis on the efficient use of urban development grants to attract private companies to invest in the areas (*The Times* 3.1.85:2).

ASSESSMENT

An assessment of the various governmental initiatives described in this chapter must start with an understanding of their limited scope. They are each concerned with circumscribed areas and provided with relatively small resources: often they are considered as 'pilot projects' for major initiatives that never occur. Merseyside, which has benefited from every new scheme, provides the starkest example of the failure of any initiative to halt, let alone reverse, the economic decline of the area. Partnership in Merseyside 'atrophied' (HC 1983:xxx). The Task Force was considered only 'a qualified success' (HC 1983:x lii) whose specific claims were often disputed by local authorities in the area (HC 1983:xxxviii–xxxix). After a decade of special initiatives the city was 'sceptical of what it was possible to achieve for Liverpool' (Parkinson and Duffy 1984:79). The problems facing Liverpool are of special severity and have been compounded by a political balance which prevented clear leadership in the local authority. The judgement in other areas, however, is scarcely less severe. One experienced observer in a review of urban policy wrote: 'Measured against the search for an ultimate solution, policy has clearly failed' (Boaden 1983:24). Such successes as the policy has achieved are, he believes, of a largely symbolic nature or concerned with the alleviation rather than the cure of urban distress.

The difficulties of assessing the more specific economic policies, however, should lead to a cautious approach even to scepticism. The EZs, for example, have a decade to prove themselves and the consequences if they are successful will continue far into the future. The problem is how success is to be measured in the various policies for industrial development. Would the firms have settled in a particular area without local authority incentives? If not, are the jobs created in one area simply lost to another? How much *additional* economic activity is generated by the efforts of local authorities to manage their local economies? Is it sometimes the case, as Professor Massey and the New Urban Left contend, that local economic policies are to be judged more on ideological than economic grounds? There is little research to throw light on such questions, but certainly the number of jobs created is very small when compared with the growth in unemployment since the 1970s. The relocation of industry to non-urban areas 'is on some accounts a tide of change as powerful as that which produced the modern industrial city. It is against such a tide that urban economic programmes must swim' (Young and Mason 1983:219). Even so, Young and Mason believe there may be some value in local authority activities. They point to the different economic fortunes of cities that have similar industrial backgrounds. Such differences may depend on 'a complex of economic and non-economic factors' which may include 'the cumulative activities of local authorities' (Young and Mason 1983:221).

DISCUSSION – THE NEW URBAN LEFT AND LOCAL ECONOMIC POLICY

In a review of the mainstream approaches to local economic policy, Martin Boddy concludes that they have 'been property-led, business and market orientated and competitive, with economic development rather than employment the primary focus' (Boddy 1984:163-4). Such a strategy was obviously unsatisfactory from the point of view of the more radical Labour councillors who took power in some of the major urban areas in the early 1980s. They were concerned to change the basis of the economic system in pursuit of a more equal and just society. Local economic policies were part of a general alternative economic strategy that they hoped would be implemented by a future Labour government. Local economic policy for the New Urban Left was not, therefore, simply a matter of underpinning the local economy. They had a concern with the employment and democratic implications of local economic policy as well as with its consequences for economic development. They were concerned also to avoid the competitiveness that may cause a successful economic development policy in one local authority area to be achieved at the expense of other localities. They saw their policy within a framework of general economic growth and social change.

The New Urban Left adopted a twofold strategy to implement their policies. First they began to use the economic potential of local authorities as employers and customers. By the size of their own workforce and by their expenditure on worthwhile services, local authorities make a direct contribution to relieving unemployment. In 1983, for example, Sheffield City Council provided employment for around 31,000 local people and spent about £20 million on goods and services from 900 local firms (Blunkett and Green 1983:11). Moreover, by adopting equal opportunity employment policies both for their own workforce and in contracts placed with outside suppliers, local authorities can achieve broader policy objectives concerned with overcoming racial and sexual discrimination. Contracts can also include clauses encouraging trade union membership and improvements in wages and conditions of employment.

Second, a few socialist local authorities, notably Sheffield, the GLC and the West Midlands Metropolitan County, adopted a different approach to economic development (Boddy 1984:165-75). The GLC, for example, instead of providing assistance to private industry from the perspective of a free market economy, expected assistance to depend upon 'local Planning Agreements' arising from 'three-way talks between GLEB, the enterprise and the Unions concerned' (GLC 1981:17). The Greater London Enterprise Board (GLEB) was created as a limited company in 1982 to provide investment either in new industries or in existing industries threatened with closure. The major part of GLEB's income for investment came from Section 137 rate revenue. Investment was linked to more general policy objectives such as the establishment of workers' co-operatives or assistance to groups who found it difficult to obtain access to more orthodox sources of funds (Marks 1983:8). The investment was not intended, however, to be an act of charity. GLEB had to demonstrate that the investment would produce economically viable and socially useful jobs. A similar approach was adopted in the West Midlands (Boddy 1984:168-71).

In Sheffield, the new economic strategy was retained within the normal local authority structure. The policies are co-ordinated by an Employment Committee and Department established in 1981. The committee, the first of its kind in Britain, is chaired by a senior councillor. The first head of the new department had been director of one of the CDPs in the 1970s. He thus embodied the links between the themes explored in this chapter. The aims of the Employment Department are ambitious; to co-ordinate everything that the City Council can do to help:

i) to prevent further loss of jobs in the City;
ii) to alleviate the worst effects of unemployment, and to encourage effective training for new skills and jobs;
iii) to stimulate new investment, to create new kinds of employment, and to diversify job opportunities in the City;
iv) to explore new forms of industrial democracy and co-operative control over work (Sheffield 1982:1).

The Employment Department approaches its task first on the basis of research into 'the structure of local industry – its products and processes, ownership and control – to see how it might be bent to meet social priorities efficiently' (Blunkett and Green 1983:9). Second, there is a recognition 'that the Department cannot have much impact on job numbers within an established industrial sector, so the emphasis should be on reforming ... the working conditions of those who remain employed' (Blunkett and Green 1983:13). In developing employment prospects in the areas of 'new technology', 'a "user centred" design approach [is emphasised] so that the final product meets a real community need, as opposed to developing a product and *then* searching for a market' (Blunkett and Green 1983:13). Product development companies have been formed jointly with the local university and polytechnic.

An assessment of the economic policies adopted by the New Urban Left may be approached in two ways. First, we may ask whether the policies have been effective on their own terms. Have the jobs been created? Have the conditions and control of employment changed? The answer to these questions is yes – to a very limited extent. In its first two years GLEB claimed to have saved or created 2,000 jobs at an average direct investment per job of £4,500. This is a much lower cost than is estimated for the creation of jobs through central government regional incentives or EZs. The number of jobs involved, however, must be placed against the 400,000 unemployed in London in 1985 (GLC 1985:12). Similarly, the number of jobs created in Sheffield between 1981 and 1984 was estimated at 1,000 which only matched the number of jobs lost through redundancies in *each month* of that three-year period (Child and Paddon 1984:22).

Local authorities cannot be expected to have the resources to tackle major unemployment problems on their own. The GLC believed, however, that GLEB had demonstrated a demand for the financial assistance it could make available to job-creating enterprises. They had to turn away many sound projects for lack of funds. The provisions of the Local Government (Interim Provisions) Act 1984, however, made the continuation of GLEB, and other similar agencies in the metropolitan counties, uncertain. Under this Act the GLC and MCCs required the consent of the Secretary of State for the Environment for all Section 137 expenditure incurred after April 1985, thus the source of funding for agencies such as GLEB could be curtailed. The local authorities themselves, of course, were abolished in 1986. Any future initiative for the whole of a metropolitan area will depend on the success of cooperative efforts by the boroughs or districts concerned.

The jobs created by the New Urban Left policies have been subject to careful control to ensure good working conditions. In some cases co-operatives or other innovative forms of ownership have been supported. Despite these policies for improving working practices, however, there may be nothing particularly *socialist* about the outcome. Local authority funds may end up 'meeting a gap in the capital market and contributing to the better management of capitalist enterprise – municipal capitalism rather than municipal socialism' (Boddy 1984:181) – albeit a municipal capitalism with a welfare tinge.

The New Urban Left recognise that it would be unrealistic to expect local authorities to solve the employment problems created by a major economic recession, or to change the economic and social structure in a fundamental way in only one part of the country. The limited resources and powers available to local authorities preclude such possibilities. The approach adopted needs, therefore, to be assessed in a more general way than simply by counting the number and quality of the jobs created. This second way interprets the alternative economic policies as part of a general *political* strategy of showing 'why the economics of the market place and private enterprise itself create an unacceptable society, and how the concept of community can form an alternative to that of greed and self-interest as the only motivator of innovation and initiative' (Blunkett and Green 1983:28). The contrast between the approach adopted by central government through the creation of UDCs and EZs and the perspectives of the New Urban Left obviously reflects a fundamental difference in political attitude. The success or otherwise of either set of policies must be assessed in some measure, therefore, by the effect they have on the ideological commitment of the electorate. 'Hence', as Duncan and Goodwin explain, 'all the fuss about a set of apparently minor policies; hence all the conflict over the form of local government, about how it does things and who it does them for' (Duncan and Goodwin 1984:27).

Chapter thirteen

THEORIES OF THE LOCAL STATE

The tratitional complaint that we lack a theory of local government was referred to in Chapter 1. But though local government may lack a theory, there is no lack of theories about politics. What has happened over the past few years is that these general theories are increasingly involved in academic discussions about local government and urban politics. Local government is being incorporated into more general theories of the state. Nor is the discussion only the concern of academia. The theories, and sometimes the theoreticians, have an effect on the policies pursued by political parties; and are at the heart of some of the major debates within the left both in Britain and in other countries in Europe. The developing interest in theoretical approaches adds intellectual excitement to the study of urban politics, but it can make difficulties for students taught in a more traditional manner; or who are mainly concerned with professional examinations in local government or administration. For such students, an advanced course in political theory may appear necessary before some of the journal articles on the subject can be understood. In this final chapter we cannot do justice to the richness of the theoretical debates which are taking place; but, as in the rest of the book, we hope to guide the student through some of the literature and to provide an understanding of the language being used.

The discussion of theoretical issues is included in this final section because the major recent controversies have taken place in the context of a structuralist interpretation of local government. This does not mean, of course, that other interpretations have no theory. Some approaches adopt an atheoretical stance which causes their underlying assumptions to remain implicit rather than explicit; but a theory must be present if order is to be brought to the infinity of empirical reality. Without such an order understanding will not develop. Gramsci writes of everyone being a philosopher. Each person 'participates in a particular conception of the world, has a conscious line of moral conduct, and therefore contributes to sustain a conception of the world or to modify it . . . ' (Hoare and Smith 1971:9; cf. Joll 1977:91). The structure of this, or any other, book is a 'theory': it governs the material, or facts, to be presented and the relationship of parts of the whole to each other. We may tell 'nothing but the truth' but we cannot tell 'the whole truth'; the act of selection implies a 'theory' or basis for selection: it also affects the questions asked or considered important enough for discussion. Such considerations affect the presentation of an outline of the theories themselves, of course, and students need to retain their scepticism in good order as they approach areas where supporting facts are rare and sometimes appear as mirages rather than firm reality.

The basic theoretical question with which we are concerned is the relationship of local government to the state: and in what respects the concept of 'the local state' can have meaning. The nature of the state is, of course, at the heart of political theory and we shall range more widely than the local government and urban politics literature during our discussion. It is as well to start with definitions. The state is an organisation of individuals living within a defined territory who are subject to a common rule. This common rule will take priority over all other arrangements within the territory of the state. Within this territory, in Weber's defining characteristic, the state 'claims the monopoly of the legitimate use of physical force' (Gerth and Mills 1948:78). 'The state is thus a society of individuals submitted, if necessary, by compulsion, to a certain way of life' (Laski 1961:11). Every word and phrase in these definitions is subject to controversy (see for example Rose 1982), much of which need not detain us in the present context. There are two issues, however, that are important for our subsequent discussion.

First, there is the problem of how the state should be conceptualised. One tradition of political philosophy has reified the abstract concept of the state. In other words, the concept has been converted into a thing: sometimes philosophers in this tradition have even given human attributes such as self-awareness to the insensate abstraction. Within this tradition the individual citizen achieves his being as part of a greater unity and has no rights, perhaps even no meaning, except as an expression of the purpose of the state. When outlined in this way, this approach may appear implausible, but such a view is implicit in many everyday statements. Such phrases as 'the interests of the state' should always be examined closely to discover their true meaning. Is the state being assumed to have interests over and above the interests of the citizens who comprise it? And if not, are the interests of all citizens capable of compression into a single, consensual, statement of this kind?

Another tradition of political philosophy gives a negative answer to both the questions which end the previous paragraph. The second approach to the conceptualisation of the state describes its manifestations in the institutions and relationships of government and administration. Thus Ralph Miliband argues 'that "the state" is not a thing. ... What "the state" stands for is a number of particular institutions which, together, constitute its reality, and which interact as parts of what may be called the state system' (Miliband 1973:46). These institutions comprise 'the government, the administration, the military and the police, the judicial branch, sub-central government and parliamentary assemblies' (Miliband 1973:50;cf. Dearlove and Saunders 1984:Ch. 11). 'Sub-central government' includes both local government and the single-purpose authorities which were discussed in chapter 11.

The second problem we must mention in this preliminary discussion concerns the control of the state. In the more extreme versions of the first tradition mentioned above, the state itself adopts a godlike position of control: the citizens can only act within its purpose. When the state is described as a set of institutions, however, the question of who controls them becomes important. From the many answers to this question we may mention three that correspond to the framework of this book. First, there is the constitutional approach. The state is controlled, in British terms, by the Queen acting within the confines of the parliamentary system. Second, there is the pluralist approach that allows within the political process for the pressures and influences operating alongside the formal structures. Third, there is the Marxist position which starts a lengthy, and at times esoteric, debate with 'the famous formulation of the *Communist Manifesto*: "The executive of the modern state is but a committee for managing the common affairs of the whole bourgeoisie"' (Miliband 1973:7). Each of these approaches will be examined in turn in relation to the study of local government and urban politics. We end with a discussion of the 'dual state thesis'.

THE CONSTITUTIONAL APPROACH

The constitutional approach to the nature of the state rests on a basis of law. Indeed, textbooks in this tradition seldom mention the state in so many words. They are concerned with such questions as the nature of parliamentary sovereignty, that is, the legal right of the Queen in Parliament 'to make or unmake any law whatsoever on any matter whatsoever' (Smith 1971:67). A quick glance at any of the older textbooks concerned with local government (or central government for that matter) will show the predominance of this approach. There is an emphasis on institutional arrangements and formal electoral processes. The question of control is treated as unproblematic: the elected representatives support a government within the framework of the constitution. The Crown is perceived as the embodiment of the state: but as the head of the Home Civil Service has reminded civil servants, 'For all practical purposes the Crown in this context means ... the Government of the day' (*The Times* 27.2.85:1).

Local government is regarded within the constitutional approach as a creature of Parliament: created for certain purposes which may be developed or amended according to the policies of the central government. There is, within this tradition, a circumspect debate as to whether local government acts as an *agent* or a *partner* of central government in fulfilling its responsibilities, but this debate is resolved by reference to the legal rule of *ultra vires* (see Ch. 1). Only the most adventurous of the advocates of the partnership position draw attention to the difficulties of enforcing the law. Examples of central state power are drawn from the big set pieces of history – Poplar and Clay Cross – while the mutual adjustments of practical administration are given less prominence.

The summary contained in the previous paragraph is of course, a caricature – although one that is easily recognisable. The strengths of the approach are in its careful exposition of the law and formal arrangements. The weaknesses are in its avoidance both of the realities of political conflict and of the disposition of social forces that leads to the adoption of one set of constitutional arrangements rather than another. Nevertheless, it is an approach that dominates not only the older textbooks but both the measured arguments of official reports and the rhetoric of central politicians in their attempts to exert greater control over local authorities.

THE PLURALIST APPROACH

Whereas the constitutionalists emphasise the importance of law, the pluralists concentrate on political processes. Peter Saunders suggests three fundamental principles underlie pluralist theory: 'First, the state is independent of any one section of the population. ... Second, those who control state policy-making are elected ... and are therefore accountable to the population as a whole. ... Third, the political power ... is exercised on the basis of a fundamental value consensus in society ... ' (Saunders 1981:130). Thus the state, though again the word is seldom used, is understood as a framework within which competing interests may struggle to achieve their purposes. In some versions of pluralist theory the state becomes even less significant: simply one pressure group among many. The theory, therefore, 'argues that power in western industrialised societies is widely distributed among different groups. No group is without power to influence decision-making, and equally no group is dominant' (Ham and Hill 1984:27).

Pluralist theory underlies most of the case-studies of local politics in Britain. These case-studies, particularly the earlier ones, were strongly influenced by Robert Dahl's book on New Haven in which he developed pluralist theory through a detailed study of a local community. Dahl believed that over the previous two centuries New Haven had 'gradually changed from oligarchy to pluralism' (Dahl 1961:11). In other words, power had been dispersed from the few to a large number of competing groups. The reason for this 'revolution' was, in Dahl's view, to be found in the shift from 'a system of *cumulative inequalities* in political resources to a system of non-cumulative or *dispersed inequalities* in political resources' (Dahl 1961:228, original emphasis). Again we need to translate these phrases into less technical language for the point to become clear. Dahl argues that political resources such as wealth, access to information, social standing, the legitimacy of public office, or mass support are dispersed in such a way that no one group in a community can secure a monopoly. Moreover, the various resources differ in their significance from one issue to another causing an even greater fragmentation of power. The system is not anarchic, however, for it operates 'within that vague politial consensus, the prevailing system of beliefs, to which all the major groups in the community subscribe' (Dahl 1961:84). This consensus develops 'through those complex processes of symbiosis and change that constitute the relations of leaders and citizens in a pluralistic democracy' (Dahl 1961:325).

Many people have criticised the sanguine assumptions upon which pluralism is based and have pointed to the manifest inequalities in power that exist in our society. From Patrick Dunleavy's critique of Dahl we may point to two other difficulties in accepting the analysis of local decision-making upon which the theory is based. First, the analysis leads 'directly to an institutional definition of urban politics as no more than the politics of city or local government' (Dunleavy 1980a:31). This exaggerates the autonomy of the locality and excludes from the analysis the full influence of regional or national actors: 'For example, most economic and social "notables" in New Haven lived in suburban areas beyond the city boundaries and consequently had no stake in two of Dahl's three key issues ... ' (Dunleavy 1980a:31). Second, the emphasis on issues which become a matter of public debate ignores 'the possibility that power may be most effectively used in preventing an issue from being politicised or made public' (Dunleavy 1980a:32). Such power may be exerted covertly; but it is even more effective when it does not need to be used at all: when 'the vague political consensus, the prevailing system of beliefs' prevents a potential political issue being recognised as such. In these circumstances the dominance of a particular group may not need to be expressed through the cumulation of political resources. Rather it will be expressed through the general acceptance of a particular view of the world. This ability 'to shape, directly or indirectly, the cognitive and affective structures whereby men perceive and evaluate problematic social reality' (Femia 1975:31) is Gramsci's concept of hegemony.

The critique of pluralism forms the starting point of much of the recent work on urban politics. Justified as the criticisms are in many respects, they should not obscure the contribution made to the study of local politics by many of the case-studies of particular localities. They rescued the subject from the arid concerns of the constitutional approaches and introduced sociological techniques to examine political processes. They provide a mass of detailed information to assist more general reflection. They cannot be said, however, to have contributed much to the theory of the state – unless one takes the view that the concept of the state is itself an ideological construct reflecting a particular view of social reality. In this case the pluralist's denial of a centralised location of power becomes a basis for questioning the validity of any general theory of the state.

THE MARXIST APPROACH

Scholars who adopt a Marxist, or quasi-Marxist, approach deny the basic premises of pluralism: the neutral stance of the state, the dispersal of power and the existence of a basis for consensual politics. They interpret the state as an expression of the interests of the dominant class in any given society. The role of the capitalist state, therefore, is to create the conditions for capital accumulation through the production of profit. The state is engaged in the continuing struggle between classes which forms the dynamic of social change. Attempts to relate this approach to existing capitalist societies have led to considerable theoretical debate from which we have chosen three themes for more extended discussion: the nature of the capitalist state, collective consumption and the role of urban social movements in generating social change.

THE NATURE OF THE CAPITALIST STATE

Marx identified the basis of particular forms of society in the nature of the economic production process appropriate to that stage of historical development. Thus he discussed slave-owning, feudal and capitalist societies and foresaw a future transformation to socialism. The dynamic of social change from one system to another arose in the class conflict between the owners of the means of production and those they exploited. Within capitalism this meant between capitalists (bourgeoisie) and workers (proletariat). Within this theoretical system, the state has the role of managing and protecting the interests of the dominant class. The precise way in which this is achieved has been a source of much disagreement among Marxists.

The formulation from the *Communist Manifesto* quoted earlier in the chapter is obviously too crude to be applied to the real world, but there has continued to be a tradition of Marxist analysis which emphasises the identity of personnel and purpose within the dominant class and the state. From this perspective, the state can have no interests separate from the interests of the ruling class – or dominant fraction of the ruling class. The reason for this identity of interest rests in the economic basis of society: the structure of the economy itself constrains the actions of the state. In other words, a capitalist state that acted against the interests of capitalism would find itself in economic crisis. The structuralist model of the state outlined here has been developed and modified by Poulantzas (1973). He argues that class struggle 'determines to some extent how the state in fact functions and creates policy. The state has, therefore, a degree of autonomy – a "relative autonomy" – because it ... may intervene ... and may make concessions to non-capitalist interests as a means of regulating the class struggle. ... This accounts for the growth of welfare states and increased spending on social consumption' (Lowe 1986:Ch. 1).

The modifications to the structuralist model that Poulantzas introduced made the theory less rigid but the publication of his views led to a famous exchange with Ralph Miliband in the columns of the *New Left Review*. Miliband accused Poulantzas of turning Marxism into 'but another form of determinism' (Miliband 1977:73) removing any possibility of freedom of action from individuals – who became simply the agents of impersonal objective forces. The reason for this tendency in Poulantzas was, in Miliband's view, his 'failure to make the necessary distinction between *class power* and *state power*' (Miliband 1983:41, original emphasis). This prevented further analysis of the relationship between the two concepts in the context of concrete historical examples. Miliband extends the concept of the 'relative autonomy' of the state by arguing that 'while the state does act, in Marxist terms, *on behalf* of the "ruling class", it does not for the most part act *at its behest* ... it enjoys a high degree of autonomy and independence in the matter of its operation as a class state ... ' (Miliband 1977:74, original emphasis).

Whether the emphasis is placed upon 'structural determinism' or 'relative autonomy', the theories outlined above lead to further difficulties. Cynthia Cockburn, in her book *The Local State*, approaches the 'determinist' end of the continuum. She describes local government as 'an aspect of national government which in turn is a part of the state' (Cockburn 1977:2). This formulation, which bears a passing similarity to the constitutional approach discussed earlier, denies the possibility of independent action by local authorities. Moreover, despite the title, the book scarcely considers the concept of the local state. Cockburn usually uses the phrase as a synonym for local government, thus robbing it of a broader content which includes other local manifestations of the state apparatus. Cockburn argues that local councils, whether Labour or Conservative controlled, are unable to respond to any interests but those of the ruling class: even 'the services which we ourselves need and struggle to win from the state must also be seen as "servicing", we are serviced for our labour power' (Cockburn 1977:2). This idea of local government servicing the labour force is one we shall come back to later in our discussion of 'collective consumption'.

Cockburn's main theme, however, is the relationship between *corporate management* and *community development* – both of which have been considered in earlier chapters. She sees community development, and the various forms of public participation associated with it, as the 'tender' aspect of 'tough' corporate management. Public participation is a way of incorporating prospective protest into the strategies of the state. Although she mentions in her last paragraph the possibility of using the contradictions within the local state as a lever for social advance, there is little encouragement in the book for the New Urban Left in their attempts to exercise local elected power in this respect. There is even less support for the policies of decentralising local power that form part of the campaign manifestos of several left-wing local parties.

There is much evidence to support Cockburn's points about public participation. A review of the various initiatives in the 1960s and 1970s concluded: 'élite perspectives have won out, and participation has served the purposes of building up a consensus for the proposals of those in power, thereby legitimating them' (Boaden *et al.* 1982:179). Cockburn's approach, however, goes much further than an analysis of what has happened. She attempts a theoretical explanation for why it will continue to happen. In the course of this explanation she criticises approaches which tend 'to give the state too much importance and apparent detachment from the economic base' (Cockburn 1977:163).

The difficulty with the 'determinist' approach is its rigidity; the difficulty with the 'relative autonomy' approach is to define the extent of the state's autonomy. By introducing the idea that the state responds to pressure from exploited classes, an opening is offered to pluralist thinking. The state becomes a focus for struggle rather than an instrument of the ruling class within that struggle. The distinction is important in the debate among Marxists about the possibility of achieving social change through democratic rather than revolutionary means. There is also the difficulty that the relative autonomy approach 'enables its adherents to "explain" both those situations where capital benefits as a result of state policies and those where interests opposed to capital prevail. . . . It is, in short, a tautology' (Saunders 1981:207–8).

COLLECTIVE CONSUMPTION

Manual Castells has referred to 'the organisation of the means of collective consumption' (Castells 1978:3) as fundamental to an understanding of 'the urban question'. It is necessary, therefore, to spend a little while elucidating his general approach during a discussion of this central concept. Castells criticises previous approaches to urban sociology as being ideological in character and unspecific about the content of its subject-matter (Castells 1976a). He attempts a re-construction on the basis of historical materialism – or Marxism. In the course of this reconstruction he dismisses geographic or area-specific definitions of the urban and seeks the location of the concept within the dynamic of the class relations of society. 'Urban' is then defined as the arena within which labour-power is reproduced. The conditions of this reproduction are, of course, the normal consumption goods such as food, clothing, housing, transport and so on which are necessary for people both to live and to care for children until they can enter the productive process as workers. The extent of the provision necessary for this process is affected by several factors. Among these are the demand for more specific types of labour which may require longer periods of education or training and the 'growing bargaining power of the workers ... [which] changes the historical definition of "need", both qualitatively and quantitatively, ... ' (Castells 1978:17). Some of this demand for consumption goods forms the basis of new profitable investment, but in other cases ' ... the intervention of the state becomes necessary in order to take charge of the sectors and services which are less profitable ... but necessary for the functioning of economic activity and/or the appeasement of social conflicts' (Castells 1978:18). The state is thus acting in ways which are both structurally determined, in providing for the necessary reproduction of labour-power, and relatively autonomous, in appeasing social conflicts: in both instances it is acting in the interests of the dominant class.

'Urban' is not, therefore, defined simply as what goes on in towns and cities. It is defined in terms of its content as the location of state-provided or 'collective' consumption. This gives the study of urban politics a new importance both with regard to the economic function the local state performs for the capitalist relations of production, and with regard to the conflicts over the quantity and quality of goods and services entering collective consumption.

The concept of collective consumption has stimulated much new thinking about urban politics but it has also been subject to criticism. In Peter Saunders's view: 'Three problems in particular need to be considered. First, can collective consumption be equated with spatial units as Castells suggests? Second, can collective consumption be defined in terms of its function in producing labour-power as Castells argues? And third, what sort of provisions does the term "collective consumption" actually refer to?' (Saunders 1981:210). The first problem relates to the difficulty of equating every form of collective consumption with a spatial aspect of the state. Some 'have a spatial reference (public housing, hospitals, schools), others do not (social security payments, family allowances, pension schemes)' (Saunders 1981:211). We may be concerned with the theoretical problems posed by collective consumption, therefore, without necessarily having a theoretical concern for spatial units. The second problem refers to the difficulty of defining urban in terms of its role in reproducing labour-power when this 'is only one aspect of urban processes. ... Socialised provisions may function not only in aiding the reproduction of labour-power ... , but also in ... investment in necessary but non-profitable economic infrastructure such as roads, telecommunications, ports and so on' (Saunders 1981:211). Collective provision, and the urban process, may in other words have a far wider significance for the productive process than is implied through the use of the term 'collective consumption'.

The third problem relates to the actual content of the concept of collective consumption. Does it refer to all goods that are collectively provided or to those that are collectively consumed? (Saunders 1980:121–7). A few examples may make the distinction clear: health care is collectively provided through the NHS, but individually consumed by patients; preventative public health measures are both collectively provided and collectively consumed. That is, there is no immediate way of distinguishing between those who benefit from preventative public health policies and those who do not. The complexity of this problem, with the endless possibilities of arguing about definitions and typologies, has occupied much academic writing over the past few years (Saunders 1981:215–18). It is not simply a technical point, however. The proper understanding of the concept of collective consumption becomes important as we move to the analysis of urban social movements within which Castells locates a new dynamic of social change.

URBAN SOCIAL MOVEMENTS

In view of the difficulty of much of the writing we are considering, it is as well to summarise and reiterate the main points of the argument as a basis for proceeding further. Castells started from the classical Marxist assumption that located the dynamic of social change in a class conflict between the owners of the means of production and the workers. In the course of this conflict, a balance would be reached that allowed the workers to retain sufficient of their produce to reproduce the labour-power necessary for the system to continue – plus a little extra if they were well organised in a militant labour movement. Under modern conditions these necessities for the 'reproduction of labour-power' – housing, health care and so on – became increasingly the responsibility of the state. Hence the concept of 'collective consumption' arose.

Castells then went on to argue that conflicts over the distribution of goods of collective consumption were assuming as great an importance for the understanding of social change as conflicts in industry over the distribution of output. In his earlier work, Castells remained close to a structuralist perspective that emphasised the primary contradiction in society between capital and labour at the point of production. Conflicts over consumption issues could not assume importance in generating social change unless they were linked to these primary contradictions. He distinguished, therefore, between 'social movements' which are simply 'an instrument of participation within general, dominantly institutional objectives' (Castells 1977:378) and 'urban social movements' which 'are drawn into the advanced sections of the working class movement ... through the mediation of a political organisation following a "correct line"' (Lowe 1986:Ch. 1). The first category obviously refers to the type of organisations found in the pluralist literature. Their actions are contained within the prevailing system and are even conducive to its continued existence (Cockburn 1977; Boaden *et al.* 1982). Castells had more difficulty in discovering examples of his second category and in his later work he modified his position considerably in response to both the results of his empirical research and changes in his political thinking.

Stuart Lowe has identified three phases in the development of Castell's approach to urban social movements. The first phase we have already outlined. Phase two is associated with the publication of *City, Class and Power* (1978). Lowe identifies two main areas of development in this book. First, Castells attributes much greater importance to the 'new forms of social cleavage arising from collective consumption. . . . They do not supplant the primary capital/labour contradiction, but . . . there is much greater parity between the two levels' (Lowe 1986:Ch. 1). Second, the urban social movements associated with these new forms of social cleavage are allowed much greater autonomy in effecting social change.

The autonomy of urban social movements is further extended in the third phase of Castells's thinking. In *The City and the Grassroots*, he separates urban social movements from political parties while still retaining the need – in an ill-defined way – for links to be developed between the two if fundamental social change is to occur (Castells 1983:284). His new position may be summarised – with the inevitable distortions caused by compression – in the following few sentences. He starts by arguing that the numerous organisations emerging in recent years to challenge existing forms of society are founded in civil rather than political society: 'and are not necessarily limited to, or bound by, the rules of the game and the institutionalisation of dominant values and norms' (Castells 1983:294). He also emphasises 'the importance of space as a material basis for all forms of social organisation' and in particular the significance of cities for the development of protest movements (Castells 1983:69). These movements are concerned not only with consumption issues, but with cultural, gender and ethnic issues as well. They therefore challenge the dominant social values, or hegemony, that maintain the stability of the existing social order *and they do so by organising across the class divisions of classical Marxist theory*. As might be expected, these views have caused much controversy, particularly as they can be linked to arguments within left-wing political parties. The earlier, structuralist, position conforms to the traditional communist view of the necessity for a 'vanguard' party to identify on the basis of Marxism the correct policy for working-class progress. *The City and the Grassroots* is closer to the Eurocommunist position that argues for a 'democratic road to socialism' through the creation of an alliance between working-class organisations and other protest movements. The alliance will be influenced by but not under the control of a communist party. Castells's new position is also compatible with the growing importance of the women's movement and organisations based on ethnic rather than class divisions.

During the academic discussion of urban social movements several weaknesses in Castells's original exposition have been identified (Saunders 1980:119–21). Some of these have become redundant by the change in stance represented in his later work. Others remain matters of current debate. Of particular significance is the question of whether political cleavages based upon consumption issues lead to organisation across social class lines. In some cases this may occur, but there are other examples where 'consumption issues may in fact be highly *divisive* not only separating say middle class owner occupiers from working class council tenants but ... by dividing the workers among themselves – in this instance manual worker home owners and non-home owners' (Lowe 1986:Ch. 1, original emphasis). The significance of Lowe's point has been well understood by political parties who have differed substantially over the Conservative government's policy of encouraging the sale of council houses.

Lowe's argument can be used to indicate the growing salience of political cleavages which are not class based. Patrick Dunleavy has developed a theory of sectoral cleavages that cross-cut occupational class divisions. These cleavages may be based on whether a person works for the private or public (including local government) sector (Dunleavy 1980b) or on 'how people gain access to goods and services, such as housing, transport, health care and education' (Dunleavy 1984a:52). He shows how voting in the 1979 parliamentary election was affected by whether people depended mainly on the private or public sectors for these goods and services irrespective of their social class. Such results are consistent with at least one version of the collective consumption thesis, though, of course, the congruence depends upon selecting the appropriate definition of collective consumption.

THE DUAL STATE THESIS

The theoretical positions discussed so far in this chapter have all sought an explanation of the role of the local state within a unitary view of state activities. Peter Saunders has developed a different approach. He starts by rejecting theories of the state 'which attempt to explain the various operations of the different branches and levels of the state system in terms of a single general theory' (Saunders 1984:23). He believes 'two different types of political process ... have developed side by side in the modern British state. These ... can be distinguished on four main dimensions – ... organisational ... functional ... political ... and ... ideological' (Saunders 1984:24). A few more words on each of these will be helpful before we return to the general conclusions drawn from the analysis.

Recent work in relating organisational theory to intergovernmental relations relies heavily on the model developed by Rod Rhodes (see Ch. 10). In this model, organisations such as local authorities exist within an environment in which they compete with other organisations on the basis of a differential access to various sources of power. Some of the criticisms of this essentially pluralistic approach have been mentioned in Chapter 10: Saunders believes 'such organisational interests can only be the starting point for our analysis ... it is necessary to consider the different functional responsibilities of central and local government ... ' (Saunders 1984:25).

Saunders provides an analysis of the functions of the state by drawing on a classification by J O'Connor (1973). Three different areas of expenditure are distinguished on the basis of the primary function they perform: 'social expenses (policies designed to maintain social order), social investment (policies that contribute principally to private sector profitability through provision of necessary means of production), and social consumption (policies that contribute mainly to the social and material support of the working population)' (Saunders 1981:260). As with any classification, there are problems of overlap between categories, but Saunders believes the distinction between the last two is particularly significant in an analysis of central–local relations. He locates 'the principal sphere of local government responsibility in Britain today ... in control over certain key areas of consumption provision' (Saunders 1984:27). The link to Castell's concept of collective consumption is obvious.

Saunders also distinguishes between central and local government on the basis of their relationship with other sources of pressure within the political process. Central government in his view has become increasingly remote even from elected parliamentary institutions. Decisions are made within a closed group of powerful corporate interests who are consulted regularly by central government. The institutions appropriate to this process are the various QUANGOS appointed at a national level or regional bodies of the kind discussed in Chapter 11. Local government, on the other hand, is open to a wide range of popular interests through its relative closeness to the public. The enthusiasm for 'corporate' explanations of British politics has declined from the high point of tripartite institutions in the 1970s. At that time many policies were apparently determined through discussions between the government, the Confederation of British Industry and the TUC (Warde 1982:Ch. 8). Nevertheless, the rise of the New Urban Left and the resistance to central government policies by many other local authorities, both Labour and Conservative controlled, is consistent with the point Saunders is making.

The ideological dimension Saunders uses to distinguish central from local government is the tension 'between the principles of market organisation and the rights of private property on the one hand, and those of collectivism and the rights of citizenship on the other. These two core components of political ideology are, of course, polarised to a large extent in different levels of government' (Saunders 1984:29). Central government is concerned with economic efficiency and prosperity within an individualised market economy. Local government is concerned with the maintenance of a certain quality of life through providing collectively for the needs of various sections of the population. Once again, there can be many arguments about the detail of this dichotomy, but the main point is clear.

From his analysis Saunders concludes that state intervention at the central and local level is esentially of a different character. The national state is concerned with the process of production and maintaining profitability within a framework of private property on the basis of a mobilisation of interests concerned with the social organisation of production. The local state is concerned with the process of consumption 'where policies are developed through a process of competitive political struggle ... typically formed on the basis of specific consumption sectors' (Saunders 1984:31). He draws two important theoretical implications from this analysis. First 'we cannot apply the same general theory to both levels of government, since different processes can be seen to be operating at each level. ... Second ... class analysis is generally inappropriate if we wish to understand local struggles around issues of consumption' (Saunders 1984:31). Within the dualistic framework, he sees the possibility of reconciling theoretical approaches previously thought incompatible by stressing the relevance each has in different situations. He suggests, 'in over-simple terms ... that pluralistic approaches may be most relevant to the analysis of local competitive consumption processes, ... Marxist approaches may be most relevant to the analysis of corporate investment processes ... ' (Saunders 1981:277).

In a careful critique of the dual state thesis, Dunleavy points to some of the difficulties of applying the model. In particular he argues that 'O'Connor's distinction between social expenses, investment and consumption is, as Saunders recognises, a set of "ideal types" ' (Dunleavy 1984b:71). The typology has never been successfully applied to an analysis of any state budget. In practice there are great difficulties in allocating public expenditure between categories which are not mutually exclusive: 'Education, for example, could be seen as a legitimation form of social expenses, or as social investment in human capital, or as a type of collective consumption' (Dunleavy 1984b:71). Such difficulties do not, of course, remove the interest of the dual state thesis. If education, for example, serves several purposes, the analysis may help in understanding the increasing central governmental intervention in aspects of educational provision. The role of the Manpower Services Commission is clearly concerned with 'social investment in human capital' and its location outside the realm of local government is significant. Dunleavy produces figures to show how social consumption has become more dominant among local authority functions since the Second World War as other forms of expenditure have been transferred to central or regional agencies (Dunleavy 1984b:75). The dual state thesis can stimulate our thinking about both the causes and consequences of these developments.

CONCLUSION

At the end of Chapter 1 we admitted 'a deep scepticism of attempts to develop a theory to cover all eventualities'. At the same time, we recognised the importance, indeed the inevitability, of theory in presenting and seeking explanations for empirical reality. The growing acceptance of this combined perspective of scepticism and interest in theory has informed many of the contributions to the debates about the local state in recent years. The discussions of 'pure theory', which have much in common with medieval disputations concerning the number of angels who could be accommodated on the point of a pin, have given way to attempts at theoretical explanations of current practice. Increasingly, academic authors 'recognise that *different* kinds of theory may be appropriate to the analysis of *different* kinds of politics at *different* levels of generality' (Dearlove and Saunders 1984:435, original emphasis). All theories, of course, are not equal: we may discriminate between them on the basis of both their accord with the facts and the breadth of explanation they offer. Nevertheless, many different theories can offer important insights for the structuring of reality. The variety of these theoretical explanations, and the lively arguments between their exponents, should not detract from the interest of the endeavour: quite the contrary. By engaging in the debate we gain a greater understanding of the subject-matter of local government and urban politics.

Chapter fourteen
CONCLUSION

Local government has become a major centre of political controversy in recent years and much of the current literature reflects the polemical arguments involved. The major themes of these debates are interwoven throughout the previous pages but it is necessary in conclusion to draw together more clearly the economic and political threads that hold the pattern in place. Such a conclusion is bound to be a very personal statement. Students should, therefore, use this final chapter as a basis for discussion and be aware that their teachers and examiners may differ even more sharply from the conclusions than from the preceding description and analysis.

The British economy is in a period of substantial structural change. The major industries upon which its previous strength was based are in decline: the emerging pattern of post-industrial economic activity is as yet not clearly defined. In one sense, of course, such change is a continuous process. The period between 1918 and 1939, for example, saw a rapid growth in industries based upon the new understanding of electricity and the beginnings of mass communications. The wireless, moving-picture houses and motor-car production lines were as symbolic of the 1930s as are television, video films and micro-computers of our own period. Then, as now, unemployment rose above 3 million; and the economic changes were accompanied by substantial movements of population. People from declining areas in Wales, Scotland and the north-east of England helped the growth of new centres of population in the Midlands and the South-east. The detailed analysis of the relative significance of the present changes must, therefore, be left to economic and social geographers, or perhaps more realistically to future economic historians. There are two aspects of these changes, however, which are undoubtedly having major effects on local government: the run-down of our great industrial cities and the fragmentation of the two-party consensual politics that has dominated electoral processes for over fifty years.

Earlier periods of rapid economic change have been accompanied by the growth of urbanisation. In the nineteenth century Birmingham,

Sheffield, Manchester and other northern industrial centres grew from collections of villages into major cities. Their demand for civic recognition was accepted first by the Municipal Corporations Act of 1835 and consolidated with the establishment of the county boroughs in 1888. The inter-war changes, referred to in the previous paragraph, were again associated with urban growth, this time with the development of large suburban estates of both private and council housing. The problems that economic change brought for local government in the past, therefore, were those of managing urban growth. The corollary of rural depopulation, and the decline of small towns based on primary industries such as coal; was not a major preoccupation for most of the population: the areas were isolated and by definition few people lived in any one settlement.

Current economic changes are producing a quite different effect. All the major cities, from London to Glasgow, are losing population as their industrial base deteriorates. And this time the industry and population are not simply moving from the nineteenth-century centres to suburban peripheries – though that caused problems enough. Whole industrial areas are suffering. Naturally, the effect varies from one area to another, but every industrial city has patches of dereliction which grow in some cases into vast wastelands of abandoned property and cleared sites. The economic growth that is occurring is taking place far away in the small towns of the South-east and East Anglia. For the first time, therefore, our major local authorities are faced not with the problems of growth but with the task of managing economic decline. It is a task for which they are ill-equipped.

During the century and a half since the beginning of modern local government in 1835, local authorities have been concerned to provide expanding services. First, there was the need to develop the sanitary infrastructure such as sewage disposal, clean water supply and the like, which is necessary for modern urban life. This challenge had been largely met by the beginning of the twentieth century. Local authorities were then encouraged in their second growth area: the provision and expansion of education, social welfare and other services necessary for the social infrastructure of their areas. Since their inception, therefore, local authorities have *expected* a steady expansion and improvement in the services they provide. When the minister then responsible for local government, Anthony Crosland, indicated to a local government gathering in the early 1970s that 'the party is over', neither he nor they had a full understanding of the hangover that lay ahead.

Industrial decline and loss of population cause problems no less severe than those associated with expansion and growth but they do not provide the resources with which these problems can be tackled. Moreover, the local authorities concerned understandably feel the need to present an optimistic front so as to retain and attract any industrial development that becomes available. A local authority is not like an industrial concern that can simply close down or move its operations to a site with better opportunities. The cities have a duty to care for the population remaining within their boundaries and the civic pride to wish their former glories to continue. To fulfil these expectations, however, they need assistance from outside their own areas. Such assistance depends upon a political will which successive central governments have found neither the economic resources, nor more latterly, the ideological commitment to maintain.

The political developments associated with the changes in economic structure have effected local government in both electoral and ideological terms. The industrial economy within which modern local government developed provided the basis for two powerful political parties. The Labour Party was unchallenged in the mining areas and among the organised industrial workers: the Conservative Party found support in the rural areas and among professional and business people. The result in local government terms was a settled pattern of political control. Particular localities could be controlled by one party or another for generations. Individual councillors who had served for thirty or more years were not uncommon. In the past few years this settled pattern has been disturbed. Employment has been reduced in the industries providing a bedrock of Labour Party support: mining, the railways, steel and manufacturing generally. The new employment prospects are in the provision of services, micro-electronics and other occupations removed both in ethos and often in location from the working-class communities of the past. The nature of Conservative support has changed also. The leadership once given by the traditional professions and the proprietors of long-established family firms has given way to a more thrusting approach by young executives from the emerging professions associated with the new economic developments. The formation of the Social Democratic Party and the revival of the Liberal Party has enhanced the electoral impact of a more fluid political environment. The controlling party on many local authorities changes more frequently and councils without a clear majority have become more common. As electoral success becomes less secure so the turnover of councillors becomes greater, thus reducing the period of socialisation that helped to moderate the political attitudes of our former 'city fathers' – and very occasional 'mothers'. The new generation of councillors are more determined in their political beliefs and the consequences of this change in attitude are accentuated by the ideological changes taking place within the two major parties.

Mrs Thatcher came to the leadership of the Conservative Party determined to break the consensus that had dominated political thinking since 1945. Her governments shifted the centre of political debate away from the previous acceptance of a substantial public sector and an all-embracing Welfare State. That the success, or even the existence, of many of the attributes claimed for the post-1945 welfare settlement could be doubted is not important. The myths were being challenged and political myths are a powerful factor in reinforcing political stability. The new Conservative approach was one of self-sufficient individualism; the attitude expressed in the antipodes by the frequently heard injunction to 'stand on yer own feet cobber'. Within such an approach there was no room for corporate intermediaries between the individual and the state. The attack on QUANGOS, the trade unions, tripartite collective bargaining, the scale of welfare provision, *and local government* were part of the endeavour 'to set the people free' to pursue their own purposes. Once again the success of particular policies in achieving the intended aims is immaterial: we are dealing in ideologies whose strength is undeterred by contrary empirical evidence.

Within the Labour Party a similar move from a pragmatic to a more ideological stance could be observed – particularly at the local level. The younger Labour councillors who came to prominence in several of the major cities devoted themselves to the development of local expressions of socialism. They had a deep commitment to local public services – within which they were frequently employed – and to forms of community politics involving the encouragement of mass political consciousness through local community interest groups. Some of these groups received financial grants from the local authority. Such grants were frequently tied to an acceptance of the 'established policy objectives of the council' – that is, the views of the controlling faction among the councillors. This ideological approach was far removed from the insistence on pragmatic efficiency in the management of local services with which Herbert Morrison had captured the LCC for Labour in the 1930s. It was removed also from the centralised decision-making style adopted by Morrison and other Labour leaderships in the industrial cities they controlled. As in the case of the Conservative Party, an element of fantasy often entered into the working out of the local socialist ideology: the 'mass support of working people and trade unionists', for example, was seldom forthcoming; but also as with the Conservatives, some of Labour's main themes received electoral support. The electorate responded positively to the Conservatives' *generalised* attack on 'too generous welfare provision' and to their promises of reduced personal taxation. They also supported the Labour Party's defence of *particular* health and welfare services and resented attacks on long-established local policies and constitutional privileges.

Within the context of the ideological division which has been sketched in the previous two paragraphs, the set-piece battles of the early 1980s took place. The Conservative government insisted on their right to determine the level of local spending: Labour councillors resisted the 'cuts' and defended 'local jobs and services'. In reality the financial arguments were a façade behind which the political debate was conducted. The rate-capping provisions, for example, were so loosely drawn that the Secretary of State could vary his formula to pinpoint particular local authorities. The criteria used were in fact manipulated in such a way as to produce a 'widespread belief that political discrimination is regularly involved in Government action' (Newton and Karran 1985:119). Certainly very few Conservative local authorities fell foul of the new restrictions even when they appeared to come within the original *financial* intentions of the legislation. The financial arguments for abolishing the GLC and the metropolitan counties were even less convincing. Few commentators believed that the new arrangements would be less expensive and the government itself avoided any prediction of the savings its policy would produce. The local authorities concerned were all, at the time of abolition, under the control of the Labour Party.

More detailed support for the generalisations contained in the previous pages will be found scattered throughout the earlier chapters. We may expect in a conclusion, however, to become more speculative in our anticipation of the consequences of current developments. To start with we must be quite clear that there are no easy solutions to the economic difficulties facing many of our major urban areas. Nor can their problems be solved within their own local boundaries. The difficulties affecting our major urban areas are national in scope and demand national policies to resolve them. There is, unfortunately, no indication that the major parties are producing such policies.

The Conservative Party is relying upon private initiatives in other more prosperous areas of the country to create a favourable economic climate within which the fortunes of the older industrial areas will begin to revive. The condition of the declining areas will, in other words, be alleviated as the economy as a whole begins to expand. In the meantime, the Conservatives continue the procession of 'special measures' which have proved totally inadequate in relation to the scale of the economic changes taking place. The Labour Party, on the other hand, often appears unwilling to accept the full social and political implications of these changes. By denying the problem they preclude themselves from developing a policy for its solution. Labour traditions and support have been strong within the declining industries and regions. There is a tendency for party activists to suggest, therefore, that the decline is simply a consequence of malign policies pursued by either Conservative governments or large-scale capitalism – or more probably both! From this point of view, there is no true reason for the decline. There is no need, therefore, to consider the consequences. A 'socialist economic policy' will restore the demand for coal, steel and manufacturing in general and bring prosperity back to the industrial areas. Such attitudes in both parties prevent a rigorous analysis of present economic developments and the production of a policy to accommodate them.

Although the economic changes taking place are real ones, we do not have to adopt a fatalistic attitude. Nor are the problems restricted to the declining areas in the north of the country. The rapid growth in some parts of the South and South-east is already producing pressure on land for development and for the housing, schools and other facilities necessary for an expanding population. Where is the recognition that the local authorities concerned need the resources to provide for growth? Strategic planning is out of favour following the extravagances of the structure plans, but some form of regional planning is needed to guide us through the changes taking place. Such planning would also provide a better basis for central–local relations than the present ideological posturing. It is a tragedy that 'it took a riot' to bring a recognition from the government that Liverpool has serious economic and social problems (Parkinson 1985:15). It is bizarre that the response has been to reduce the resources available to the local authority and to abolish the Merseyside MCC – the one agency with strategic planning responsibilities.

The social and political perspectives arising from the present crisis in central–local relations are no less serious than the failure to confront the local and regional implications of economic change. Once again it is necessary to go beyond the immediate stories that captured the headlines in the early 1980s and look at the longer-term consequences. The 'New Urban Left' that came to power after 1980/81 in several of our major urban centres continues to affect local government policies in those areas; but the confrontation that some councillors hoped would lead to the fall of the government failed in its objectives. The government retained a parliamentary majority for its principal policies: the GLC and MCCs have been abolished; 'rate-capping' has been introduced without the political upheavals predicted in several cities. Indeed, the upheavals that did occur were *within* local Labour parties as the New Urban Left struggled to carry the support of the Labour movement for its policy of refusing to implement the legislation. Moreover, some of the leading personalities of the New Urban Left, including Ken Livingstone and David Blunkett, have been adopted as candidates for safe Labour constituencies and will presumably pursue their future political careers in Parliament. In such circumstances the government might find grounds for complacency; but its 'success' may have been won at too high a cost.

In *The City and the Grassroots*, Castells (1983) draws attention to the continued importance of place for social and political cohesion. The significance of this insight has largely been ignored in the policies pursued in respect of local government over the past two or three decades. First, many of the social communities in our major cities were destroyed by the major redevelopment schemes of the late 1950s and 1960s. The consequences of social malaise and individual isolation that followed have now been recognised but the previous social structure is difficult to re-create artificially. Second, the 1970s and 1980s have witnessed a complete upheaval in local political communities. Many long-established communities were absorbed into the larger units of local government established in the early 1970s without proper provision being made for a continuation of their social and political role. The community councils in Scotland provide a partial exception to this generalisation. The basis for local political communities was further eroded in the early 1980s when the independence of the newly created local authorities was severely curtailed by tighter government controls and eventually by 'rate-capping'. Whether the government finds it desirable, or necessary, to use its new powers very widely or not is immaterial to their effects on central-local relations. There has been a major shift in the balance of power towards greater centralisation of our governmental system.

The effects of these developments on social and political processes cannot be predicted from a simple analysis of legal forms. The reiteration of the legal fact that the United Kingdom is a unitary state, for example, denies the more subtle constitutional relationships which contain the potential power of a 'too mighty sovereign'. British governments are expected to respect the rights of alternative centres of authority within the state. We pride ourselves on being a 'plural society', yet the measures adopted by Conservative governments of the 1980s have led us 'within sight of a form of government which is more highly centralised than anything this side of East Germany' (Newton and Karran 1985:129). This is why one distinguished public lawyer has 'no difficulty in saying of an Act to put a limit on the rates leviable by a local authority that it is politically unconstitutional ... it runs counter to the spirit and letter of the existing constitution, and makes the change quite fundamental' (Griffith in Loughlin *et al.* 1985:xii).

The current concerns of students of local government and urban politics are, therefore, of more than parochial significance. A breakdown in the social and political cohesion of our major cities could have severe consequences for national political life. For this reason, if no other, governments should be seeking to strengthen rather than weaken the place of local authorities within our system of government. The failure of governments to recognise the importance of the crisis developing from the interaction of economic change and the devaluing of local government has caused academics of all political persuasions to become less detached and more critical in their writings. The former emphasis on local forms and political processes has been supplemented by a concern for public policy in urban affairs. This text is a contribution to the new approach to the subject.

ABBREVIATIONS

APT & C	Administrative, professional, technical and clerical
AHA	Area Health Authority
ACC	Association of County Councils
ADC	Association of District Councils
AEC	Association of Education Committees
AMA	Association of Metropolitan Authorities
AMC	Association of Municipal Corporations
ATTI	Association of Teachers in Technical Institutions
CAWC	Central Advisory Water Committee
CLEA	Central Council of Local Education Authorities
CIPFA	Chartered Institute of Public Finance and Accountancy
CDP	Community Development Project
CHC	Community Health Council
CASE	Confederation for the Advancement of State Education
CCLGF	Consultative Council on Local Government Finance
COSLA	Convention of Scottish Local Authorities
DHA	District Health Authority
DOE	Department of the Environment
DMT	District Management Team
EZ	Enterprise Zones
FPC	Family Practitioner Committee
GRE	Grant-Related Expenditure
GREA	Grant-Related Expenditure Assessment
GRP	Grant-Related Poundage
GLC	Greater London Council
GLEB	Greater London Enterprise Board
GNP	Gross National Product
HMI	Her Majesty's Inspector
HMC	Hospital Management Committee
HC	House of Commons
IAS	Inner Area Study
ILEA	Inner London Education Authority

LACSAB	Local Authorities' Conditions of Service Advisory Board
LGBC	Local Government Boundary Commission
LIT	Local Income Tax
LBA	London Boroughs' Association
LCC	London County Council
LPTB	London Passenger Transport Board
LRT	London Regional Transport
LTE	London Transport Executive
MCC	Metropolitan County Council
MLG	Ministry of Local Government and Regional Planning
MEU	Municipal Employees' Union
NALGO	National and Local Government Officers' Association
NAS	National Asociation of Schoolmasters
NAS/UWT	National Association of Schoolmasters/Union of Women Teachers
NEC	National Executive Committee (Labour Party)
NHS	National Health Service
NUGMW	National Union of General and Municipal Workers
NUPE	National Union of Public Employees
NUT	National Union of Teachers
NWC	National Water Council
OU	Open University
PTA	Passenger Transport Authority
PTE	Passenger Transport Executive
PSI	Policy Studies Institute
PTP	Public Transport Plan
QUANGOS	Quasi-autonomous National Governmental Organisations
RSG	Rate Support Grant
RHA	Regional Health Authority
RHB	Regional Hospital Board
RWA	Regional Water Authority
RIPA	Royal Institute of Public Administration
SDD	Scottish Development Department
SOLACE	Society of Local Authority Chief Executives
SELNEC	South East Lancashire and North East Cheshire
SYCC	South Yorkshire Councy Council
TUC	Trades Union Congress
TPP	Transport Policies and Programmes
TSG	Transport Supplementary Grant
UDC	Urban Development Corporation

FURTHER READING

Students who wish to follow specific topics will find references in the text which can be located in the bibliography. The bibliography will appear daunting, however, to those who intend to pursue some more general reading at this stage rather than specialise. The following list comprises two or three items for each chapter that will introduce the student to the main themes covered. In some cases, of course, the relevant material will form only a part of the reference given. In other cases a reference will contain material relevant to more than one chapter. The list provides, however, a good introductory library on the subject.

Chapter 1. Introduction
Sharpe L J 1970, Theories and values of local government. *Political Studies* 18:153–74
Hill D M 1974, *Democratic Theory and Local Government*. Allen and Unwin

Chapter 2. The structure of local government: Origins to 1970
Redlich J, Hirst F W 1958, *The History of Local Government in England*, ed B Keith-Lucas. Macmillan
Keith-Lucas B, Richards P 1978, *A History of Local Government in the Twentieth Century*. Allen and Unwin

Chapter 3. The structure of local government: 1970 to the present
Wood B 1976, *The Process of Local Government Reform 1966–74*. Allen and Unwin
Alexander A 1982, *The Politics of Local Government in the United Kingdom*. Longman

Chapter 4. The services provided by local government
Elcock H 1982, *Local Government*. Methuen
Newton K 1982, Is small really so beautiful? Is big really so ugly? Size, effectiveness, and democracy in local government. *Political Studies* 30:190–206

Chapter 5. Internal organisation
Dearlove J 1979, *The Reorganisation of Local Government*. Cambridge University Press
Stewart J 1983, *Local Government: the conditions of local choice*. Allen and Unwin

Chapter 6. Local government finance
Foster C D, Jackman R, Perlman M 1980, *Local Government Finance in a Unitary State*. Allen and Unwin
Rose R, Page E 1982, *Fiscal Stress in Cities*. Cambridge University Press
Newton K, Karran T J 1985, *The Politics of Local Expenditure*. Macmillan

Chapter 7. Local councillors, parties and people
Gyford J 1984, *Local Politics in Britain* (2nd Edn). Croom Helm
Boaden N, Goldsmith M, Hampton W, Stringer P 1982, *Public Participation in Local Services*. Longman

Chapter 8. Group activity in the local political process
Newton K 1976, *Second City Politics*. Clarendon Press
Thomson A 1982, Local government as an employer. In Rose and Page (eds) *Fiscal Stress in Cities*. Cambridge University Press, pp 107–36

Chapter 9. The national local government system
Gyford J, James M 1983, *National Parties and Local Politics*. Allen and Unwin
Rhodes R A W 1986, *The National World of Local Government*. Allen and Unwin

Chapter 10. Central–local government relations
Griffith J A G 1966, *Central Departments and Local Authorities*. Allen and Unwin
Jones G 1980, *New Approaches to the Study of Central–Local Government Relationships*. Gower
Jones G, Stewart J 1983, *The Case for Local Government*. Allen and Unwin

Chapter 11. Special purpose authorities
Jordan A G, Richardson J J, Kimber R H 1977, The origins of the Water Act of 1973. *Public Administration* 55:317–34
Klein R 1983, *The Politics of the National Health Service*. Longman
Wistrich E 1983, *The Politics of Transport*. Longman

Chapter 12. Local government and the local economy
Higgins J, Deakin N, Edwards J, Wicks M 1983, *Government and Urban Poverty*. Basil Blackwell
Young K, Mason C 1983, *Urban Economic Development*. Macmillan

Boddy M, Fudge C 1984, *Local Socialism*. Macmillan

Chapter 13. Theories of the local state
Dunleavy P 1980, *Urban Political Analysis*. Macmillan
Saunders P 1981, *Social Theory and the Urban Question*. Hutchinson
Lowe S 1986, *Urban Social Movements*. Macmillan.

BIBLIOGRAPHY

Adams R J 1977, Bain's theory of white-collar union growth: a conceptual critique. *British Journal of Industrial Relations* **15**: 317–21

Alexander A 1982a, *Local Government in Britain Since Reorganisation.* Allen and Unwin

Alexander A 1982b, *The Politics of Local Government in the United Kingdom.* Longman

Arthur P 1980, *Government and Politics of Northern Ireland.* Longman

Ashford D E (ed) 1980, *Financing Urban Government in the Welfare State.* Croom Helm

Ashford D E 1982, *British Dogmatism and French Pragmatism.* Allen and Unwin

Bacon W 1978, *Public Accountability and the Schooling System.* Harper and Row

Bailey S J 1982, Do fewer pupils mean falling expenditure. In Rose R, Page E (eds) *Fiscal Stress in Cities.* Cambridge University Press, pp 137–67

Bain G S 1970, *The Growth of White-Collar Unionism.* Oxford University Press

Bains M (Chairman) 1972, *The New Local Authorities: management and structure.* HMSO

Banfield E C 1975, Foreword to *Essays on the Study of Urban Politics,* Young K (ed). Macmillan, pp vii–xi

Barker A 1976, *The Local Amenity Movement.* The Civic Trust

Barratt Brown M 1984, *Models in Political Economy.* Penguin Books

Barrett S, Fudge C 1981, *Policy and Action.* Methuen

Bealey F, Sewel J 1981, *The Politics of Independence: a study of a Scottish town.* Aberdeen University Press

Benington J 1975, The flaw in the pluralist heaven: changing strategies in the Coventry CDP. In Lees R, Smith G (eds) *Action Research in Community Development.* Routledge and Kegan Paul, pp 174–87

Bennett R J 1982, *Central Grants to Local Governments.* Cambridge University Press

Birch A H 1959, *Small-town Politics.* Oxford University Press

Birch A H 1967, *The British System of Government.* Allen and Unwin

Birrell D 1982, Policy-making in Northern Ireland under direct rule. Paper presented to Political Studies Association Work Group on United Kingdom politics.

Blaydon S 1974, *Municipal Review* **45**: 90

Blowers A 1977, Checks and balances: the politics of minority government. *Public Administration* **55**: 305–16

Blowers A, Brook C, Dunleavy P, McDowell L (eds) 1981, *Urban Change and Conflict*. Harper and Row

Blunkett D 1981a, Towards a socialist social policy. *Local Government Policy Making* **8**: 97–103

Blunkett D 1981b, Struggle for democracy. *New Socialist* Sept/Oct

Blunkett D, Green G 1983, *Building from the Bottom: the Sheffield Experience*. Fabian Tract 491

Boaden N 1971, *Urban Policy Making*. Cambridge University Press

Boaden N 1982, 'Urban Development Corporations – Threat or Challenge?' *Local Government Studies* **8** 4: 8–13

Boaden N 1983, Review of Higgins *et al. Government and Urban Poverty. Housing and Planning Review* **38**: 24

Boaden N, Goldsmith M, Hampton W, Stringer P 1980, Planning and participation in practice. In *Progress in Planning* Vol 13 parts 1/2 pp 1–102

Boaden N, Goldsmith M, Hampton W, Stringer P 1982, *Public Participation in Local Services*. Longman

Boddy M 1982, *Local Government and Industrial Development*. School for Advanced Urban Studies, Occasional Paper No 7.

Boddy M 1983, Changing public–private sector relationships in the industrial development process. In Young K, Mason C (eds) *Urban Economic Development*. Macmillan, pp 34–52

Boddy M 1984, Local economic and employment strategies. In Boddy M, Fudge C (eds) *Local Socialism*. Macmillan, pp 160–91

Boddy M, Barrett S 1979, *Local Government and the Industrial Process*. School for Advanced Urban Studies, WP6

Boddy M, Fudge C (eds) 1984, *Local Socialism*. Macmillan

Bone T 1974, The General Teaching Council for Scotland: its achievements. *London Educational Review 3:* 51–9

Bonner G A 1977, The case against local income tax. *Public Administration* **55**: 27–31

Bowman M, Hampton W (eds) 1983, *Local Democracies: a study in comparative local government*. Longman Cheshire, Melbourne.

Bramley G, Stewart M, Underwood J 1978, *Local Economic Initiatives*. School for Advanced Urban Studies, WP1

Brand J 1974, *Local Government Reform in England, 1888–1974*. Croom Helm

Branson N 1979, *Popularism, 1919–1925*. Lawrence and Wishart

Bristow S 1982, Rates and votes – the 1980 district council elections. *Policy and Politics* **10**: 163–80

Bristow S, Kermode D, Mannin M 1983, *The Redundant Counties?* G W and A Hesketh

Brown R G S 1975, *The Management of Welfare*. Fontana/Collins

Brown R G S 1979, *Reorganising the National Health Service*. Basil Blackwell and Martin Robertson

Bruce A, Lee G 1982, Local election campaigns. *Political Studies* **30**: 247–61

Bruce M 1968, *The Coming of the Welfare State* (4th edn). Batsford

Buchanan C (Chairman) 1963, *Traffic in Towns*. Report of a Working Group appointed by the Ministry of Transport. HMSO

Bullock Lord (Chairman) 1977, *Report of the Committee of Inquiry on Industrial Democracy* Cmnd 6706. HMSO

Burgess T, Travers T 1980, *Ten Billion Pounds*. Grant McIntyre

Burns P, Doyle M 1981, *Democracy at Work*. Pan Books

Burns W (Chairman) 1980, *Review of Local Authority Assistance to Industry and*

Commerce. Report of the Joint Group of Officials of Local Authority Associations and Government Departments. DOE

Bush T 1982, *Rhetoric and Reality: relationships between central government and local authorities.* Society of Education Officers

Butcher H, Collis P, Glen A, Sills P 1980, *Community Groups in Action: case studies and analysis.* Routledge and Kegan Paul

Byrne T 1981, *Local Government in Britain.* Penguin Books

Carroll B, Carroll T 1980, Britain: Northern Ireland. In Rowat DC (ed) *International Handbook on Local Government Reorganisation.* Aldwych Press

Castells M 1976a, Is there an urban sociology? In Pickvance C G (ed) *Urban Sociology.* Methuen and Tavistock, pp 33–59

Castells M 1976b, The service economy and post-industrial society: a sociological critique. *International Journal of Health Services* **6**: 595–607

Castells M 1977, *The Urban Question.* Edward Arnold

Castells M 1978, *City, Class and Power.* Macmillan

Castells M 1983, *The City and the Grassroots.* Edward Arnold

CDP 1974, *The national community development project; inter-project report* 1973. CDP Information and Intelligence Unit

Central Policy Review Staff 1977, *Relations between Central Government and Local Authorities.* HMSO

Chapman E J 1982, Local government reorganisation and public library provision in West Yorkshire, 1971–1974. Sheffield University: unpublished MA in Librarianship

Cherry G E 1974, *The Evolution of British Town Planning.* Leonard Hill

Cherry G 1982, *The Politics of Town Planning.* Longman

Child D, Paddon M 1984, Sheffield: steelyard blues. *Marxism Today* **28**(7):18–22

Clegg H A 1954, *General union: a study of the National Union of General and Municipal Workers.* Basil Blackwell

Clegg H A 1976, *Trade Unions under Collective Bargaining.* Basil Blackwell

Coates R D 1972a, *Teachers' Unions and Interest Group Politics.* Cambridge University Press

Coates R D 1972b, The teachers' associations and the restructuring of Burnham. *British Journal of Educational Studies* **20**: 192–204

Cochrane A, Hamnett C, McDowell L (eds) 1981, *City, Economy and Society.* Harper and Row

Cockburn C 1977, *The Local State.* Pluto Press

Cole G D H, Postgate R 1961, *The Common People.* Methuen University Paperbacks

Community Action 1984, Special feature on decentralisation in local government, No 66

Conservative Newsline Jan 1984

Coopers and Lybrand associates 1983, *Streamlining the Cities: an analysis of the government's case for reorganising local government in the six metropolitan counties.* Coopers and Lybrand associates

Coopers and Lybrand associates 1984, *Streamlining the Cities: an analysis of the costs involved in the government's proposals for reorganising local government in the six metropolitan counties.* Coopers and Lybrand associates

Cousins P 1977, Theories of democracy and local government. *Public Administration Bulletin* No 23: 40–53

Cox H, Morgan D 1973, *City Politics and the Press.* Cambridge University Press

Cox K R, Johnston R J (eds) 1982 *Conflict, Politics and the Urban Scene.* Longman

Craik W 1955, *Bryn Roberts and the National Union of Public Employees.* Allen and Unwin

Craik W 1968, *Sidney Hill and the National Union of Public Employees.* Allen and Unwin

Crispin A 1983, Comment on Kogan M, The case of education. In Young K (ed) *National Interests and Local Government.* Heinemann, pp 75–81

Cullingworth J B 1966, *Housing and Local Government.* Allen and Unwin

Cullingworth J B 1972, *Town and Country Planning in Britain* (4th edn). Allen and Unwin

Currell M 1974, *Political Woman* Croom Helm

Dahl R A 1961, *Who Governs?* Yale University Press, New Haven

Darke J, Darke R 1979, *Who needs Housing?* Macmillan

Davies J G 1972, *The Evangelistic Bureaucrat.* Tavistock

Davies P 1982, Territory and function; the electric supply industry in Great Britain. Paper presented to Political Studies Association Work Group on United Kingdom Politics

Davies T 1980, *Building Bridges: linking economic regeneration to inner city employment problems.* School for Advanced Urban Studies, WP8

Davies T 1981, Implementing employment policies in a district authority. In Barrett S, Fudge C (eds) *Policy and Action.* Methuen, pp 105–21

Dawson D 1976, Determinants of local authority expenditure. *Local Government Finance.* Appendix 7. HMSO

Dawson D 1983, Financial incentives for change. In Young K (ed) *National Interests and Local Government.* Heinemann, pp 11–31

Dearlove J 1973, *The Politics of Policy in Local Government.* Cambridge University Press

Dearlove J 1979, *The Reorganisation of Local Government.* Cambridge University Press

Dearlove J, Saunders P 1984, *Introduction to British Politics.* Polity Press

Department of the Environment 1971, *Local Government in England.* Cmnd 4584. HMSO

Department of the Environment/Welsh Office 1972, *Town and Country Planning Act, 1971: part II development plan proposals: publicity and public participation.* Circular 52/72

Department of the Environment/Welsh Office 1974, *Local Government in England and Wales: a guide to the new system.* HMSO

Department of the Environment 1977a, *Unequal City.* Final report of the Birmingham Inner Area Study by Llewellyn-Davies Weeks Forestier-Walker and Bor. HMSO.

Department of the Environment 1977b, *Change or Decay.* Final report of the Liverpool Inner Area Study by Hugh Wilson and Lewis Womersley, Roger Tym and Associates and Jamison Mackay and Partners. HMSO

Department of the Environment 1977c, *Inner London: policies for dispersal and balance.* Final report of the Lambeth Inner Area Study by Graeme Shankland, Peter Wilmott and David Jordan. HMSO

Department of the Environment 1977d, *Policy for the Inner Cities.* Cmnd 6845. HMSO

Department of the Environment 1977e, *Local Government Finance.* Cmnd 6813. HMSO

Department of the Environment 1979, *Organic Change in Local Government.* Cmnd 7457. HMSO.

Department of the Environment/Welsh Office 1983a, *Rates*. Cmnd 9008. HMSO

Department of the Environment 1983b, *Streamlining the Cities*. Cmnd 9063. HMSO

Development Plans. A manual on form and content 1970. HMSO

Donnison D 1983, *Urban Policies: a new approach*. Fabian Tract 487

Donoughue B, Jones G 1973, *Herbert Morrison: portrait of a politician* Weidenfeld and Nicolson

Drucker H, Dunleavy P, Gamble A, Peele G (eds) 1984, *Developments in British Politics*. Macmillan

Dunbabin J P D 1963, The politics of the establishment of county councils. *Historical Journal* **6**: 226–52

Dunbabin J P D 1965, Expectations of the new county councils and their realisation. *Historical Journal* **8**: 353–79

Duncan S S, Goodwin M 1984, *The Local State and Local Economic Policy: why the fuss?* University of Sussex Department of Urban and Regional Studies, Working Paper 40

Dunleavy P J 1980a, *Urban Political Analysis*. Macmillan

Dunleavy P 1980b, The political implications of sectoral cleavages and the growth of state employment. *Political Studies* **28**: 364–83 and 527–49

Dunleavy P J 1981, *The Politics of Mass Housing in Britain: corporate power and professional influence in the Welfare State*. Clarendon Press

Dunleavy P 1984a, Voting and the electorate. In Drucker H *et al.* (eds) *Developments in British Politics*. Macmillan, pp 30–58

Dunleavy P 1984b, The limits to local government. In Boddy M, Fudge C (eds) *Local Socialism*. Macmillan pp 49–81

Edwards J, Batley R 1978, *The Politics of Positive Discrimination*. Tavistock

Elcock H 1972, Opportunity for ombudsman: the Northern Ireland Commissioner for Complaints. *Public Administration* **50**: 87–93

Elcock H 1979, Politicians, organisations and the public: the provision of gypsy sites. *Local Government Studies*, New Series **5**: 43–54

Elcock H 1982, *Local Government*. Methuen

Elcock H 1983, Disabling professionalism: the real threat to local democracy. *Public Money* June: 23–7

Elliott M 1983, Constitutional continuity and the position of local government. In Young K (ed) *National Interests and Local Government*. Heinemann, pp 35–57

English J, Martin F M 1983, *Social Services in Scotland*. Scottish Academic Press

Fairbairn N 1983, Case proved – by the Scots. *The Times* 4 July

Femia J 1975, Hegemony and consciousness in the thought of Antonio Gramsci. *Political Studies* **23**: 29–48

Fletcher D P C 1972, The peak in road passenger transport: a comment. *Journal of Transport Economics and Policy* **6**: 211–12

Foster C D, Jackman R, Perlman M 1980, *Local Government Finance in a Unitary State*. Allen and Unwin

Fraser, D 1976, *Urban Politics in Victorian England: the structure of politics in Victorian cities*. Leicester University Press

Fudge C 1981, Winning an election and gaining control: the formulation and implementation of a 'local' political manifesto. In Barrett S, Fudge C (eds) *Policy and Action*. Methuen, pp 123–41

Fudge C 1984, Decentralisation: socialism goes local? In Boddy M, Fudge C (eds) *Local Socialism*. Macmillan, pp 192–214

Gerth H H, Mills C W 1948, *From Max Weber: essays in sociology*. Routledge and Kegan Paul

Gibson J G, Game C H, Stewart J D 1982, The measurements of central control in England and Wales. *Political Studies* **30**: 432–6

GLC 1981, *Manifesto of the Labour Party for the GLC elections 1981*.

GLC 1985, *Jobs for a Change*. No 14

Goffin N A 1979, Decision-making in residential renewal. Unpublished MPhil thesis, Sheffield City Polytechnic

Goldsmith M 1980, *Politics, Planning and the City*. Hutchinson

Gordon P 1980, *Policing Scotland*. Scottish Council for Civil Liberties

Gosden P H 1977, The origins of cooptation to membership of local education committees. *British Journal of Educational Studies* **25**: 258–67

Gosden P 1982, The educational system of England and Wales since 1952. *British Journal of Educational Studies* **30**: 108–21

Grant W 1977, *Independent Local Politics in England and Wales*. Saxon House

Gray C 1982, Regional water authorities. In Hogwood B W, Keating M (eds) *Regional Government in England*. Clarendon Press, pp 143–67

Green D G 1981, *Power and Party in an English City*. Allen and Unwin

Green G 1972, National, City and Ward Components of Local Voting, *Policy and Politics* **1**: 45–54

Greenwood R 1982, Pressures from Whitehall. In Rose R, Page E (eds) *Fiscal Stress in Cities*. Cambridge University Press, pp 44–76

Greenwood R, Norton A, Stewart J 1969, Recent changes in the Internal organisation of county boroughs. *Public Administration* **47**: 151–67 and 289–306

Greenwood R, Stewart J D 1974, *Corporate Planning in English Local Government*. Charles Knight & Co Ltd

Griffith J A G 1966, *Central Departments and Local Authorities*. Allen and Unwin

Griffith J A G 1974, *Local Authorities and Central Control*. Barry Rose Publishers

Gyford J 1976 and 1984, *Local Politics in Britain*. Croom Helm

Gyford J 1983a, The implications of local socialism. *Local Government Studies* **9**: 13–17

Gyford J 1983b, *The New Urban Left: origins, style and strategy*. University College London, Town Planning Discussion Paper No 38

Gyford J 1983c, The New Urban Left: a local road to socialism? *New Society* 21 April: 91–3

Gyford J 1985, *The Politics of Local Socialism*. Allen and Unwin

Gyford J, James M 1983, *National Parties and Local Politics*. Allen and Unwin

Hain P 1980, *Neighbourhood Participation*. Temple Smith

Ham C, 1982 and 1985, *Health Policy in Britain*. Macmillan

Ham C, Hill M 1984, *The Policy Process in the Modern Capitalist State*. Wheatsheaf Books

Hambleton R 1980, *Engaging the Private Sector*. School for Advanced Urban Studies, WP 10

Hampton W 1966, The county as a political unit. *Parliamentary Affairs* **19**: 462–74

Hampton W 1970, *Democracy and Community*. Oxford University Press

Hampton W 1972, Political attitudes to changes in city council administration. *Local Government Studies* **1**: 23–35

Hampton W 1978, *Providing the Posh Words ...* DOE

Hampton W 1981, Who calls the tune. *Public Administration Bulletin* No 36:63–6

Harvey C 1982, *Against Metropolis*. Fabian Tract 484

Haynes R J 1980, *Organisation Theory and Local Government*. Allen and Unwin

Haywood S 1977, Decision-making in local government: the case of an independent council. *Local Government Studies*, New Series **3**: 41–55

Haywood S C, Elcock H J 1982, Regional health authorities: regional government or central agencies? In Hogwood B W, Keating M (eds) *Regional Government in England*. Clarendon Press, pp 119–42

Hepple B, O'Higgins P 1971, *Public Employee Trade Unionism in the United Kingdom: the legal framework*. Institute of Labor and Industrial Relations, University of Michigan – Wayne State University, Ann Arbor

Herbert Sir E (Chairman) 1960, *Report of the Royal Commission on Local Government in London 1957–60*. Cmnd 1164. HMSO

Higgins J 1978, *The Poverty Business: Britain and America*. Basil Blackwell and Martin Robertson

Higgins J, Deakin N, Edwards J, Wicks M 1983, *Government and Urban Poverty*. Basil Blackwell

Hill D M 1974, *Democratic Theory and Local Government*. Allen and Unwin

Hoare Q, Smith G N (eds) 1971, *Selections from the Prison Notebooks of Antonio Gramsci*. Lawrence and Wishart

Hoggart K 1983, Changes in education outputs in English local authorities 1949–1974. *Public Administration* **61**: 169–78

Hogwood B W, Keating M (eds) 1982, *Regional Government in England*. Clarendon Press

Hood C, Wright M (eds) 1981, *Big Government in Hard Times*. Martin Robertson

Houlihan B 1983, Conceptualising central local relations. Paper presented to Political Studies Association Conference, Newcastle

HC 1983. *The Problems of Management of Urban Renewal (Appraisal of the Recent Initiatives in Merseyside)*. Third Report from the Environment Committee of the House of Commons, Session 1982–83

HC Debates (Hansard) 1984, 17 Jan and 18 Dec

Hovell P J, Jones W H 1975, Planning and passenger transport executives. *Local Government Studies*, New Series **1**: 27–38

Humble S 1984, Neighbourhood councils in England. Unpublished PhD thesis, University of Birmingham.

Ilersic A R 1975, *Local Government at the Crossroads*. Aims for Freedom and Enterprise

Isaac-Henry K 1975, Local authority associations and local government reform. *Local Government Studies*, New Series **l**: 1–12

Isaac-Henry K 1980, The English||local authority associations. *Public Administration Bulletin* No 33: 21–41

Jackman R 1983, Comment on Chapter 2. In Young K (ed) *National Interests and Local Government*. Heinemann, pp 31–4

Jackson M 1982, *Trade Unions*. Longman

Jackson R M 1965, *The Machinery of Local Government* (2nd edn). Macmillan

Johnson N, Cochrane A 1981, *Economic Policy-making by Local Authorities in Britain and Western Germany*. Allen and Unwin

Johnson T J 1972, *Professions and Power*. Macmillan

Joll J 1977, *Gramsci*. Fontana

Jones G (ed) 1980, *New Approaches to the Study of Central–Local Government Relationships*. Gower

Jones G W 1979, *Borough Politics*. Macmillan

Jones G W, Norton A 1978, *Political Leadership in Local Authorities*. Institute of Local Government Studies

Jones G, Stewart J 1983a, Local government – the government's record assessed. *Local Government Studies* **9**: 3–9

Jones G, Stewart J 1983b, *The Case for Local Government*. Allen and Unwin

Jordan A G, Richardson J J 1977, Outside committees and policy-making: the Central Advisory Water Committee. *Public Administration Bulletin* No 24: 41–58

Jordan A G, Richardson J J, Kimber R H 1977, The origins of the Water Act of 1973. *Public Administration* **55**: 317–34

Kantor P 1976, Elites, pluralists and policy arenas in London: towards a comparative theory of city policy formation. *British Journal of Political Science* **6**: 311–34

Kavanagh D (ed) 1982 *The Politics of the Labour Party*. Allen and Unwin

Keating M, Midwinter A 1983, *The Government of Scotland*. Mainstream Publishing

Keith-Lucas B 1952, *The English Local Government Franchise*. Blackwell

Keith-Lucas B 1980, *The Unreformed Local Government System*. Croom Helm

Keith-Lucas B, Richards P G 1978, *A History of Local Government in the Twentieth Century*. Allen and Unwin

Kellas J G, Madgwick P 1982, Territorial ministries: the Scottish and Welsh Offices. In Madgwick P, Rose R (eds) *The Territorial Dimension in United Kingdom Politics*. Macmillan, pp 9–33

Kirby A 1982, The external relations of the local state in Britain: some empirical examples. In Cox K R, Johnston R J (eds) *Conflict, Politics and the Urban Scene*. Longman, pp 88–104

Klein R 1974, Policy making in the National Health Service. *Political Studies* **22**: 1–14

Klein R 1983, *The Politics of the National Health Service*. Longman

Kogan M 1974, *Educational Policy Making*. Allen and Unwin

Kogan M 1978, *The Politics of Educational Change*. Fontana

Kogan M 1983, The case of education. In Young K (ed) *National Interests and Local Government*. Heinemann, pp 58–75

Kogan M with Eyken W 1973, *County Hall*. Penguin Books

Laffin M 1980, Professionalism in central–local relations. In Jones G (ed) *New Approaches to the Study of Central–Local Government Relationships*. Gower, pp 18–27

Laski H 1961, *An Introduction to Politics*. Unwin Books

Layfield F (Chairman) 1976, *Local Government Finance*. Report of the Committee of Inquiry, Cmnd 6453. HMSO

Leach S 1982, In defence of the rational model. In Leach S, Stewart J *Approaches in Public Policy*. Allen and Unwin, pp 6–23

Leach S, Stewart J 1982, *Approaches in Public Policy*. Allen and Unwin

Lee J M, Wood B 1974, *The Scope of Local Initiative*. Martin|Robertson

Lees R, Smith G (eds) 1975, *Action-research in Community Development*. Routledge and Kegan Paul

Levinson H 1971, *Collective Bargaining by British Local Authority Employees*.

Institute of Labor and Industrial Relations, University of Michigan – Wayne State University, Ann Arbor

Lewis N, Gateshill B 1978, *The Commission for Local Administration, a Preliminary Appraisal*. Royal Institute of Public Administration

Lewis N, Harden I 1982, Law and the local state. *Urban Law and Policy* **5**: 65–86

LGBC 1972, Local Government Boundary Commission for England Report No 1, Cmnd 5148. HMSO

LGBC 1973, Local Government Boundary Commission for England Report No 3. HMSO

Lindley P 1982, The Merseyside Task Force. Paper presented to Political Studies Association Work Group on United Kingdom Politics

Lipman V D 1949, *Local Government Areas, 1834–1945*. Basil Blackwell

Local Government (Scotland) Act 1973

Lomer M 1977, The chief executive in local government. *Local Government Studies*, New Series **3**: 17–44

Loney M, Allen M (eds) 1979, *The Crisis of the Inner City*. Macmillan

Long J 1976, *Employee Participation and Local Government*. Society of Local Authority Chief Executives

Loughlin M, Gelfand M D, Young K 1985, *Half a Century of Municipal Decline 1935–1985*. Allen and Unwin

Loveday B 1983, The role of the police committee. *Local Government Studies* **9**: 39–52

Lowe S 1986, *Urban Social Movements*. Macmillan

Lukewarm response to parent governor plans 1984, *Education* **163**: 444–5

Maass A (ed) 1959, *Area and Power*. The Free Press, Glencoe, Ill

McKay D, Cox A 1979, *The Politics of Urban Change*. Croom Helm

McLoughlin J 1973, *The Water Act, 1973*. Sweet and Maxwell

McQueen W R, Freeman I C 1978, *Community Councils in Scotland*, Scottish Office

Macrory P A (Chairman) 1970, *Report of the Review Body on Local Government in Northern Ireland*. Cmd. 546 Belfast HMSO

Madgwick P J with Griffiths N, Walker V 1973, *The Politics of Rural Wales*. Hutchinson

Madgwick P, Rose R (eds) 1982, *The Territorial Dimension in United Kingdom Politics*. Macmillan

Mair R 1983, Health services. In English J, Martin F M (eds) *Social Services in Scotland*. Scottish Academic Press, pp 48–67

Mallaby G (Chairman) 1967, *Staffing of Local Government*. Report of the Committee on the Staffing of Local Government. HMSO

Margerson C J, Elliott C K 1970, A predictive study of the development in teacher militancy. *British Journal of Industrial Relations* **8**: 408–17

Marks S 1983, Making London work. *New Statesman* **105** (1 April): 8–10

Marris P, Rein M 1967, *Dilemmas of Social Reform*. Routledge and Kegan Paul 1967 and 1972, (2nd edn); Penguin Books 1974

Martlew C 1983, The state and local government finance. *Public Administration* **61**: 127–47

Massey D 1979, In what sense a regional problem? *Regional Studies* **13**: 233–43

Massey D 1982, Enterprise zones: a political issue. *International Journal of Urban and Regional Research* **6**: 429–34

Massey D 1983, The shape of things to come. *Marxism Today* **27**(4):18–27

Masterson M 1979, The creation of Scotland's national system of official voluntarism. *Journal of Voluntary Action Research* **8**: 103–13

Maud, Sir John (later Lord Redcliffe-Maud) (Chairman) 1967, *Management of Local Government*: Vol I, *Report*; Vol II, *The Local Government Councillor;* Vol III, *The Local Government Elector*; Vol IV, *Local Government Administration Abroad*; Vol V, *Local Government Administration in England and Wales*. HMSO

Melling J 1980, *Housing, Social Policy and the State*. Croom Helm

Mercer J 1978, *Scotland: the devolution of power*. John Calder

Merrison, Sir Alec (Chairman) 1979, *Report* of the Royal Commission on the National Health Service. Cmnd 7615. HMSO

Metropolitan County Councils 1983, *The Case for Metropolitan Counties*. Published by West Yorkshire Metropolitan County Council for the metropolitan counties.

Midwinter A 1982, *Management Reform in Scottish Local Government*. Department of Administration, University of Strathclyde

Midwinter A 1984, *The Politics of Local Spending*. Mainstream Publishing

Midwinter A, Keating M, Taylor P 1983, 'Excessive and unreasonable': the politics of the Scottish hit list. *Political Studies* 31: 394–417

Miliband R 1973, *The State in Capitalist Society*. Quartet Books

Miliband R 1977, *Marxism and Politics*. Oxford University Press

Miliband R 1982, *Capitalist Democracy in Britain*. Oxford University Press

Miliband R 1983, *Class Power and State Power*. Verso

Mill J S 1900, *A System of Logic*. Longman, Green and Co.

Ministry of Local Government and Regional Planning 1970, *Reform of Local Government in England*. Cmnd 4276. HMSO

Minogue M 1979, *The Consumer's Guide to Local Government*. Macmillan

Moorhouse B, Wilson M, Chamberlain C 1972, Rent strikes – direct action and the working class. In Miliband R, Saville J (eds) *The Socialist Register 1972*. The Merlin Press, pp 133–56

NALGO 1977, *Industrial democracy*

Neve B 1977, Bureaucracy and politics in local government: the role of local authority education officers. *Public Administration* 55: 291–303

Newcastle 1983, *The Inner City: conditions within Newcastle and Gateshead*. Newcastle/Gateshead Inner City Partnership

Newton K 1969, City politics in Britain and the United States. *Political Studies* 17: 208–18

Newton K 1975, Community politics and decision-making: the American experience and its lessons. In Young K (ed) *Essays on the Study of Urban Politics*. Macmillan, pp 1–24

Newton K 1976a, *Second City Politics*. Clarendon Press

Newton K 1976b, Comparative community performance. *Current Sociology* 26: 50–5

Newton K 1980, *Balancing the Books: financial problems of local government in West Europe*. Sage Publications Ltd

Newton K 1981, *Urban Political Economy*. Frances Pinter

Newton K 1982, Is small really so beautiful? Is big really so ugly? Size, effectiveness and democracy in local government. *Political Studies* 30: 190–206

Newton K, Karran T J 1985, *The Politics of Local Expenditure*. Macmillan

Norton A 1983, Economic development and job creation. *Local Government Studies* 9: 63–7

Norton P 1984, *The British Polity*. Longman

Oakeshott M 1962, *Rationalism in Politics*. Methuen

O'Connor J 1973, *The Fiscal Crisis of the State*. St Martin's Press, New York

OU Course Team 1975, *Environmental Control and Public Health*, Unit 8 *Administrative Control*. The Open University Press

Page E 1980a, The measurement of central control. *Political Studies* **28**: 117–20

Page E 1980b, Why should central–local relations in Scotland be different from those in England? In Jones G (ed) *New Approaches to the Study of Central–Local Relationships*. Gower, pp 84–100

Page E 1983, Local government in Scotland. In Bowman M, Hampton W (eds) *Local Democracies: a study in comparative local government*. Longman Cheshire, Melbourne, pp 41–60

Page E, Midwinter A 1979, *Remote Bureaucracy or Administrative Efficiency? Scotland's New Local Government System*. Centre for the Study of Public Policy, University of Strathclyde

Page H 1971, Local government in decline. *The Three Banks Review* No 90: 3–27

Pahl R 1975, *Whose City?* Penguin Books

Pahl R E, Flynn R, Buck N H 1983, *Structures and Processes of Urban Life*. Longman

Parental Influence at School: a new framework for school government in England and Wales 1984, Cmnd 9242. HMSO

Parkinson M 1985, *Liverpool on the Brink*. Policy Journals

Parkinson M, Duffy J 1984, Government's response to inner-city riots: the Minister for Merseyside and the Task Force. *Parliamentary Affairs* **37**: 76–96

Parry R 1982, Who runs Scottish social policy? Paper presented to Political Studies Association Work Group on United Kingdom Politics

Parston G 1980, *Planners, Politics and Health Services*. Croom Helm

Pateman C 1970, *Participation and Democratic Theory*. Cambridge University Press

Paterson I V (Chairman) 1973, *The New Scottish Local Authorities: organisation and management structure*. HMSO

Pederson T 1982, On the educational function of political participation: a comparative analysis of John Stuart Mill's theory and contemporary survey research findings. *Political Studies* **30**: 557–68

Pickvance C G (ed) 1976, *Urban Sociology*. Methuen and Tavistock

Pimlott B, Cook C (eds) 1982, *Trade Unions in British Politics*. Longman

Poole K P 1978, *The Local Government Service in England and Wales*. Allen and Unwin

Poulantzas N 1973, *Political Power and Social Classes*. New Left Books and Sheed and Ward

Price R, Bain G S 1976, Union growth revisited: 1948–1974 in perspective. *British Journal of Industrial Relations* **14**: 339–55

Price R, Bain G S 1983, Union growth in Britain: retrospective and prospect. *British Journal of Industrial Relations* **21**: 46–68

Randall V 1981, Housing policy-making in London boroughs: the role of paid officers. *The London Journal* **7**: 161–76

Redcliffe-Maud, Lord (Chairman) 1969, Royal Commission on Local Government in England 1966–1969: Vol I, *Report*, Cmnd 4040; Vol II, *Memorandum of Dissent* by D Senior, Cmnd 4040 – I; Vol III, *Research Appendices*, Cmnd 4040 – II. Research studies: (1) *Local Government in South-East England*; (2) *The Lessons of the London Government Reforms*; (3) *Economics of Scale in Local Government Services*; (4) *Performance and Size in Local Government Services*; (5) *Local Authority Services and the Characteristics of Administrative Areas*; (6) *School Management and Govern-*

ment; (7) *Aspects of Administration in a Large Local Authority*; (8) *The Inner London Education Authority. A Study of Divisional Administration*; (9) *Community Attitudes Survey: England*; (10) *Administration in a Large Local Authority. A Comparison with Other County Boroughs*. HMSO

Redcliffe-Maud, Lord (Chairman) 1974, *Conduct in Local Government*. Report of Prime Minister's Committee on local goernment rules of conduct, Cmnd 5636. HMSO

Redcliffe-Maud, Lord, Wood B 1974, *English Local Government Reformed*. Oxford University Press

Redlich J, Hirst F W 1958, *The History of Local Government in England*, ed Keith-Lucas B. Macmillan

Regan D 1979, *Local Government and Education* (2nd edn). Allen and Unwin

Regan D 1980, *A Headless State: the unaccountable executive in British local government*. University of Nottingham Inaugural lecture

Regan D 1983, *Are the Police under Control?* The Social Affairs Unit

Regan D E, Stewart J D 1982, An essay in the government of health: the case for local authority control. *Social Policy and Administration* **16:** 19–43

Rex J, Moore R 1967, *Race, Community and Conflict*. Oxford University Press

Rhodes G 1970, *The Government of London*. Weidenfeld and Nicolson

Rhodes G (ed) 1972, *The New Government of London*. Weidenfeld and Nicolson

Rhodes R A W 1981, *Control and Power in Central–Local Government Relations*. Gower

Rhodes R A W 1986, *The National World of Local Government*. Allen and Unwin

Rhodes R A W, Hardy B, Pudney K 1981, Public interest groups in central–local relations in England and Wales. *Public Administration Bulletin* No 36: 17–36

Rhodes R A W, Hardy B, Pudney K 1982, '*Corporate Bias in Central–Local Relations: a case study of the Consultative Council on Local Government Finance*. University of Essex, Department of Government

Rhodes R A W, Hardy B, Pudney K 1983a, *Local Government Pay Negotiations and the National Community of Local Government*. University of Essex, Department of Government

Rhodes R A W, Hardy B, Pudney K 1983b, *Constraints on the National Community of Local Government: members, 'other governments' and policy communities*. University of Essex, Department of Government

Rhodes R A W, Hardy B, Pudney K 1983c, '*Power-dependence' Theories of Central–Local Relations:* a critical assessment. University of Essex, Department of Government

Richards P G 1975a, *The 'Reformed' Local Government System* (2nd edn). Allen and Unwin

Richards P G 1975b, *The Local Government Act 1972: problems of implementation*. Allen and Unwin

Richards P G 1983, *The Local Government System*. Allen and Unwin

Richardson J J, Jordan A G, Kimber R H 1978, Lobbying, administrative reform and policy styles: the case of land drainage. *Political Studies* **26:** 47–64

RIPA/PSI 1980, *Party Politics in Local Government: officers and members*. Royal Institute of Public Administration/Policy Studies Institute

Robinson D (Chairman) 1977, *Remuneration of Councillors*: Vol I, *Report* (Cmnd 7010); Vol II, *The Surveys of Councillors and Local Authorities*. HMSO

Robson W A 1948, *The Government and Misgovernment of London* (2nd edn). Allen and Unwin

Roche D 1982, *Local Government in Ireland*. Institute of Public Administration, Dublin

Rose R 1982, Is the United Kingdom a state? Northern Ireland as a test case. In Madgwick P, Rose R (eds) *The Territorial Dimension in United Kingdom Politics*. Macmillan, pp 100–36

Rose R, Page E (eds) 1982, *Fiscal Stress in Cities*. Cambridge University Press

Routh G 1967, White-collar unions in the United Kingdom. In Sturmthal A (ed) *White-collar Trade Unions*. University of Illinois Press, Chicago, pp 165–204

Rowat D C (ed) 1980, *International Handbook on Local Government Reorganisation*. Aldwych Press

Roy W 1968, *The Teachers' Union: Aspects of Policy and Organisation in the National Union of Teachers 1950–1966*. Schoolmaster Publishing Co.

Sainsbury E 1977, *The Personal Social Services*. Pitman

Salt J 1971, Experiments in anarchism, 1850–1854. *Transactions of the Hunter Archaeological Society* **10**: 37–53

Saunders P 1980, *Urban Politics*. Penguin Books

Saunders P 1981, *Social Theory and the Urban Question*. Hutchinson

Saunders P 1984, Rethinking local politics. In Boddy M, Fudge C (eds) *Local Socialism*. Macmillan, pp 22–48

Scotland J 1982, Scottish education, 1952–1982. *British Journal of Educational Studies* **30**: 122–35

Scottish Development Department 1973, *A Measure of Plenty: water resources in Scotland – a general survey*. HMSO

Seebohm F (Chairman) 1968. *Report* of the Committee on Local Authority and Allied Personal Social Services. Cmnd 3703. HMSO

Self P 1972, *Administrative Theories and Politics*. Allen and Unwin

Senior D 1969, *Memorandum of Dissent*. *See* Redcliffe-Maud 1969

Sewell W R D, Coppock J T (eds) 1977, *Public Participation in Planning*. John Wiley and Sons

Sharpe L J 1970, Theories and values of local government. *Political Studies* **18**: 153–74

Sharpe L J (ed) 1979, *Decentralist Trends in Western Democracies*. Sage

Sharpe L J 1982, Labour and the geography of inequality: a puzzle. In Kavanagh D (ed) *The Politics of the Labour Party*. Allen and Unwin, pp 135–70

Sharpe L J, Newton K 1984, *Does Politics Matter?* Clarendon Press

Shaw G B (ed) 1889, *Fabian Essays in Socialism*. The Fabian Society

Shaw R 1983, The Audit Commission and its role. *Local Government Studies* **9**: 19–22

Sheail J 1983, Planning, water supplies and ministerial power in inter-war Britain. *Public Administration* **61**: 386–95

Sheffield, City of 1982, *Employment Department: an initial outline*. Internal document

Sheppard M G 1982, The effects of the franchise provisions on the social and sex composition of the municipal electorate 1882–1914. *Bulletin of the Society for the Study of Labour History* No 45: 19–25

Simon H A 1957, *Administrative Behavior* (2nd edn). The Free Press, New York

Skeffington A (Chairman) 1969, *People and Planning*. HMSO

Skelcher C 1983, Towards salaried councillors? – the special responsibility allowances. *Local Government Studies*: 9 10–15

Skilbeck M 1982, What shall we do with the Schools Council? *Education* **159**: 479–80

Sklair L 1975, The struggle against the Housing Finance Act. In Miliband R, Saville J (eds) *The Socialist Register 1975*. The Merlin Press, pp 250–92

Smellie K B 1946, *History of Local Government*. Allen and Unwin

Smith D 1982, *Conflict and Compromise: class formation in English society 1830–1914*. Routledge and Kegan Paul

Smith S A de 1971, *Constitutional and Administrative Law*. Penguin Books

Solomos J 1984, Black youth and the 1980–81 riots: official interpretations and government responses. *Politics* **4**: 21–7

Spoor A 1967, *White-collar Union*. Heinemann

Stacey M 1960, *Tradition and Change*. Oxford University Press

Stacey M, Batstone E, Bell C, Murcott A 1975, *Power, Persistence and Change*. Routledge and Kegan Paul

Stacey M, Price M 1981, *Women, Power and Politics*. Tavistock

Stanyer J 1970, The Maud Committee Report. In Wiseman H V (ed) *Local Government in England 1959–69*. Routledge and Kegan Paul, pp 42–70

Stanyer J 1975, On the study of urban electoral behaviour. In Young K (ed) *Essays on the Study of Urban Politics*. Macmillan, pp 25–51

Stanyer J 1976, *Understanding Local Government*. Martin Robertson

Stanyer J, Smith B 1976, *Administering Britain*. Fontana/Collins

Stewart J 1974, *The Responsive Local Authority*. Charles Knight & Co Ltd

Stewart J 1983, *Local Government: the conditions of local choice*. Allen and Unwin

Stewart J D, Leach S, Skelcher C K 1978, *Organic Change*. INLOGOV

Stewart M 1983, The role of central government in local economic development. In Young K (ed) *National Interests and Local Government*. Heinemann, pp 105–29

Stewart M 1984, *Talking to Local Business: the involvement of chambers of commerce in local affairs*. University of Bristol, School for Advanced Urban Studies, Working Paper 38

Stewart M, Whitting G 1983, *Ethnic Minorities and the Urban Programme*. University of Bristol, School for Advanced Urban Studies, Occasional Paper No 9

Stodart A (Chairman) 1981, *Report* of the Committee of Inquiry into Local Government in Scotland, Cmnd 8115. HMSO

Sturmthal A (ed) 1967, *White-collar Trade Unions*. University of Illinois Press, Chicago

Sutherland M B 1982, Progress and problems in education in Northern Ireland, 1952–1982. *British Journal of Educational Studies* **30**: 136–49

Tarr R J 1983, Political management – the reality of local government management? *Local Government Studies* **9**: 5–11

Taylor T (Chairman) 1977, *A New Partnership for our Schools*. HMSO

Terry M 1982, Organising a fragmented workforce: shop stewards in local government. *British Journal of Industrial Relations* **20**: 1–19

The Times 27 May 1980; 5 April 1983; 18 May 1983; 27 May 1983; 16 Jan 1984; 29 June 1984; 17 July 1984; 3 Jan 1985; 27 Feb 1985; 6 Feb 1986

Thomson A 1982, Local government as an employer. In Rose R, Page E (eds) *Fiscal Stress in Cities*. Cambridge University Press, pp 107–36

Thomson A W J, Beaumont P B 1978, *Public Sector Bargaining: a study of relative gain*. Saxon House

Thomson J M 1977, The London motorway plan. In Sewell W R D, Coppock J M (eds) *Public Participation in Planning*. John Wiley and Sons, pp 59–69

Thornhill W (ed) 1971, *The Growth and Reform of English Local Government*. Weidenfeld and Nicolson

Tomlinson J 1982, *The Unequal Struggle? British Socialism and the Capitalist Enterprise.* Methuen

Townsend P 1979, *Poverty in the United Kingdom.* Penguin Books

The Transport Act 1983

Tyson W J 1970, A study of peak cost and pricing in road passenger transport. *Institute of Transport Journal* **34**: 19–24

Tyson W J 1972a, The peak in road passenger transport: an empirical study. *Journal of Transport Economics and Policy* **6**: 77–84

Tyson W J 1972b, The finance of public transport. *Local Government Finance* **76**: 273–6

Volker D 1966, NALGO's affiliation to the TUC. *British Journal of Industrial Relations* **4**: 59–76

Walker P 1979, A Conservative view. In Loney M, Allen M (eds) *The Crisis of the Inner City.* Macmillan, pp 9–21

Ward M 1983, Labour's capital gains: the GLC experience. *Marxism Today* **27**(12): 24–9

Warde A 1982, *Consensus and Beyond.* Manchester University Press

The Water Act 1973

Webb S and B 1963, *The Development of English Local Government 1689–1835.* Oxford University Press

Welsh Office 1967, *Local Government in Wales.* Cmnd 3340. HMSO

Welsh Office 1971, *The Reform of Local Government in Wales.* HMSO

Wendt R 1983, Working in a 'hung' council. *Local Government Studies* **9**: 1–6

Wheatley, Lord (Chairman) 1969, Report of the Royal Commission of Local Government in Scotland, 1966–1969. Research Studies: (1) *Administrative Costs of Local Authorities Local Taxation;* (2) *Community Survey:Scotland;* (3) *Manpower Surveys: The Ratio of Councillors to Electors in the Different Types of Local Authorities in Scotland; Percentage Polls and Contested Seats.* HMSO

Willis K G 1983, New jobs in urban areas – an evaluation of advance factory building. *Local Government Studies* **9**: 73–85

Wilson C H (ed) 1948, *Essays on Local Government.* Basil Blackwell

Wilson D J, Pinto-Duschinsky 1976, Conservative city machines: the end of an era. *British Journal of Political Science* **6**: 239–44

Wiseman H V (ed) 1970, *Local Government in England 1958–69.* Routledge and Kegan Paul

Wistrich E 1983, *The Politics of Transport.* Longman

Wolmar C 1984, Divided we stand. *New Socialist.* No 22: 13–15

Wood B 1976, *The Process of Local Government Reform 1966–74.* Allen and Unwin

Wright M 1982, Pressures in Whitehall. In Rose R, Page E (eds) *Fiscal Stress in Cities.* Cambridge University Press, pp 17–43

Ylvisaker P 1959, Some criteria for a 'proper' area division of governmental powers. In Maass A (ed) *Area and Power.* The Free Press, Glencoe Ill,. pp 27–49

Young K 1972, Political party organisation. In Rhodes G (ed) *The New Government of London.* Weidenfeld and Nicolson

Young K 1975, *Local Politics and the Rise of Party.* Leicester University Press

Young K (ed) 1975 *Essays on the Study of Urban Politics.* Macmillan

Young K (ed) 1983, *National Interests and Local Government.* Heinemann

Young K, Mason C (eds) 1983, *Urban Economic Development.* Macmillan

Young K, Mills L 1982, The decline of urban economies. In Rose R, Page E (eds) *Fiscal Stress in Cities.* Cambridge University Press, pp 77–106

Young M, Hall P 1982, *The Middle of the Night.* Tawney Pamphlet 4

Young M, Willmott P 1962, *Family and Kinship in East London.* Penguin Books

Young T 1984, The politics of public participation in planning. University of Sussex, unpublished MPhil thesis.

INDEX